THE MYTHOLOGY OF KUMBH-PARVA

कुम्भ की पौराणिक-कथा

THE MYTHOLOGY OF KUMBH-PARVA

Editor
Amit Agnihotri

VANI PRAKASHAN

vaniprakashan.com

Hardback First Edition : 2025

VANI PRAKASHAN

Head Office

4695, 21-A, Daryaganj, New Delhi-110 002, India
Phone : +91 11 23273167, 23275710

Registered Bookstores and Offices

Ashok Rajpath, Patna-800 004, Bihar
Coffee House Campus, Mahatma Gandhi Marg, Prayagraj-211 001, Uttar Pradesh
Mahatma Gandhi Antarrashtriya Hindi Vishwavidyalaya, Wardha-442 001, Maharashtra
sales@vaniprakashan.in
vaniprakashan@gmail.com

The Mythology of Kumbh-Parva
Edited by Amit Agnihotri

ISBN : 978-93-6944-347-5
Religion/History

Price : ₹ 3500

Printed and bound in City Press, Delhi-110 095

Vani Prakashan's signature motif is created by Artist Maqbool Fida Husain

Foreword

As we stand on the cusp of the grand celebration of Mahakumbh in 2025, it is only fitting to reflect on the profound significance of this sacred gathering, not just as a ritual, but also as a vibrant tapestry of culture, spirituality, and human connection. The Mahakumbh, often regarded as one of the largest religious congregations in the world, is more than just an event; it is a confluence of faith, tradition, and community that transcends borders and unites millions in a shared experience of devotion and reverence.

The origins of the Kumbh Mela can be traced back to ancient Hindu scriptures, where it is described as a divine gathering held every twelve years at four sacred locations in India. This cycle is not merely a measure of time; it is a cosmic rhythm that aligns the spiritual aspirations of humanity with the celestial movements of the universe. Each location—Haridwar, Allahabad (Prayagraj), Nashik, and Ujjain—brims with its own unique stories, rituals, and cultural nuances, yet they all share a common thread: the quest for purification and enlightenment.

In 2025, the Mahakumbh will take place in Prayagraj, a city steeped in history and myth, where the holy rivers Ganges, Yamuna, and the mythical Saraswati converge. This sacred confluence is not just a geographical meeting point; it symbolizes the unification of diverse beliefs and practices, drawing pilgrims from various walks of life. People journey from distant lands, often traversing treacherous paths, driven by an unwavering faith that a dip in the holy waters will cleanse them of sins and grant them spiritual liberation.

The Mahakumbh is a living testament to the power of faith and the resilience of human spirit. It is a space where age-old traditions

coexist with modernity, where sages and scholars share their wisdom alongside the vibrant energy of youth. This convergence creates a dynamic atmosphere that fosters dialogue, learning, and mutual respect. It is a celebration of life in all its forms—where spirituality intertwines with art, music, and cuisine, creating a sensory experience unlike any other.

This coffee table book aims to encapsulate the essence of the Mahakumbh, offering readers a glimpse into the myriad experiences that define this monumental event. Through stunning photography, insightful essays, and personal narratives, we seek to document the multifaceted nature of the Kumbh, showcasing not only the rituals and ceremonies but also the stories of the people who come together to make it a reality. From the solemn prayers of ascetics to the jubilant laughter of families, every moment at the Kumbh is a story waiting to be told.

As you turn the pages of this book, you will encounter the diverse tapestry of life that unfolds during the Mahakumbh. You will witness the intricate artistry of traditional crafts, the soulful melodies of devotional music, and the rich flavors of local cuisine that create a feast for the senses. You will meet pilgrims from all walks of life—each with their own unique motivations and aspirations—who come together to share in this collective experience of faith and hope.

Moreover, we delve into the challenges and triumphs of organizing such a monumental event. The Mahakumbh is not merely a celebration; it is a logistical marvel that involves meticulous planning, coordination, and community involvement. Local authorities, volunteers, and spiritual leaders work tirelessly to ensure the safety and well-being of millions of participants, creating an environment that fosters harmony and respect.

In a world often marked by division and discord, the Mahakumbh stands as a beacon of unity and inclusivity. It invites us to engage with one another, to listen and learn, and to celebrate our shared humanity. This gathering reminds us that despite our differences, we are all part of the same cosmic journey—seeking meaning, connection, and transcendence.

As we look forward to the Mahakumbh 2025, let us not forget the lessons it imparts. It challenges us to embrace diversity, to cultivate compassion, and to seek a deeper understanding of ourselves and one another. In these pages, you will find reflections that resonate beyond the confines of faith, echoing the universal truths that bind us all.

In closing, I invite you to immerse yourself in the pages of this book, to feel the pulse of the Mahakumbh, and to be inspired by the stories that unfold within. May this collection serve not only as a visual feast but also as a source of contemplation, reminding us of the enduring power of faith and the beauty of human connection. As we prepare for this monumental event, let us carry the spirit of the Kumbh in our hearts, celebrating the divine within each of us and recognizing the sacredness of our shared journey.

Welcome to the Mahakumbh—an experience that promises to enrich your soul and ignite your spirit.

the mythology of kumbh-parva

The word 'Kumbh' literally means 'Pitcher' that is a receptacle and is also synonymous to the human body. As water or liquid can be held and stored in a 'Pitcher', likewise soul known as 'Atma' is contained in the body. The occurrence of Kumbh-Parva and convergence of people at Sangam has very ancient origin and finds mention in ancient Vedic scriptures. Kumbh Mela litrally means 'Festival of the Pot'. There are many legends and anecdotes regarding Kumbh and its celebration. One of the most popular beliefs is the 'spilling over' of "Amrit" or nectar from the pitcher which became available after the churning of ocean (Samudra-Manthan) by the gods and demons, who together indulged in this activity in search of elixir to attain immortality on the advice of Lord Brahma.

The legend of 'Samudra-Manthan' describes that for the possession of the 'Pitcher' having elixir, there was fierce battle between 'Devas and Asuras'. As per well conceived strategy, Jayant, the son of Lord Indra slipped away with the 'Amrit-Kumbh' towards East. Thereafter demons rushed in hot pursuit of Jayant and it continued for twelve days and during these period demons tried to snatch the 'Amrit-Kumbh'. They made eight serious efforts in the sky and four determined efforts on the earth. During this ensuing flight and fight some drops of amrit fell on the

ground from the 'Amrit-Kumbh' despite best efforts of Jayant and the help of Sun, Moon, Jupiter and Saturn the celestial gods deputed by Lord Vishnu to help Jayant. The places where the drops of amrit fell on the ground are believed to be Prayag, Haridwar, Ujjain and Nasik. The Parva of Kumbh known as 'Amritotsav-Kumbh-Parva' is celebrated at these places every twelfth year when Sun, Moon, Jupiter and Saturn come into a definite conjunction. Since each day of gods is equal to one human year, the battle of twelve days determines the interval of twelve year between two Kumbhs at a place.

Another legend regarding Kumbh revolves around sage 'Durvasa' who was very short tempered 'Rishi'. Once being happy due to the prayers and penance of Lord Indra, sage Durvasa gave a 'Mala' that is a necklace to Indra but due to carelessness Lord Indra gave this necklace to his elephant named 'Airavat'. Airavat threw it on the ground and crushed it under his feet. Durvasa got very upset and cursed Indra. It results into all round misery and suffering not only for Indra but for others as well. For relief, gods and demons churned the ocean together. But when a Kumbh with amrit came out, the demons ran away with it and hid it in 'Nag-Lok'. Then gods took the help of 'Garur' who retrieved the 'Pitcher' from Nag-Lok but tired of the efforts put the pot down at Prayag, Haridwar, Ujjain and Nasik, where Kumbh is traditionally celebrated.

Another important interpretation is provided by practitioners of occult sciences. Their version is that human spine and ribs signify 'Mandaranchal' and 'Vasuki' respectively and elevating and enlightening tendencies and virtues represent gods but lust and wishful desires

stand for demonic forces and the ensuing eternal conflict and dilemma going on in human psyche is the real churning and visit to religious places in divine ambience helps a person to resolve the conflict and follow the path of salvation and enlightenment. As human body has been compared with a 'Kumbh', the above process when reaches its zenith, in worthy of great celebration.

There are many other prevalent legends and mythological stories regarding the occurrence of Kumbh but the common thread running through all of them, is the struggle between divine and demonic forces and the ultimate victory and celebration of divinity.

Kumbh-Parva is celebrated at the Prayag, Haridwar, Ujjain and Nasik when the planets Sun, Jupiter and Moon are in the same conjunction as at the time of 'Devasur' battle for possession of 'Amrit-Kumbh'.

Kumbh at Allahabad is celebrated when the Planet Jupiter is in Aries and the Planet Sun is in Aquarius. Aquarius is also known as Kumbh in Sanskrit. There is detailed descripition regarding Kumbh-Parva in 'Skand-Purana'. According to Skand-Purana, when Sun is in Aries and Jupiter in Aquarius, Kumbh is celebrated at Haridwar. Generally, this planetary position occurs in 'Vaishakh'; that is why Kumbh-Parva at Haridwar is commonly knows as 'Vaishakhi-Snan'. Likewise when Moon and Sun are in Aries, Kumbh is celebrated at Ujjain and when Jupiter is in Scorpio and Moon and Sun are in Leo position, Kumbh is celebrated at Nasik.

When Moon and Sun are in Capricorn and Jupiter enters in Aries or Taurus, as per 'Skand-Purana' Kumbh-Parva begins on 'Amavasya' at Prayag. The following 'Shlokas' of Skand-Purana very clearly indicate the positioning of planets when Kumbh is celebrated-

माघे मेशगते मकरे चन्द्र-भास्करौ। अमावस्या तदा योगः , कुंभाख्यस्तीर्थ-नायके।।

मकरे च दिवानाथे ह्य जगे च बृहस्पतौ। कुंभ योगो भवेत्तत्र प्रयागे ह्यति दुर्लभः।।

मकरे च दिवानाथे वृश-राषि गतं गुरौ। प्रयागे कुंभ योगो वै माघ मासे विधुक्षये।।

As Moon and Sun are in Capricorn every year in the month of 'Magh' (January), the date of 'Makar Sankranti' is never changed and is celebrated on 14th January. Due to this planetary position of Moon and Sun, bathing in the month of 'Magh' and especially on 'Makar Sankranti' day is considered very auspicious in Prayag.

No specific date and time can be ascribed when the celebrations of Kumbh-Prava was first held in Prayag. There is a mention of word 'Kumbh' in 'Shukla-Yajuraveda'. Likewise 'Atharva-Veda' describes about four Kumbhs and their occurrence at various places due to definite planetary position in the sky. Later on the importance of bathing at Prayag has been described in the great epic, 'Mahabharat'. Is is said that well planned arrangements for Kumbh were started during the 'Gupta' period. But there is no authentic record to prove it. The first authentic record of events of Kumbh-Parva is available in travel accounts of Buddhist-Chinese traveler Hiuen-Tsang. He visited India during the reign of Harsha Vardhan (617-647 A.D.). His descriptions have been dealt with in detail in the first chapter of the book.

Is is said that the present form of Kumbh celebration began during the period of 'Jagat Guru' Aadi Shankaracharya. He indulged into great deliberations with the Buddhist scholars and humbled then in religious discourses and propounded and re-established Acharya Sureshwaracharya, founded an ascetic order known as 'Dashnami' , who were to defend 'Advait' philosophy with 'Shastra and Shaastra' (arms and logic). It was a democratic system where scholars of different dispositions deliberated among themselves and then finally reached a conclusion. Is was compulsory for 'Dashnami' Sanyasis to visit Kumbh-Parva, meet common people and apprise them about the right conduct sanctioned by 'Dharma'.

During medieval period, there is no mention of Kumbh-Parva but occurrence of 'Magh Mela' and visits by royal personage is found. It is recorded that Birbal, one of the most important 'Nav-Ratans' of Akbar visited Prayag during 'Magh Mela'. Visits of Mughul emperors Jahangir and Aurangzeb were also recorded and it is said that Aurangzeb granted three villages to the temple of 'Someshwar-Mahadev' and donated one thousand gold coins and ten "Tolas' gold to the priest of the temple.

The various travel records and other works amply testify the congregation of pilgrims, tourists, Sadhus and common citizenry at the time of Magh Mela and Kumbh in Prayag on a regular basis. The details of the Kumbh-Parvas of 19th century and rare photographs are available in Regional Archives at Allahabad and it is recorded that millions of people visited these Kumbhs.

The first Kumbh of Independent India was organized in 1954 and there was all round enthusiasm among the people when about five million people congregated at Sangam.Dr.Rajendra Prasad, the first President of India and Pt. Jawahar Lal Nehru, the first Prime Minister of India also visited Allahabad during this period. The main stream of Ganga river had come very close to the Bund on city side and comparatively very less area was available for camping as well as movement of the people. This led to the great tragedy when on main bathing day of 'Mauni Amavasya', the crowd control system failed and resulting in the stampede, large number of people lost their lives and many more were injured.

This is a black spot on the history of Kumbh and its memory haunts whenever Kumbh arrangements are discussed and deliberated upon. A judicial enquiry commission headed by Justice Sir Kamala Kant Verma went into the causes of this tragedy and gave recommendations for proper conduct of Kumbh. This report and its recommendations became the basis of planning and preparation for incident free conduct of Kumbh-Parva.

The conduct of Kumbh in 1965 and 1966 (two Kumbhs were organized due to differences among the scholars and Akharas regarding exact occurrence of planetary positions), 1977 and 1989 were without any blemish and T.N. Mishra in his celebrated work on the Kumbh, 'Kumbh-Gaatha', has recorded that the Kumbh 1977 was unique in many respects and the visit and bathing of 10.3 million people on 'Mauni Amavasya' at Sangam was recorded in 'Guiness Book of Records'. It was very well planned and Mrs. Indira Gandhi, then Prime Minister of India also visited Allahabad during this period. Due to proper planning and efficient administration, it was again an incident free Kumbh-Parva.

Thus it is obvious that Kumbh has been an important aspect of Indian culture and people from all strata of society have been visiting it since ages. Without any invitation millions and millions of people from all corners of the world have been congregating at Sangam during Kumbh-Parva with the only desire to have a dip at the confluence. What do they get at Sangam? What makes them travel hundreds and thousands of Kilometres from the safe and secured environs of their homes and habitations to venture the hazards of not only the journey but also of the stay and security aspects? These questions have been haunting the human consciousness of many logicians and intellectuals since ages.

Prima-facie, these questions, doubts and queries appear to be quiet natural and even valid. But it is pertinent to understand that since time immemorial, human being has a tendency and strong desire to associate itself with the larger family, group, society or organization. Thus Kumbh-Parva has been an important occasion for individual members and families to associate themselves and merge their identity with the identity of multitude visiting Kumbh during this period. The question, doubts and queries remain till one reaches Prayag. As soon as one reaches the parade ground and crosses the Bund and proceeds towards Sangam; all uncertainties and doubts evaporate and the individual soul merges itself with the Universal soul and there is immediate transformation of one's existence from mundane to divinity.

The desire to have a dip at Sangam remains the most dominates desire in the minds of people and all other considerations become trivial. One forgets the troubles and tribulations of earthly life and not only connects oneself with the multitude of people visiting the place with the same desire but also with the ancestors, the divine ambience and the ultimate Power, the omnipresent God.

"True glory consists in doing what deserves to be written;

in writing what deserves to be read; and in so living as

to make the world happier and better for our living in it."

Pliny.

सन् 1861 के माघ मेला के सम्बन्ध में मजिस्ट्रेट, इलाहाबाद की रिपोर्ट

वर्ष 1858-59 में माघ मेले के आयोजन की अनुमति नहीं मिली थी, इसके कारण वर्ष 1860 के माघ मेले में सामान्य से अधिक यात्री आये थे, यह सूचना मजिस्ट्रेट (जिलाधिकारी), इलाहाबाद द्वारा आयुक्त, इलाहाबाद को प्रेषित माघ मेला सन् 1861 सम्बन्धी रिपोर्ट में दी गयी। इसमें यह भी बताया गया कि वर्ष 1861 में मेला से हुयी आय, वर्ष 1860 के मेले से हुई आय की तुलना में अपेक्षाकृत कम थी। सन् 1861 के माघ मेला में 10228/- रूपया एवं 10 आना की आय हुई थी। वर्ष 1861 में माघ मेला सकुशल सम्पन्न कराने के उपलक्ष्य में मेला प्रभारी रतन सिंह को रू0 300/- की खिलअत (सम्मान) दिये जाने का प्रस्ताव किया गया था।

क्षेत्रीय अभिलेखागार, प्रयागराज

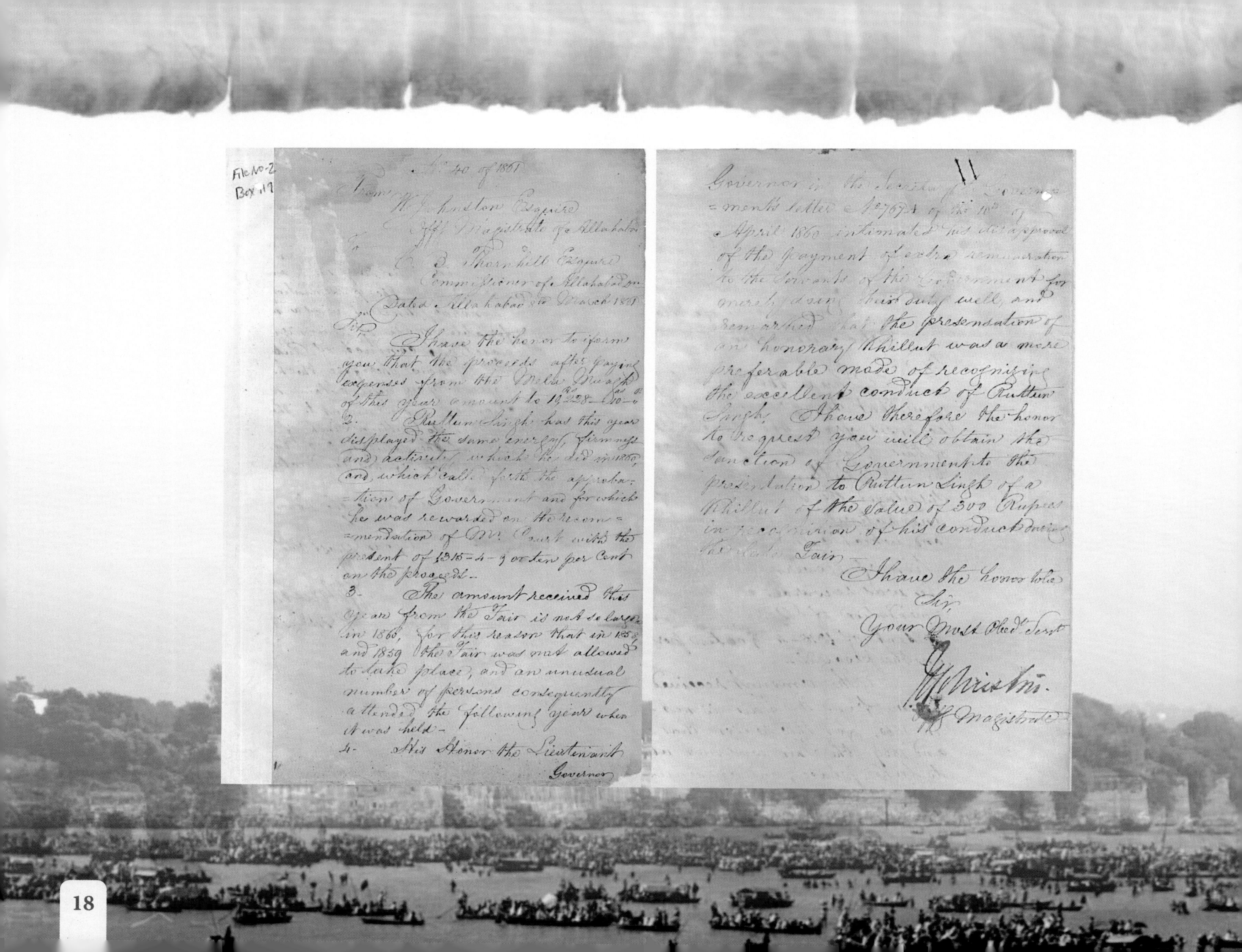

File No-2
Box 19

No. 40 of 1861

From
W. Johnston Esquire
Offg Magistrate of Allahabad

To
C. B. Thornhill Esquire
Commissioner of Allahabad Dn

Dated Allahabad 8th March 1861

Sir,

I have the honor to inform you that the proceeds after paying expenses from the Mela Magh of this year amount to Rs 10,228–as 10–p 0

2. Ruttun Singh has this year displayed the same energy, firmness and activity which he did in 1860, and which called forth the approbation of Government and for which he was rewarded on the recommendation of Mr. Court with the present of 1315–4–9 or ten per Cent on the proceeds –

3. The amount received this year from the Fair is not so large as in 1860, for this reason that in 1858 and 1859 the Fair was not allowed to take place, and an unusual number of persons consequently attended the following year when it was held –

4. His Honor the Lieutenant Governor in the Secretary of Government's letter No 767A of the 10th of April 1860 intimated his disapproval of the payment of extra remuneration to the servants of the Government for merely doing their duty well, and remarked that the presentation of an honorary Khillut was a more preferable mode of recognizing the excellent conduct of Ruttun Singh. I have therefore the honor to request you will obtain the sanction of Government to the presentation to Ruttun Singh of a Khillut of the value of 300 Rupees in recognition of his conduct during the late Fair –

I have the honor to be
Sir,
Your most Obed Servt
W. Johnston
Offg Magistrate

माघ मेला हेतु परगना चायल के ग्राम विरोही पटटी की 261 एकड़ भूमि के अधिग्रहण के सम्बन्ध में जारी अधिसूचना- 3 जनवरी-1866

पत्रा0 संख्या - 25 डिफरेन्ट डिस्ट्रिक्ट बोर्ड आफ रेवेन्यू

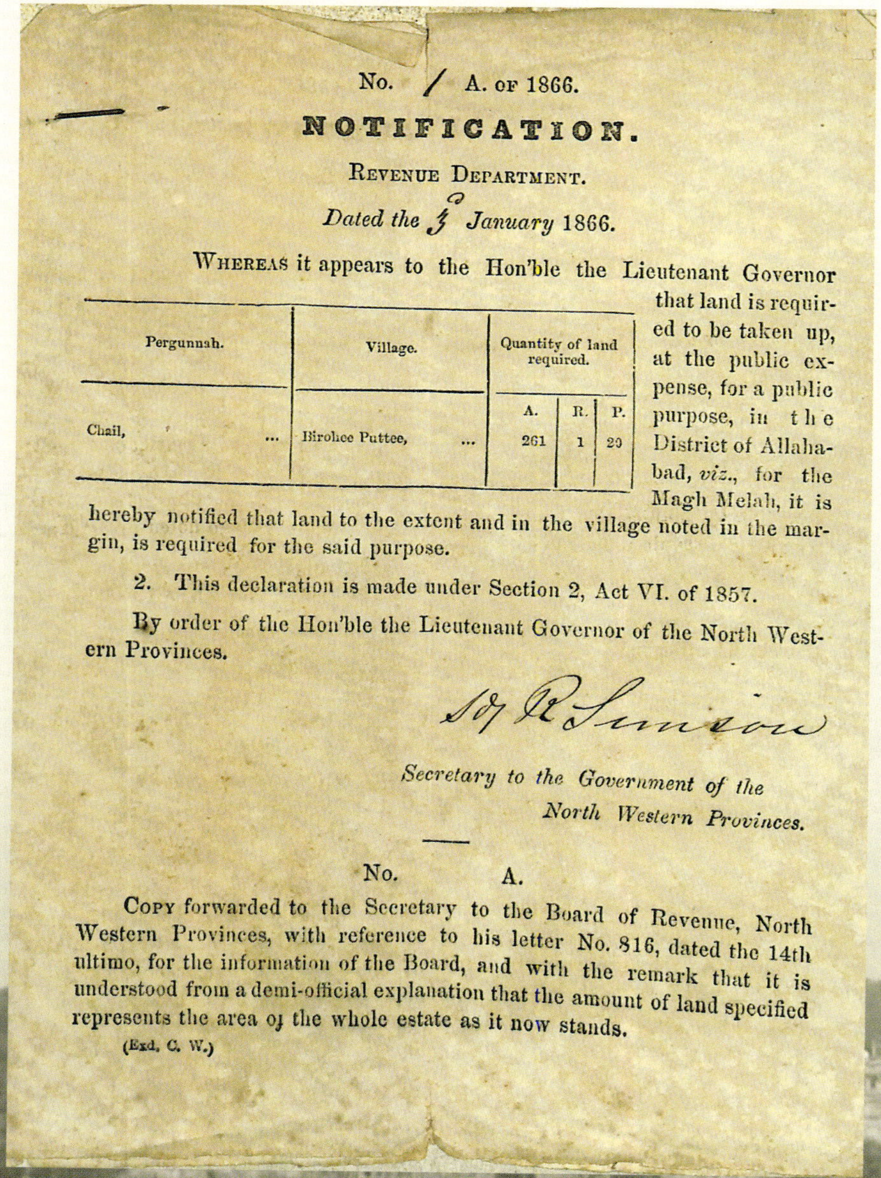

No. / A. of 1866.

NOTIFICATION.

Revenue Department.

Dated the 3 January 1866.

Whereas it appears to the Hon'ble the Lieutenant Governor that land is required to be taken up, at the public expense, for a public purpose, in the District of Allahabad, *viz.*, for the Magh Melah, it is hereby notified that land to the extent and in the village noted in the margin, is required for the said purpose.

Pergunnah.	Village.	Quantity of land required.		
		A.	R.	P.
Chail, ...	Birohee Puttee, ...	261	1	20

2. This declaration is made under Section 2, Act VI. of 1857.

By order of the Hon'ble the Lieutenant Governor of the North Western Provinces.

Sd/ R Simson

Secretary to the Government of the North Western Provinces.

No. A.

Copy forwarded to the Secretary to the Board of Revenue, North Western Provinces, with reference to his letter No. 816, dated the 14th ultimo, for the information of the Board, and with the remark that it is understood from a demi-official explanation that the amount of land specified represents the area of the whole estate as it now stands.

(Exd. C. W.)

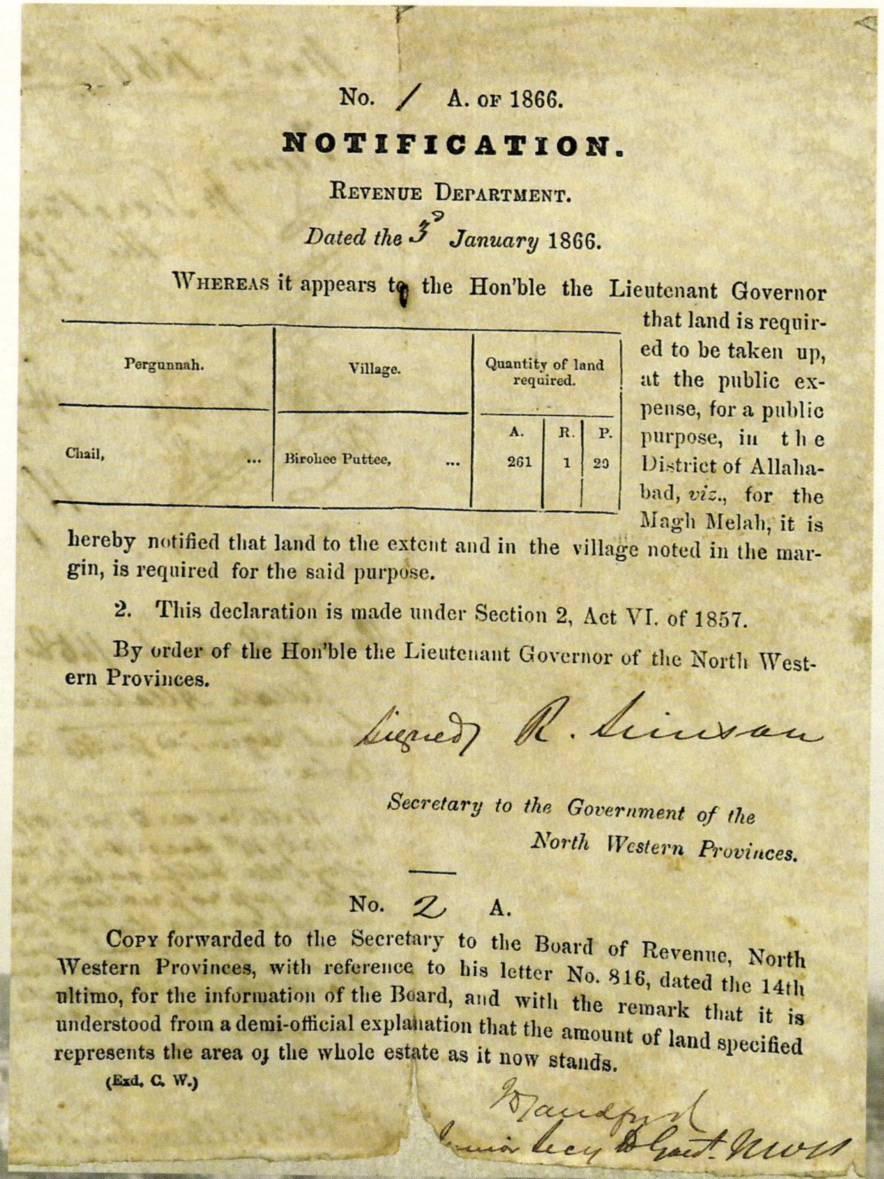

No. / A. of 1866.

NOTIFICATION.

Revenue Department.

Dated the 3 January 1866.

Whereas it appears to the Hon'ble the Lieutenant Governor that land is required to be taken up, at the public expense, for a public purpose, in the District of Allahabad, *viz.*, for the Magh Melah, it is hereby notified that land to the extent and in the village noted in the margin, is required for the said purpose.

Pergunnah.	Village.	Quantity of land required.		
		A.	R.	P.
Chail, ...	Birohee Puttee, ...	261	1	20

2. This declaration is made under Section 2, Act VI. of 1857.

By order of the Hon'ble the Lieutenant Governor of the North Western Provinces.

Signed) R. Simson

Secretary to the Government of the North Western Provinces.

No. 2 A.

Copy forwarded to the Secretary to the Board of Revenue, North Western Provinces, with reference to his letter No. 816, dated the 14th ultimo, for the information of the Board, and with the remark that it is understood from a demi-official explanation that the amount of land specified represents the area of the whole estate as it now stands.

(Exd. C. W.)

Sandford
Junior Secy to Govt. N.W.P.

कुम्भ मेला सन् 1870 के सकुशल सम्पन्न होने पर मजिस्ट्रेट, इलाहाबाद द्वारा कमिश्नर, इलाहाबाद को लिखा गया पत्र

इलाहाबाद के कार्यवाहक मजिस्ट्रेट ने मण्डलायुक्त, इलाहाबाद को सन् 1870 कुम्भ मेला के सकुशल सम्पन्न होने की सूचना पत्र के माध्यम से दी। पत्र में यह अवगत कराया कि छोटी-मोटी घटनाएं छोड़कर मेले में तीर्थ यात्रियों का अभूतपूर्व जन समूह उपस्थित हुआ तथा कोई अप्रिय घटना नहीं हुयी। बताया गया है कि ईस्ट इण्डिया रेलवे ने मुख्य स्नान पर्व में इलाहाबाद के लिए 39505 टिकटों का विक्रय किया था। मेला स्थल पर चिकित्सा, जनसुविधाओं, पुलिस तथा प्रशासनिक प्रबन्ध का विस्तार से उल्लेख करते हुए बताया गया है कि मेला में विभिन्न स्रोतों से कुल रू0 41824/- की राजस्व प्राप्ति हुई थी।

क्षेत्रीय अभिलेखागार, प्रयागराज

No 32 of 1870 (177)

From,

J. C. Robertson Esqr
Offg Magistrate of Allahabad

To

F. O. Mayne Esqr C.B.
Commissioner of 4th Division

Dated Allahabad the 24th March 1870

Sir,

I have the honor to inform you that the Magh Mela which this year being a "Koombh" attracted an unprecedented crowd has passed without any serious accident to life or property and without any crime in the fair itself beyond petty thefts. a fire broke out and destroyed some huts but very little property and Rs 66-„-„ were refunded to those persons whose huts were destroyed. On the 31st „ which was the great bathing day on which the several sects went in procession there was an immense concourse of people, the E. I. Railway Company for that day alone issued 39505 Tickets for Allahabad and from what I have heard there is no doubt that several persons were left

left at the different Railway stations owing to there being no accomodation for them - the roads on all sides were crowded with travellers. -

2nd Fortunately the river had this year receded towards the Jhoosee Bank leaving a large tract of land available for the fair and also the water being very shallow at the junction of the Rivers proved a great assistance in prevention of accidents - The ground on this side was marked off in streets and let out for shops &ca in the usual manner while at rear of each street mat latrines were erected on the trench principle - and a very large number of sweepers entertained. - The result was a most complete success as far as conservancy was concerned - and though I visited the fair almost daily and one of my assistants held his Court there the whole day for about a month - no complaints were made to us - and I believe that Dr. Irving agrees with me as to the completeness of the Conservancy. -

3rd / 4

(173)

3rd. A Dispensary was erected on this side of the river in the centre of the fair with a large supply of Medicines – but it seemed adviseable to Dr. Irving and myself considering the enormous number of persons collected that the hospital for infectious diseases should be on the opposite side of the river – For this purpose a hut was erected and a Native Doctor appointed while a boat painted white was kept for the special purpose of taking over infected persons – The Hospital Returns show that of 22 persons sent to hospital 12 died but it must be remembered that several of these never had been in the fair at all for any person on the road near there who was attacked, was at once sent in to the Hospital –

4th. The watch and ward and all other Police arrangements were carried out by special police enlisted as Chowkedars under the management of Inspector Narain Singh whom I cannot sufficiently praise for the admirable arrangements made by him for Police, Conservancy and general management, and also for the great tact shown by him on the bathing days in arrangeing the order for the different processions to pass, and so preventing any disturbance between rival sects of Faquers – Having been personally present during those days I can vouch for the difficulties which he had to encounter and for the ability shown by him in over-coming them and I have much pleasure in again recommending him for a reward of Rupees 500 " " –

5th. The whole collections amounted to Rupees 41,824-10-0 and expenditure of which detail is submitted to Rs. 12,815-4-1 leaving a balance of Rs 29009-5-11 credited to the Nuzool Fund – These accounts were tested on the spot by Mr. R. Smeaton assistant Magistrate who reported them as satisfactory and that to the best of his belief the details given in the Books of account faithfully represented the state of affairs and that he failed, after a searching examination, to discover any discrepancy –

6th. As it appeared inadvisable to

(175)

to have any cultivation on the land below the Bund situated within Cantonments but close to the Fair arrangements were made with the Cantonment Magistrate that he should for this year forego cultivation of it receiving in lieu the sum for which he had farmed it last year Vizt Rs 1175-0-0 also owing to this being a 'Koombh fair' I considered it necessary to relieve Narain Singh of charge of the City and a police inspector was appointed in his place for whose services Rs 350-0-0 have been charged to this account.-

7th The details of expenditure are as follows.-

	Rs.	as.	p.
Police charges	5,023	15	"
Conservancy &c	2,559	14	6
Public Works - Vizt Levelling Roads - making Latrines &c	1,916	10	6
×Miscellaneous	3,314	12	1
	Rs 12,815	4	1

The latter item includes

	Rs.	as.	p.
Compensation for land	Rs 1,877	10	"
Do Loss by fire & payment for extinguishing &c	731	8	"
Medical attendance & Medicine	324	6	1
Printing and Stationery	52	"	"
Lighting	106	"	"
Cost of Tools	63	12	"
Dieting Prisoners	92	"	"
Petty items	67	"	"

8th The item of Rs 1,877-10-0 includes Rs 1,175-0-0 paid to Cantonment Magistrate referred to in para: 7 and Rs 702-10-0 paid to the Zemindar of Berahee Puttee under Board of Revenues No 513 dated 30th October 1869.-

I have the honor to be
Sir,
Your Most Obedt St.
[illegible signature]
Offg Magistrate

अर्द्ध कुम्भ मेला सन् 1876 के सम्बन्ध में मजिस्ट्रेट (जिलाधिकारी) इलाहाबाद द्वारा दी गयी रिपोर्ट

जे0सी0 राबर्टसन मजिस्ट्रेट (जिलाधिकारी), इलाहाबाद ने कमिश्नर, इलाहाबाद को 23 मार्च, 1876 को लिखे पत्र में अवगत कराया कि सन् 1876 में सम्पन्न हुए अर्द्ध कुम्भ में मुख्य स्नान दिवस अर्थात् 26 जनवरी तक लगभग 150000 लोग उपस्थित हुए।

कुम्भ मेले हेतु सरकार द्वारा 10220/- रू0 आवंटित किए गए जिसके सापेक्ष सरकार द्वारा मेले की व्यवस्थाओं में 9368 रू0 14 आना 1 पैसा व्यय हुआ। सरकार को कुम्भ मेले में करों से 30881/- रू0 की आय हुयी। इस प्रकार कुम्भ मेले में समस्त व्यय करने के बाद भी 11292 रू0 3 आना 5 पैसे का लाभ हुआ। उक्त धनराशि का उपयोग सामान्य कार्यों हेतु किया जा सकता था। साथ ही कुम्भ मेले में उच्च स्तरीय प्रबन्धन हेतु इन्सपेक्टर लियाकत हुसैन को रू0 500 का पुरस्कार भी दिए जाने की अनुशंसा की गयी।

पत्रावली संख्या 21/1876 क्षेत्रीय अभिलेखागार, प्रयागराज

PROCEEDINGS

OF THE

GOVERNMENT OF THE N.-W. PROVINCES,

IN THE

GENERAL DEPARTMENT,

FOR THE MONTH OF

MAY 1876.

INDEX No.		PROGS. No. AND DATE.
Nos. 1 TO 4.	From Commissioner, Allahabad Division, to Officiating Secretary to Government, North-Western Provinces, (No. 47.)—Dated Allahabad, the 29th March, 1876.	APRIL 29, 1876.
No 1.		Nos. 29 TO 32.
		No. 29.

SIR,—I have the honour to forward the Magistrate of Allahabad's report on the last Magh Mela.

2. It was the half Kumbh fair, and the attendance was far greater than usual: there was no sickness, no unusual crime, and with the exception of the fire, which has already been reported, all went off well.

3. Mr. Robertson recommends a reward of Rs. 500 to Leakut Hussain, the City Inspector, who had charge of the fair; it is a large sum, but half Kumbh fairs only occur in every seventh year, and as the duties are far heavier in these years, I think he has earned the larger reward.

3. There are unusual charges for revenue and malikana, but they must be passed, for they cannot be contested.

4. There is a surplus of Rs. 11,000 at the disposal of Government, which I hope may be spent in Allahabad.

I have, &c.,
G. H. M. RICKETTS.
Commissioner.

No. 2. From Magistrate of Allahabad, to Commissioner, Allahabad Division, (No. 31.)—Dated Allahabad the 23rd March, 1876. No. 30.

SIR,—The past Magh Mela, of which the statement of receipts and disbursements is herewith submitted, having been a half Kumbh one, was more numerously attended than on ordinary occasions, and it is calculated that on the chief bathing day, 26th January, about 150,000 persons were present, but there was no disturbance of order and no crime, beyond a few petty thefts, while there were no robberies in the district of persons coming to or returning from the fair, also there was no sickness. Unfortunately, on the 26th a fire occurred, which resulted in heavy loss of life, but as has already been reported, no blame is attributable to any one,—the fire having been purely accidental, and rendered more serious by a very high wind which was blowing at the time.

No. 7, dated 2nd February, 1876.

2. The total collections amounted to Rs. 30,881-1-6, and expenditure Rs. 9,368-14-1, leaving a balance Rs. 21,512-3-5, of which, after deducting Rs. 10,220 already allotted by Government, Rs. 11,292-3-5 are available for general purposes. The accounts were examined by Mr. Pears, and certified by him as having been correct and properly prepared. Under the heading of compensation for land, is an increased charge which requires explanation, viz.:—Formerly, the land on which the fair is usually held not having been on the touzi, there was no charge for land revenue, but the land in ques-

(2)

GENERAL DEPARTMENT.

NORTH-WESTERN PROVINCES, MAY 1876.

INDEX No.		PROGS. No. AND DATE.
No. 2.	tion having recently been assessed by the Se[illegible] Officer at Rs. 1,145, it became necessary to charge this item, and also [illegible] 99, malikana, payable to the zemindar under the Sudder Dewani Adalat's decision, 8th August, 1862. Against the receipts from the fair, the remainder consists of Rs. 350, paid annually to the Cantonment Magistrate.	APRIL 29 1876. No. 30.

3. Mr. Pears, who was in charge of the fair, has recorded very strongly his opinion as to the excellent arrangements which were made by Inspector Liakat Hussain, on whom devolved the direct superintendence. Taking into consideration the fact that the fair being a half Kumbh, was much more largely attended and consequently more difficult to manage than an ordinary one, and that the management of the processions which take place at the Kumbh and half Kumbh fairs is a business which, if not managed with great tact and firmness, might easily cause disturbance. I would suggest that in the present instance Liakat Hussain receive a reward of Rs. 500, he having in my opinion earned it fairly by hard work and by being careful that the collections were properly made, and that excessive expenditure was not incurred.

I have, &c.,
J. C. ROBERTSON,
Magistrate.

इलाहाबाद में आयोजित हुए कुम्भ-सन् 1882 में सम्मिलित हुए अखाड़ों का विवरण

इलाहाबाद में आयोजित हुए सन् 1882 के कुम्भ मेले में विभिन्न अखाड़ों ने भाग लिया। जो निम्नवत् हैं:-

1. निर्वाणी (नागा गोशाई)
2. निरंजनी (जूनी से सम्बद्ध)
3. बैरागी-इनके तीन सम्प्रदाय हैं

i. निर्वाणी
ii. दिगम्बरी
iii. निर्मोही

4. छोटा अखाड़ा पंचायती (उदासी)
5. बड़ा अखाड़ा पंचायती (बधुआ अखाड़ा)
6. निर्मली (सिक्ख), इनके साथ थे बिन्द्रावनी

सामान्य प्रशासन विभाग -प्रोसीडिंग, सन्-1882

74/81

179

No. 3295 of 1882.

RESOLUTION.

General Department.

Dated Naini Tal, the 21st September, 1882.

Read—

Letter from the Commissioner, Allahabad Division, No. $\frac{2818}{81}$, dated 16th June, 1882, and enclosures, being the report on the Mágh Mela held at Allahabad during the month of January, 1882.

Read also—

Report by the Sanitary Commissioner, North-Western Provinces and Oudh, as contained in paragraphs 166 to 220 of his Provincial Sanitary Report for the year 1881.

Observations.—The reports on the Mágh Mela of 1882 place the history of the fair before Government in a clear and connected manner. On the present occasion, the Mela was of a special character, deriving peculiar importance from certain planetary conjunctions which recur every twelfth year; and the attendance was consequently very large. From the figures given it would appear that on the great day, which fell on the 19th of January, nearly a million of people were present, completely filling the space set apart at the confluence of the rivers Ganges and Jumna, and overflowing into the adjoining tracts; while the number who remained on the spot from first to last probably somewhat exceeded 100,000. All parts of India and all varieties of caste were represented in the enormous crowd; and although the fair was primarily a religious gathering, it became for the time being a huge commercial bazar, in which a very large trade in all kinds of articles appropriate to the occasion was carried on.

2. Mr. T. Benson, C.S., Joint-Magistrate of Allahabad, was the officer in immediate charge of the entire fair. Under his orders, which were chiefly carried out through Saiyid Liákat Husain, the City Inspector of Police, who has for many years held subordinate charge of the Mágh Mela, the necessary arrangements were commenced in good time, and by the close of December streets had been laid out, roads metalled, sites leased, camps arranged, latrines erected, bathing platforms constructed, a hospital and dispensary prepared, and a temporary court-house and police offices constituted. The conservancy arrangements would seem to have been capable of improvement, but on the whole the system adopted worked fairly well. On future occasions, however, care should be taken to act on the recommendations of the Sanitary Commissioner in regard to the latrine arrangements on the site of the fair; and special attention should be given to the cleanliness of the ground adjoining the site, as well as in and round about the city of Allahabad, where large numbers of the pilgrims were accommodated.

3. The police force entertained consisted of between five and six hundred men, and cost Rs. 3,567. A head-office (kotwáli) and two police-stations were constituted within the precincts of the fair, and excellent

order was maintained throughout. In the prevention and detection of such crime as occurred (only 50 cases of theft were reported) the police were successful; and they were also found efficient in assisting generally in the management of the fair and in supervising the conservancy. It is satisfactory that in a gathering so large, and with elements of danger so numerous, only one fatal accident occurred.

4. The medical arrangements were made by Dr. H. S. Smith, the Civil Surgeon of Allahabad. A dispensary, with an hospital attached, was erected in the main street of the fair and put in charge of a Native Doctor, assisted by five subordinates specially deputed by the Surgeon-General, the whole being supervised by Assistant Surgeon Babu Kali Das Nundy. A detached hospital was also provided for contagious or epidemic diseases, but it was found to be inconveniently situated as regards accessibility. An outbreak of cholera, which at one time threatened to be very severe, marred the otherwise successful conduct of operations. The first case was reported on the 16th of January; and to provide for the expected influx of cholera patients, supplementary hospitals were at once organised. The number of cholera admissions at the several dispensaries (11 were opened altogether) was 443, and of these cases 231 proved fatal. It is certainly matter of satisfaction that the mortality was, in the circumstances, comparatively small. Apart from cholera patients, the number of cases of disease and injury treated at the dispensary and hospitals was 1,472. The total medical cost was only Rs. 1,323. On future occasions care should be taken that the hospitals for the treatment of epidemic disease are conveniently located and easy of access, and that a sufficient number of persons are employed to inspect and report on the health of the people residing on the site of the fair and to remove promptly the sick from the midst of the crowd. In the event of an outbreak of epidemic disease, District Officers along the lines of road and rail over which the pilgrims return to their homes should be promptly communicated with (demi-officially) by the Magistrate in charge of the fair. On the recent occasion the fears entertained regarding the spread of the epidemic throughout the country by returning pilgrims were happily not realised; but none the less should District Officers along the return routes have been warned of the danger.

5. The receipts and charges of the fair, as compared with those of the last *Kumbh* Mela, were as under:—

	1870.			1882.		
	Rs.	a.	p.	Rs.	a.	p.
Receipts	41,824	10	0	49,840	4	3
Charges	12,815	4	1	20,228	0	7
Surplus ...	29,009	5	11	29,612	3	8

The income was mainly derived from indirect taxation on pilgrims visiting the fair, the chief sources being leases of monopolies, rents of sites, and taxes on callings. Apart from monopolies, on which the Lieutenant-Governor and Chief Commissioner's views will be found below, the items of receipt seem legitimate and unobjectionable. The price of food and other neces-

(3)

saries was certainly high, but this was due to the sudden and abnormal demand. The expediency of raising an income so much in excess of the actual requirements will be separately discussed. The items of expenditure marginally noted call for no comment. The amount for Public Works, which seems high, includes Rs. 1,590 for the construction of a new road across the Fort esplanade, and Rs. 3,028 paid to the Military Public Works Department as compensation for the damage done by the immense traffic to the roads in the vicinity of the Fort.

	Rs.	a.	p.
Police	3,567	5	4
Conservancy ...	4,237	7	7
Medical	1,323	7	2
Public Works ...	9,203	6	6
Miscellaneous ...	1,896	6	0

6. From the surplus the Lieutenant-Governor is pleased to sanction the immediate disbursement of the following grants:—

	Rs.
Alfred Park	3,000
Allahabad Library and Museum	3,600
Colvin Dispensary	2,600
Honorarium to City Inspector	500
Compensation to toll contractor	1,700
Boat for bathing-ghát	84
Total ...	11,484

The surplus is thus Rs. 18,128-3-8; and this sum is available for credit, under standing orders, as an item of provincial revenues. Deducting the balance of the debt on the Mayo Hall, amounting to Rs. 4,076, there remains a net sum of Rs. 14,052-3-8 at the disposal of the Government.

7. It remains to consider the several recommendations made by the officers who have reported on the fair, and to deal with special points calling for notice. In such matters as the cutting down of high crops, inspection of *Prágwáls'* premises, issue of railway tickets, &c., it seems unnecessary for the Government to interfere, as these may safely be left to the discretion of local authorities. But on the following questions the Lieutenant-Governor and Chief Commissioner desires to place his views on record.

(*a*) *The future management of the fair.*—As the fair is held within the limits of the municipality of Allahabad, the municipal committee should be consulted in all important matters connected with the general management of the fair. Proposals as to supervision, taxation, conservancy, police, and medical arrangements, should then be prepared and submitted to the Commissioner, who can refer to the Government if he considers it necessary to do so. The entire executive responsibility must, however, rest with the Magistrate of the district.

(*b*) *Taxation.*—The system of disposing to the highest bidder of monopolies for the sale of certain articles, without reservation as to prices, can hardly be justified, and should not again be adopted. The plan of letting shops by auction to the highest bidder ought also to be discontinued. Tenders should be invited, and shops should be let to persons who tender fair rents and are known to be of respectable character.

(4)

(*c*) Connected indirectly with the preceding question, and important in the interests of the public, is that of the alleged adulteration of the food sold at the fair. The only safeguard against this is careful inspection of the stores by responsible officers, and the public expulsion from the fair of persons detected in selling adulterated articles. Public notice of this arrangement should be given beforehand.

(*d*) *Disposal of the surplus proceeds of the fair.*—Under existing orders, the surplus, which falls under the account head of nazúl, lapses to provincial revenues, and is at the disposal of the Government. But the Lieutenant-Governor and Chief Commissioner hopes that it may eventually be found possible to place the surplus funds at the disposal of the Allahabad municipality, to be expended on municipal works directly or indirectly connected with the fair. No definite orders can at present be passed on this matter, as the whole question of district and municipal finance is under separate consideration.

8. In conclusion, Sir Alfred Lyall desires to record his appreciation of the services of the several officers engaged in the management of the fair. To Mr. Benson in particular, as the officer in general charge of the entire arrangements, the thanks of the Government are due for his successful management and excellent report; while the valuable assistance rendered by Dr. Smith, Civil Surgeon, Mr. Alone, District Superintendent of Police, Inspector Liákat Husain, and Assistant Surgeon Kali Das Nundy, in their respective departments, merits full acknowledgment.

J. R. REID,
Offg. Secretary to Government,
N.-W. Provinces and Oudh.

ORDER.—Ordered that copies of the above Resolution be forwarded to the Commissioner, Allahabad Division, for his own information, and for communication to the gentlemen concerned.

Ordered also that a copy be forwarded to the Accountant-General, North-Western Provinces and Oudh, for information.

Extracts from letter from Commissioner, Allahabad Division, No. $\frac{2818}{81}$, dated 16th June, 1882, and from report by Mr. T Benson, C.S., Joint-Magistrate, Allahabad, dated 28th April, 1882.

Ordered further that the above Resolution, together with the documents noted on the margin, be published in the *North-Western Provinces and Oudh Government Gazette,* for general information.

By order, &c.,
R. SMEATON,
Junior Secy. to Govt., N.-W. P. and Oudh.

इलाहाबाद में आयोजित हुए कुम्भ-सन् 1882 में सम्मिलित हुए अखाड़ों का विवरण

इलाहाबाद में आयोजित हुए सन् 1882 के कुम्भ मेले में विभिन्न अखाड़ों ने भाग लिया। जो निम्नवत् हैं:-

1. निर्वाणी (नागा गोशाई)
2. निरंजनी (जूनी से सम्बद्ध)
3. बैरागी-इनके तीन सम्प्रदाय हैं
   - i. निर्वाणी
   - ii. दिगम्बरी
   - iii. निर्मोही
4. छोटा अखाड़ा पंचायती (उदासी)
5. बड़ा अखाड़ा पंचायती (बधुआ अखाड़ा)
6. निर्मली (सिक्ख), इनके साथ थे बिन्द्रावनी

सामान्य प्रशासन विभाग -प्रोसीडिंग, सन्-1882

SERIAL No.

GENERAL DEPARTMENT.

NORTH-WESTERN PROVINCES AND OUDH, OCTOBER, 1882.

PROGS. No. AND DATE.

No. 3. — Sep. 23, 1882. — No. 67.

Fakírs.

8. The most conspicuous attendants at the fair were the *fakírs* or religious ascetics, who on these occasions only (*Kumbh* Melas) attend by their corporate bodies. A number of mendicant *fakírs*, common *bairagis*, always camp about Tribeni, and increase in number at the Mágh Mela, but the corporations of the other sects only assemble formally on these great festivals. To each corporation was assigned a space of ground, within which it erected a temporary village or town for the accommodation of its members, in the centre of which moved the standards of the guild on a lofty flagstaff. These encampments were orderly and well laid out, and of a comfortable description, fitted for the accommodation of the fat monks who temporarily occupied them. The camp of the *bairagis* however was very different, being merely a space of ground, about 12 acres in extent, marked off on the side of the main street opposite the kotwali, and known as the "Khak Chauk." It was with difficulty that these low class mendicants were confined to this space and induced to preserve any order: their habits are filthy and disgusting, and their devices for extorting money, such as sitting on spikes, swinging themselves by the feet, of the commonest description.

The various camps formed were—

(1) *Nirbani*, a Nanga Goshain.

(2) *Niranjani*, with whom were associated the *Junni*.

(3) *Bairagis* (already alluded to), including three sects—*Nirbani*, *Nirmohi*, and *Digambari*.

(4) *Chhota Akhara Panchayati* (*Udasi*).

(5) *Bara Akhara Panchayati*, with which was also the *Bandhua Akhara*.

(6) *Nirmali* (Sikhs), with whom were the *Bindrabani*.

All of these sects (except the *bairagis*, who are wandering homeless mendicants, though each man may have his own *localé*) have permanent houses—(whether monasteries or banking houses, such as those of the *Akhara Panchayati*) in various parts of Allahabad, and from those they move to their temporary camps in formal procession at the beginning of the month, and put up the standard, round which collected all the adherents of the sect coming to the fair from all parts. On the three great days (*Sankarant*, *Amawas*, and *Basant*) each of the six sects went separately down to bathe in formal procession. The most noticeable features being the body of naked *fakírs* closing the procession of each of the two first sects (the *Nirbani* and the *Niranjani*), and the gorgeous silken banners and elephant trappings of the wealthier guilds. The marshalling and conduct of these processions was a tedious matter, and in particular disputes amongst the three rival sects of *bairagis* caused difficulty; but this difficult and tedious matter was well got through by the City Kotwal, with only one slight disturbance in the *Niranjani* procession on the 19th. Besides the above sects camped in the fair, there were a large number of *sanyásis* camped on the Ganges sands on the left or north bank in Jhúsi: these too formed a village, with many outlying single huts. They are regarded with great reverence, and chose this locality in order to be free from the sanitary and other regulations of the fair. Coming round by Rájghát bridge-of-boats, they had nearly four miles to go to bathe at Tribeni, though by boat the distance was nothing.

Trades.

9. The majority of the frequenters of the fair are of course religious pilgrims, but those who come to pray remain to buy. Besides the confectioners and grain-sellers who supply the immediate wants

SERIAL No.

GENERAL DEPARTMENT.

NORTH-WESTERN PROVINCES AND OUDH, OCTOBER, 1882.

PROGS. No. AND DATE.

No. 3. — Sep. 23, 1882. — No. 67.

of the pilgrims, the most noticeable shops are those of the coral necklace-sellers, who occupied 225 linear cubits of shop front space, and who came mainly from Calcutta and Bombay; the country cloth merchants (*lohiwálas*) from Muttra and Bindraban, occupying 132½ cubits; and book-sellers from Benares and Lucknow, 100 cubits. Braziers and dealers in metal, mostly local, and also from Hassanpur, Benares, Fyzabad, and Moradabad had several shops. There were too what might be called ecclesiastical shops, were rosaries, shells, pebbles from the Nerbadda, and other sacred objects were for sale in quantities, as also huge images of all sorts and sizes by the score, sacrificial lamps and spoons, and so on. Besides these, cap-sellers, dealers in Moradabad wares, in ivory from the Punjáb, some Kashmir and Cabul merchants, Brummagem jewellery, and cheap toys and other gim-crack goods, and the ordinary local retailers of stone cups and saucers.

A Parsi company opened a theatre, which failed to attract any audiences: a travelling giant, and an exhibition of the decapitation trick did better. Missionaries had their stalls as usual for the sale of books and for preaching; while the Government post-office and a dispensary were opened for the use of the public.

Management and superintendence of the fair.

10. It has of late years been always customary to entrust the management and superintendence of the fair to the City Inspector of Police, or Kotwal, acting under the general supervision of the Joint-Magistrate in charge of the city. Similar arrangements prevailed at the last *Kumbh* Mela in 1870, when Inspector Narayan Singh managed the fair under the superintendence of the Officiating Magistrate, Mr. James Robertson. The question of how the *Kumbh* Mela of 1882 should be managed came up when I was officiating as Magistrate for a short time in October, 1881, and on 26th October I passed an order directing that the City Inspector, Saiyid Liakat Husain, who has managed the Magh Melas successfully for some years past, should also make the arrangements for the present year, acting under my supervision (I foreseeing that when the fair came on, I should be Joint-Magistrate of the city), and this arrangement was confirmed by Mr. Neale, who took charge as Magistrate on 14th November. Some agitation was already on foot against this appointment, and Mr. Markham had already made inquiries into some anonymous petitions against the Kotwal; but I believe the objection to the appointment of a Musalman Inspector was more sentimental than real: a good deal of the agitation was no doubt due to various parties who were anxious to get the leasing arrangement and management into their own hands. In view of the fact that the Police Inspector was the only person conversant with the ordinary arrangements of the fair (for neither myself nor any other of the district staff had managed a Magh Mela before), I felt no hesitation in passing the above order, which had the approval of Mr. Markham, the regular Magistrate of the district. At the same time, I would now say that the magnitude of the *Kumbh* Fair (which I did not then foresee) would have fully warranted the deputation of a special officer for the duty, and that it might possibly be desirable that the superior officer in charge should himself superintend more closely the putting up to auction of the various farms and other money matters, and also the conservancy arrangements.

Site of the fair.

11. The site of the fair is the Ganges bed to the east of the Fort, and of the embankment which runs northward from the Fort to Daraganj; on the south runs the Jumna, and on the east the Ganges. In the present year the main Ganges stream took its course to the extreme east of its bed, leaving an ample space for the fair. When I first visited the site on 4th November, the middle space where the fair would be, was soft treacherous mud, and there was a channel of water running along underneath the *bandh* to west. Nothing

SERIAL No.

GENERAL DEPARTMENT.

NORTH-WESTERN PROVINCES AND OUDH, OCTOBER, 1882.

PROGS. No. AND DATE.

No. 3. much could be done beyond draining off this channel (or rather pool) of water into the Jumna on the south as much as possible. I again visited the fair on 22nd November, when flags had been put up to mark out the roads, but did not see it again till 22nd December, as I was absent in camp. Preparations were then in full swing: the road across the Fort Esplanade, by which conveyances drive up to the *bandh*, was being metalled, and the fair roads laid out. The mud bed mostly dried up, leaving the ground full of deep wide fissures, a regular net-work; and to make a practicable road across it was a work of some difficulty: a considerable embankment too had to be constructed across the pool at the foot of the *bandh;* and at other places owing to quicksands, quantities of *karb* had to be thrown down, and what were in fact floating bridges formed. Sep. 23, 1882. No. 67.

12. The fair consists of one wide road, leading from the enbankment semi-circularly to a point where in October the Jumna and Ganges met, at the end of the soft mud tract already spoken of, a distance of about a mile; but by the end of December the Ganges had receded so far eastwards and southwards, as to leave beyond this point a wide tract of firm sand, on a lower level, extending out on both sides towards the two rivers: the *sangam* or confluence had shifted half a mile off (and moved further during the fair), and this wide open space formed a most valuable open dressing space for the bathers. The main street described is entirely devoted to shop sites, but on each side of it run out side-streets, along which were marked off spaces let out for the erection of *baras* or lodging-houses kept by the various *prágwáls* and *pándas* for the accommodation of their clients, the pilgrims. With a view to the size of the fair this year all the roads were made much wider than usual. On the right hand or west side of the street, approaching the river end of the street, is the kotwali, where the City Inspector resides during the fair, and where the police head-quarters are. There too I had a temporary kutcherry. Beyond it, on the same side of the road, are five shops only, known as those within the gate. On the opposite side of the road are the Khak Chauk and the enclosure for standing horses and conveyances. At the rear of the kotwali is the barbers' enclosure. The whole district, lying west of the main road, between it and the *bandh*, is known as "Jumna patti," and that on the east as "Ganga patti." Beyond the end of the street, towards the river, no encampments are allowed to be formed. At the river's edge, where the bathing takes place, are placed the dressing platforms of the *prágwáls*, each with the gay standard waving above it. For the processions of *fakírs* a wide street was marked out down to the water's edge, and the platforms ranged in order on each side of it. As I have said, the receding of the water left a large tract of firm sand open to the bathers, and this rendered bathing easy and safe for the multitudes. There was never any dangerous crowding, and the water was shallow and safe to bathe in. A few narrow channels of water crossed the wide space, and these the people had to wade through, but the inconvenience was very slight. The only exception to the rule of placing no encampments beyond the end of the street is the favour of erecting tents or *kanats* for bathing purposes only granted to a few Rájas and persons of distinction on payment of suitable fee.

सन् 1882 में इलाहाबाद में आयोजित कुम्भ मेला सम्बन्धी व्यय विवरण

सामान्य प्रशासन विभाग -प्रोसीडिंग, सन्-1882

SEP. 23, 1882.

No. 67.

much could be done beyond draining off this channel (or rather pool) of water into the Jumna on the south as much as possible. I again visited the fair on 22nd November, when flags had been put up to mark out the roads, but did not see it again till 22nd December, as I was absent in camp. Preparations were then in full swing : the road across the Fort Esplanade, by which conveyances drive up to the *bandh*, was being metalled, and the fair roads laid out. The mud bed mostly dried up, leaving the ground full of deep wide fissures, a regular net-work ; and to make a practicable road across it was a work of some difficulty : a considerable embankment too had to be constructed across the pool at the foot of the *bandh ;* and at other places owing to quicksands, quantities of *karb* had to be thrown down, and what were in fact floating bridges formed.

12. The fair consists of one wide road, leading from the enbankment semi-circularly to a point where in October the Jumna and Ganges met, at the end of the soft mud tract already spoken of, a distance of about a mile ; but by the end of December the Ganges had receded so far eastwards and southwards, as to leave beyond this point a wide tract of firm sand, on a lower level, extending out on both sides towards the two rivers : the *sangam* or confluence had shifted half a mile off (and moved further during the fair), and this wide open space formed a most valuable open dressing space for the bathers. The main street described is entirely devoted to shop sites, but on each side of it run out side-streets, along which were marked off spaces let out for the erection of *baras* or lodging-houses kept by the various *prágwáls* and *pándas* for the accommodation of their clients, the pilgrims. With a view to the size of the fair this year all the roads were made much wider than usual. On the right hand or west side of the street, approaching the river end of the street, is the kotwali, where the City Inspector resides during the fair, and where the police head-quarters are. There too I had a temporary kutcherry. Beyond it, on the same side of the road, are five shops only, known as those within the gate. On the opposite side of the road are the Khak Chauk and the enclosure for standing horses and conveyances. At the rear of the kotwali is the barbers' enclosure. The whole district, lying west of the main road, between it and the *bandh*, is known as " Jumna patti," and that on the east as " Ganga patti." Beyond the end of the street, towards the river, no encampments are allowed to be formed. At the river's edge, where the bathing takes place, are placed the dressing platforms of the *prágwáls*, each with the gay standard waving above it. For the processions of *fakírs* a wide street was marked out down to the water's edge, and the platforms ranged in order on each side of it. As I have said, the receding of the water left a large tract of firm sand open to the bathers, and this rendered bathing easy and safe for the multitudes. There was never any dangerous crowding, and the water was shallow and safe to bathe in. A few narrow channels of water crossed the wide space, and these the people had to wade through, but the inconvenience was very slight. The only exception to the rule of placing no encampments beyond the end of the street is the favour of erecting tents or *kanats* for bathing purposes only granted to a few Rájas and persons of distinction on payment of suitable fee.

SEP. 23, 1882.

No. 67.

No. 3.

14. The total income of the fair was Rs. 49,840-4-3, as compared with Rs. 41,824-10-0 at the last *Kumbh* of 1870, the principal items being—

Head of receipts.	1882.			1870.		
	Rs.	a.	p.	Rs.	a.	p.
Shop-rents	17,399	0	0	13,323	14	0
Ground-rents	7,206	3	0	7,542	4	0
Farms	11,455	0	0	7,041	0	0
Barbers' fees	10,752	0	0	12,196	8	0
Ahír and gardeners	1,240	0	0	1,700	0	0
Fines	67	15	3	21	0	0
Other items	1,720	2	0	...		
Total ...	49,840	4	3	41,824	10	0

The income is about double that of an ordinary year.

Farms.

15. I have followed above the arrangement of account given in the accounts of 1870. Including the " Ahírs and Malís," the amount realised by farms in 1882 was Rs. 12,695. This sum embraces 25 separate contracts, the amount of which was fixed (with five exceptions) by the prices bid at public auction held by the Kotwal, and the amounts of which were enhanced this year by the knowledge of the extra profits to be derived from a large fair. I think it desirable to detail these contracts :—

Number.	Kind of farm or contract.	Amount.	REMARKS.
		Rs.	
1	Sole right to hawk provisions at bathing place... ...	220	
2	Sole right to sell earthen vessels in the fair	225	
3	Sole right to sell pindas in the fair	1,700	
4	Sole right to sell wood in the fair	600	
5	Sole right to sell straw, chaff, and fodder in the fair ...	450	
6	Sole right to sell bamboos in the fair	200	
7	Sole right to sell oil in the fair	150	
8	Sole right to sell leaf dishes in the fair	70	
9	Sole right to sell glass bottles in the fair	500	
10	Sole right to hawk milk and flowers at the bathing places...	1,240	Ahírs and gardeners.
11	Sole right of selling ready-made huts in the fair ...	150	} A new farm, and amount
12	Sole right of selling five colour rings	40	} fixed by agreement.
13	Sole right of hawking sugarcane	50	Fixed by agreement.
14	Sole right of soldering up *lotas* of Ganges water ...	250	
15	Sole right of closing up with clay bottles	350	
16	Sole right of searching for money in the river... ...	350	
17	Sole right of removing hair from the barbers' enclosure ...	200	Fixed by agreement.
18	Sole right of conveying pilgrims to bathe by boat ...	1,200	
19	Sole right of ferrying pilgrims across to Arail ...	1,450	
20	Lease of site of sweetmeat-sellers' shop at end of street beyond the kotwali.	1,450	
21	Lease of site of sweetmeat-sellers' shop, No. 1, Jumna patti.	600	
22	Lease of site of sweetmeat-sellers' shop, No. 190, Ganga patti.	600	
23	Lease of site of money-changers' shop beyond kotwali ...	350	
24	Lease of site of pán-sellers' shop beyond kotwali ...	100	
25	Farm of collections from petty hawkers	250	Fixed by agreement.

The contracts or farms Nos. 2 to 13 are what are mostly in the way of monopolies, and to which objection may be made on that score, and of those Nos. 2 to 7 will probably appear most objectionable, Nos. 2, 4, 5, and 6 having further attached to them the privilege of a site, Nos. 2 and 4 being specially valuable, beyond the kotwali. These monopolies are enforced by the monopolist being empowered to charge a duty of 2 annas per rupee ($12\frac{1}{2}$ per cent.) on the value of articles brought into the fair for use, if not bought at his shop ; and of course the monopolist has the control of prices within

SERIAL No.

GENERAL DEPARTMENT.

NORTH-WESTERN PROVINCES AND OUDH, OCTOBER, 1882.

PROGS. No. AND DATE.

No. 3. — SEP. 23, 1882. — No. 67.

the fair. I confess that these farms do seem to me objectionable in principle, and that it would be better in the case of earthen vessels, wood, and so on, to let out any number of sites, so that all the pilgrims would have to pay would be the extra cost due to the cost of carriage and of the rent, and not the monopolists' fancy price: in any case if a monopoly is granted, it should only be for selling at a fair price as fixed by authority. In other cases (Nos. 1, 10, as well as 14 and 15) what is auctioned is really the right of collecting dues from all the persons following a particular calling: and does not seem so objectionable, it being taken for granted that this indirect taxation of the pilgrim is desirable, and that some hold must be kept over the followers of each craft; but it is necessary that the amount of dues to be collected should be fixed by authority: at present the farmer collects all he can manage to get. Lease No. 18 is of the same nature: owing to the high price bid this year, the farmer raised his fee per boat (which he collects from the *mallahs* who work the boats, they recouping themselves from the passengers) so high as to cause a strike amongst the *mallahs*; it was, however, speedily adjusted. If anything can be got for No. 16, there can be no objection. The objection to No. 17 is that the hair is sanctified, and should be otherwise disposed of: and this might certainly be done if Hindu feeling generally dictates it. No. 19 is an ordinary farm of a ferry: and the remainder, Nos. 20-24, are prices bid for favourable sites at open auction, and therefore wholly unobjectionable, except so far as they have been unduly raised by the fixed rents charged for other shops: while No. 25 is the most convenient way of collecting the fees levied on the petty hawkers who squat on the roads and move about with trays of combs, pins, caps, &c., and is in the same category as Nos. 1, 10, 14, and 15.

Shop-rents.

16. It will be seen that the rental realised for shop sites, as for farms, this year largely exceeded the amount paid in 1870. The majority of the shops let at so much the cubit, according to the length of street front occupied; but besides the sites let at auction already noted, Nos. 3 to 27 in Jumna patti, nearly all of which are sweetmeat-sellers' shops, and where all the sweet-sellers' shops are situated, and Nos. 191 to 197, 212 to 223, and 254 and 255 (corner shops) in Ganga patti, these being nearly all grain-sellers' (baniahs) shops, are let for lump sums, varying of course with the size of the shop. The rents charged give rates for the sweetmeat-sellers in Jumna patti of about Rs. 16 per linear cubit, the corner shops running to Rs. 20 and more; and for the green-grocers and grain-sellers in Ganga patti opposite them, of about Rs. 20 per linear cubit. For the rest of the shops the rates paid were so much per linear cubit, the rates charged being generally higher for the shops further up the street (nearer the kotwali than the *bandh*), and rather higher for Jumna patti than for Ganga patti, some regard too being paid to the class of shop and the consequent means of the shopkeeper, as also to the taking of a large frontage by one firm. Thus the coral necklace-sellers in Jumna patti (next the sweet-meat-sellers) paid Rs. 11 per cubit, the cloth-sellers Rs. 8, and the rest Rs. 8 and Rs. 10. At the extreme outer end, the common stone-ware-sellers paid Rs. 5 and Rs. 6. On the other side the baniahs and green-grocers paid Rs. 15 per cubit, book-sellers Rs. 6, braziers Rs. 10 and Rs. 12, necklace-sellers Rs. 8, and the rest of the shops Rs. 7 and Rs. 5.

These rentals were all on a higher scale than ordinary, being on the average 50 to 75 per cent. more. Looking to the probability of the traders getting larger receipts than usual, I instructed the Kotwal to do this before the fair commenced. At an early period of the fair, and I think before I was known to them by sight, I went quietly amongst the shopkeepers and enquired what they were going to pay. They know the change, and few complained of it. Owing to the early breaking up of the fair they cannot have realised what they expected and hoped, but the rents have all

SERIAL No.

GENERAL DEPARTMENT.

NORTH-WESTERN PROVINCES AND OUDH, OCTOBER, 1882.

PROGS. No. AND DATE.

No. 3. — SEP. 23, 1882. — No. 67.

been collected without difficulty. I may remark here that the complaints of articles of food being taxed are quite unfounded. The large demand for food, and the scarcity of it of course raised prices (as well as the shop-rents); but any pilgrim was at liberty to bring his own food with him (as thousands of them did, and picniced in the fair). Considering the protection afforded to the shopkeepers and to the fair-goers, a rent on shop sites seems a perfectly legitimate and desirable source of income; but if it is considered that the income of the fair is unnecessarily large, and the pilgrims unduly taxed, lower rents could of course be charged.

Ground-rents.

17. The rental realised for sites for the *baras* or inns erected by the *prágwáls* and *pándas* is slightly less than in 1870. Only the ordinary rents were charged, which were very moderate in view of the enormous crowds that congregated in their enclosures, and the trouble they caused in the way of conservancy and sanitation. The rents charged vary according to situation, running from Rs. 85 to Rs. 100, Rs. 110, Rs. 125, Rs. 135, and Rs. 150 per bigha. These *baras* are grass or straw enclosures, arranged ordinarily like sarais, with straw huts round them inside: in some cases temporary bungalows were erected, and in several *shouldaries*, *pals*, and other tents. They were all very much crowded and built closely together. There were side-streets running at right-angles to the main street through the midst of this city of straw, but it would have been desirable had there been also a number of cross streets parallel to the main one. The sites were marked out by the Kotwal, and the *baras* built before I learnt that these cross streets had not been provided for. In future years they should be, and the *baras* arranged in more orderly fashion. It is in this quarter that the great danger of fire arose, and necessitated the forbidding of cooking except at night on days of high wind. Luckily, there were only a few days of high wind at the beginning of the fair, and no accidents occurred; but the deputation of a patrol of constables to go round on windy days and see the fires put out has provoked complaints, which will probably be deemed unjustified in the light of the necessity of the occasion.

Sahas of 28th January, received with Government Memo. No. 550.

Barbers' fees.

18. Two thousand six hundred and eighty-eight barbers paid Rs. 4 each for the right of exercising their calling within the fair, thereby giving an income of Rs. 10,752. Though so large as to be twice the amount collected in 1881, this income is not so large as was expected, nor so large as that shown in 1870 (which may however include also the separate *mundan* fees). The rule of the fair—and a most salutary one—is that all persons wishing to have their heads shaved must have it done in the *nae bara*, a large enclosure to the west of the kotwali: and no barber is admitted to the enclosure without his ticket, for which he has paid Rs. 4. For this sum he can ply his calling there throughout the fair. The tax is a most equitable one, as it falls on the pilgrims for whose benefit the expenses of the fair are involved. The shaving being confined to this area, it is possible in some measure to deal decently with the masses of human hair which are removed. The desire of all pilgrims is to have their heads shaved at the river side, and commit the hair to the Ganges: were this ordinarily allowed, the untidiness and filth along the river side would be indescribable; as it was, owing to the long extent of river shore, I believe some surreptitious shaving outside the enclosure went on, especially close to Rájghát bridge, outside the fair, and the tax was I expect evaded. The passengers over the bridge on 19th had their feet covered with hair.

Mundan.

For those who most desire it, the privilege of having their heads shaved by the river side is conceded on payment of a fee of 8 annas, and Rs. 350 from 700 persons were so collected this year for

No. 3.

Sep. 23, 1882.

No. 67.

mundan, and included in the miscellaneous receipts: when man and woman go through the ceremony together, a fee of Re. 1 is paid, and Rs. 209 were this year collected for *banidan*.

Banidan.

Miscellaneous items.

19. Besides the fees for *banidan* and *mundan*, fees are charged for tents and *kanats* put up at the river side: Rs. 50 for a tent, and Rs. 10 for a *kanat*. Under this head Rs. 400 were realised this year. The rest of the miscellaneous receipts is made up of Rs. 352-8-0, realised by the sale of materials used for the various enclosures, and huts sold after the fair, and Rs. 410-10-0 realised by sub-letting for cultivation a strip of land just under the *bandh*, included in the lands leased from cantonment at Rs. 600 for the fair.

The income of the fair.

20. I have now dealt in detail with the income of the fair, which is in effect derived from a system of indirect taxation on the pilgrims, and therefore probably less felt than a direct poll-tax would be. It is of course open to odium in some respects, inasmuch as on it is cast the entire reproach of the high prices of food and other common necessaries; whereas the rise (see prices in the city) is in great part due to the sudden extraordinary demand, and the complete command of the market by the sellers. When great crowds of strangers assemble, the local shops will always demand and obtain unusual prices. There would not appear to be any possible objection to charging such shop-rents as can be obtained under free competition for the advantage of a site in the fair over shop sites elsewhere; nor again to making such charges (such as the exaction of barbers' fees) as fall on the pilgrims true and proper for whom the fair income is expended; nor again to charging ground-rent for the sites of lodging-houses. It may however be thought desirable to modify the system of monopolies (see para. 15), to which the great objection is that the monopolist may get an unfair advantage, and get more from the people than he pays to Government. For the rest, as the income always largely exceeds the expenditure, it would be possible to lower the charges,—a benefit which should become felt indirectly by the pilgrims,—to such a scale as would just provide for the necessary expenditure. It is to be considered, however, whether the encouragement of such large gatherings is desirable, and whether it is not wise in some way to discourage them by rendering attendance at them expensive. The general system of taxation for the purposes of providing funds for police and other purposes was approved in Government No. 407A., dated 26th April, 1870 (para. 4).

Facility of collecting the income.

21. That the charges made are not in any sense extravagantly excessive is, I think, proved by the way in which the whole demand falling due was collected and paid by 10th March, 1882, without any difficulty, with scarcely a remonstrance or complaint, despite the fair being broken up when it was. The municipal octroi returns, as per margin, show the unusually large imports of January, 1882, mainly due to the Magh Mela. The income from octroi was Rs. 10,000, better in January, 1882 than in January, 1881: food, fuel, cloth, and metal showing large increases. The refunds of 15th January to 15th February, 1882, were only Rs. 2,854-2-3, as against Rs. 2,628-0-11 in 1881; and it is to be concluded therefore that the goods brought for

		January, 1881.			January, 1882.		
		Rs.	a.	p.	Rs.	a.	p.
Articles of food and drink	...	9,513	6	9	15,131	3	4
Animals for slaughter	...	628	12	8	798	11	7
Fuel, lighting or washing	...	928	4	7	1,255	7	6
Building materials ...	...	919	12	9	877	4	4
Drugs, spices, and gum	...	224	8	11	463	7	9
Tobacco ...	...	104	14	9	88	7	9
Cloth and leather articles	...	2,636	7	11	5,657	2	3
Metal ...	...	672	11	6	1,426	2	11
Total	...	15,628	15	10	25,697	15	5

No. 3.

Sep. 23, 1882.

No. 67.

the fair were mostly sold there, for the foreign traders began to leave about 24th January, and were certainly all gone by 10th February. Trade was therefore good. Money was plentiful, and sales brisk: large sales were made on the *Sankarant*, and the traders had to get a fresh stock for the *Amawas*, and they had not much to remove from the fair.

Expenditure.

22. The expenditure, to meet which the income already described is collected, is that incurred on the police establishment deputed to the fair; on the establishment and other charges incurred for conservancy purposes; on public works, *i.e.*, the making of roads, police-stations, latrines, hospitals, and so on; on medical salaries and medicines; and on rent of land and other miscellaneous charges. The total expenditure this year amounted to Rs. 20,228-0-7,* as compared with Rs. 12,815-4-1 in 1870.

* *Viz.*,		Rs.	a.	p.
Police	...	3,567	5	4
Conservancy	...	4,237	7	7
Medical	...	1,323	7	2
Public Works	...	9,203	6	6
Miscellaneous	...	1,896	6	0

Police.

23. Police charges amount to Rs. 3,567-5-4, as compared with Rs. 5,023-15-0 in 1870. Large as the Mágh Mela always is, and specially large as *Kumbh* fairs are, it has never been considered necessary to depute a special police officer to the fair, or to call in drafts from other districts. All the police arrangements are made by the Police Inspector in charge of the fair, who constitutes a force consisting in part—*(a)* of men specially entertained by himself; in part *(b)* of police borrowed from the reserve, whose pay comes out of the Fair Fund; in part *(c)* of municipal chaukidárs deputed from the city, in whose place substitutes are entertained, and their pay as well as an allowance to the chaukidárs so deputed paid from the same source; and in part *(d)* of drafts from the various police-stations in the Inspector's divisions, and also from outside police-stations with permission of the District Superintendent of Police. It is in the latter way that the Inspector procures his best subordinate officers in the fair. These drafts are remunerated by allowances and rewards.

Besides the kotwali under the charge of the City Inspector, two police-stations—one in Ganga patti under a Sub-Inspector, and one in Jumna patti under a head-constable—are opened: and there is a station at the entrance to the fair under a head-constable, and numerous out-posts (30) at various points. The total force regularly employed in the fair was—

1	Inspector.	
2	Sub-Inspectors,	class *(d)*.
2	Head-constables,	„ *(d)*.
4	Ditto	„ *(b)*.
52	Constables	„ *(b)*.
60	Ditto	„ *(d)*.
38	Chaukidárs	„ *(c)*.
385	Jemadárs and chaukidárs, class *(a)*.	
Total ... 544		

but besides these 18 chaukidárs were entertained outside the fair, owing to the crowds at the railway station and at Jhúsi; and on the *Amawas* aid was largely called in all round, to the number of 170, and the police and chaukidárs so called in rewarded with allowances for the day.

Of the sum above shown, Rs. 3,346-0-7 represents the pay and allowances of this force, with some small expenses for informers or detectives.

No. 3. — Sep. 23, 1882. — No. 67.

Order.

24. The order maintained was throughout good, broken only by one slight incident in one of the *fakírs'* processions on the 19th, which was speedily dealt with. The marshalling of the processions was a difficult task as already mentioned, but successfully carried out by the Kotwal, he being much aided in this by the Brahmin Sub-Inspector of Daraganj, Brij Lal. On the 19th, about 10 A.M., the crowds returning across the Rájghát bridge (and meeting the still incoming crowd) were so great, that the Tahsildár of Allahabad, who was on duty there, became apprehensive and reported the matter to me; and I had to leave the fair on this the principal day, and remain at the bridge all day, controlling the traffic, in which I was assisted by Mr. Steel and Mr. Brownrigg. The throng was so great, that from 11 to 3-30 it was impossible for the contractor to issue or collect tickets, and the multitudes passed free. It was proposed to give him Rs. 1,000 from the Fair Funds, as some sort of consolation to him for this unavoidable loss; but he has declined it, preferring to have the affair borne in mind when the time comes to renew his contract, which will be in September, 1884, and he will then be entitled to the consideration which is due to a man who has worked his farm fairly and given satisfaction.

As I have said, the order maintained was good throughout. Some complaints have been made of the way in which sticks were taken from all persons entering the fair. But there can be no doubt that the regulation—forbidding the wearing of arms of any sort or the carrying of sticks—is a most salutary one in the interests of peace and order, and that in this matter no respect can be paid to persons, except indeed to the infirm. Owing to the ample space there are none of the difficulties at the bathing gháts, which are experienced at Hardwár. Order and safety is easily preserved: police boats are stationed so as to prevent bathers going into deep water and any danger to life. Two attempts at suicide were frustrated. The number of people who lose their friends in the fair is large, and these are always brought to the kotwali, and generally find their friends again. A few old women had to be sent to their homes after the fair, their friends being missing: most of them were penniless. There were one or two persons missed whose friends failed to find them in the fair. One old woman was accidentally run over by a cart and killed.

Crime.

25. In the way of prevention and detection of crime the police were most successful. A careful watch is kept for suspicious characters, and the measures usual in all such assemblages for precluding the possibility of their committing offences taken. The security of property in the fair became, I think, I may say proverbial. The amount of property recovered in proportion to stolen is most favourable: it includes three large robberies, one of Rs. 386 in jewellery, another of Rs. 152 cash, and another of Rs. 100 ornaments. Another large loss of about Rs. 700 in notes and other property was not reported at the fair kotwali, as the loser suspected the thief to be of his own family party; but the notes were recovered through the sharpness of a constable watching the persons leaving the fair by the Rájghát bridge. The following is a statement of the results:—

Cases reported	50		
Criminals accused	60		
Ditto convicted	51		
	Rs.	a.	p.
Stolen property	1,113	0	7½
Property recovered	903	3	1½

There were no robberies from shops or houses at night.

The Kotwal.

26. Besides the maintenance of order and the prevention and detection of crime, the police were the efficient agents in securing conservancy: and indeed, under the Kotwal's order, in carrying out all the

No. 3. — Sep. 23, 1882. — No. 67.

working arrangements of the fair. The subordinate police, and in particular Sub-Inspector Brij Lal, have all been sufficiently rewarded by the Kotwal on his own responsibility. For his own exertions I think the Kotwal is entitled to the reward of Rs. 500 which was given to Inspector Narayan Singh at the last *Kumbh*, and also to some permanent badge of distinction, an honor which he would prefer to the money grant. The orders of Government are solicited on this point.

Conservancy: latrines.

27. The main inhabited site of the fair, lying in the centre of the dry river bed as described, the ordinary provision for conservancy (besides the employment of sweepers to keep the roads and bathing gháts clear) consists in a series of latrines on the outskirts of the fair. These latrines are enclosures made with straw (*karb*) mats and on the trench principle. When first made, and before used, the first set of trenches are dug by beldárs, but the trenches subsequently made have to be dug by the sweepers in charge, who are also responsible for the cleanliness of the latrine and for filling up the trenches with earth as required.

The latrines were located, on the west, between the lodging-houses of Jumna patti and the Fort and the embankment; on the north at the edge of the cultivation in the Daraganj *kachhar*; and on the east towards the Ganges, between Ganga patti and the river; to the south lay the bathing place. The sites were selected and the latrines prepared in the first instance by the Kotwal; but Mr. Neale, the Magistrate of the district, and Dr. Smith, the Civil Surgeon, visited the fair with me on 3rd January, and the sites chosen were then approved by Dr. Smith; while Mr. Neale, foreseeing the large numbers that would assemble, directed the preparation of a very much larger number of latrines than had been provided for. These were erected from time to time as required, and the total number was not insufficient for the number of persons who frequented them.

The site of the western or Jumna patti latrines was from the first objectionable, owing to the damp and muddy nature of the soil in which they were made. Dr. Smith, however, was of opinion that, lying as they did to some extent sheltered from the Fort by the bank (cultivated) which ran underneath the Fort and embankment, they would not be objectionable to the Fort authorities. They did, however, prove generally objectionable; and in fact, owing to the wetness of the soil, quite unfit for use: and Dr. Planck, the Sanitary Commissioner, North-Western Provinces, who was on duty at the fair from 12th to 23rd January, advised their removal, and removed they accordingly were to the higher bank nearer the Fort, some fields being taken up for the purpose. There the nature of the soil proved suitable for trenches, but objections were raised by the military authorities to the location of latrines so near the Fort, and within sight of the barracks: this was, as far as possible, obviated by moving the latrines northwards, under the embankment and not under the Fort walls. The latrines to north of the fair were in sandy soil, and did fairly well; there was a good supply of them, but they were not sufficiently used, the people slipping by in the early morning, and preferring to resort for purposes of nature to the open plain under cultivation lying to north towards Daraganj and Rájghát. The *akharas* of *fakírs*, who were camped to north-west and north, had their own separate latrines close to the public ones; but many of the *fakírs* persisted in resorting to the fields. To east and south-east the latrines were numerous and much used, and had frequently to be renewed. The soil was sandy and fairly favourable to cleanliness and deodorisation, except to south-east, where, owing to the lowness of the situation and the nearness of the river course, water was met with in the sand at a foot's depth. Here was a large open tract of wet sand lying underneath a raised bank (the end of the fair site), and to this open space the *bairagis* of the Khak Chauk (and other inhabitants of the south-east end of

SERIAL No.

GENERAL DEPARTMENT.

NORTH-WESTERN PROVINCES AND OUDH, OCTOBER, 1882.

PROGS. No. AND DATE.

No. 3.

SEP. 23, 1882.

No. 67.

the fair) persisted in resorting, despite numerous punishments; and gangs of sweepers had to be kept constantly collecting and covering up the filth. This part of the outskirts of the fair was objectionably dirty.

Establishment of sweepers.

28. To work all these latrines and preserve general cleanliness in the fair a very large force of sweepers had to be entertained, but the difficulties as to conservancy within the fair site itself were overcome with fair success. The vast crowds, however, coming in and assembling all round caused great pressure. No more sweepers were to be got from Allahabad city, which with all its suburbs was overcrowded; few were to be got in the district: and so on 16th January, 40 were procured from Cawnpore; and on 19th January, 50 from Benares. Including the 40 Cawnpore men the conservancy force employed in the fair, including superintendents, jemadárs, and sweepers, was 539, besides 8 beldárs and 11 bhistis. Owing to the crowds outside latrines had to be erected, and sweepers entertained at the camping grounds at Nynee and Allahabad railway stations, and at Jhúsi (Rájghát bridge): 49 sweepers were so entertained: and extra bullocks for the filth carts in the city were also supplied out of the Fair Funds, and latrines erected at Alopi Bágh, Bharadwáj, and other points.

Uncleanliness outside the fair.

29. But the immense surplus population which suddenly poured on for one night and day (18th-19th January) proved far too much for any latrine accommodation: indeed it has been exceeding it for some days; and the crowds of pilgrims, who thronged Daraganj and camped all over the Fort Esplanade and about Alopi Bágh, could not be prevented from resorting for the purposes of nature to the large tract of level cultivation, chiefly *arhar* and *bájra* fields, lying between Colonelganj and Daraganj, and to the plain of *kachhar* rabi crops in the river bed north of the fair and east of Daraganj, already spoken of as resorted to by the people living in the fair. All those localities became covered with impurities, and it was only by the employment of large gangs of sweepers and beldárs, mostly deputed from the fair, including the 50 Benares sweepers, and also of municipal sweepers working under the Tahsíldár and the Municipal Overseer, that these localities were cleansed, and the filth collected and buried in shallow pits at various points. It is to be hoped that this purification has been effectual, and at any rate as yet no evil effects have supervened.

Total cost of conservancy.

30. All this large establishment and the numerous outside charges, which have been paid without demur from the Fair Fund, has run up the cost of conservancy to Rs. 4,237-7-7, a large sum compared with the Rs. 2,559-14-6 of 1870; and which does not include the cost of the latrines made and put up in the fair, and of the labour done by beldárs in digging trenches and pits at the beginning, the rest of which is included in the general charges on works.

Medical charges.

31. The usual medical provision made for the fair is the establishment of a dispensary in the main street of the fair, at which a native doctor is in attendance, and a detached hospital for contagious or epidemic diseases is also provided. The total medical expenditure of last year was Rs. 146-9-6, and in 1870 it appears to have been about Rs. 324. This year Rs. 1,323-7-2 has been expended.

Hospitals and establishment.

32. The usual dispensary was erected, and attached to it was a hospital intended for the immediate treatment of any surgical cases that might arise, such as from burning, which, if a fire takes place, may be numerous: while a cholera hospital was also erected in the sands on the bank of the Ganges in Jhúsi, near the *sanayási* encampment. With a view to the anticipated largeness of the gathering, the Officiating Magistrate (Mr. Neale) applied to the Surgeon-General for the services of five native doctors in addition to the native doctor

SERIAL No.

GENERAL DEPARTMENT.

NORTH-WESTERN PROVINCES AND OUDH, OCTOBER, 1882.

PROGS. No. AND DATE.

No. 3.

SEP. 23, 1882.

No. 67.

who ordinarily attended the fair; and these five men* arrived on various dates after 9th January, and remained on duty to 13th February. Their duties were at first light, and they assisted somewhat in supervising sanitation; but on the outbreak of cholera their services were utilised, one being placed in charge of the fair cholera hospital at Jhúsi, one sent to Nynee station, where a hospital had to be opened, and one as well as the regular dispensary man being sent for duty to the city cholera hospital at Khurdabad: this left two on duty in the fair, who were constantly on their rounds, and as soon as a case of cholera occurred, despatched it to the fair cholera hospital. Kahars and doolies were kept in readiness for this purpose at the kotwali, while four boats were provided to carry the sick across the river. The dispensary and the operations of the native doctors in the fair was supervised in the mornings by the native doctor of Kydganj dispensary, and in the afternoons by Babu Kali Das Nundy, Assistant Surgeon, all acting of course under the orders of the Civil Surgeon. Under this officer's orders too seven native doctors with medicines were despatched to the principal camping places along the routes frequented by the departing pilgrims, and remained out on duty for periods ranging between 21st January and 9th February.

*Viz.,—
4 hospital assistants.
1 native doctor.

Cholera.

32A. From his first coming on 12th January, the Sanitary Commissioner evinced an extreme apprehension of cholera breaking out; and cholera there was, but it was not of a virulent type; and considering the vast numbers assembled, the mortality may be considered extremely slight.

The first case of cholera in the fair occurred on 16th, and on the succeeding days, especially 19th and 20th, the cases were somewhat numerous, but there was not a single case after the 23rd in the fair itself. I have already mentioned the way in which the multitudes flocked out of the fair on the morning of 19th January; and this movement may no doubt have been promoted in part by the rumour of sickness prevailing, as well as by the desire to get away from a place where the crowd was so great as to make any lengthened stay undesirable if possible. After this, on the 21st sickness increasing, the people were warned to depart; and on the 22nd measures were taken to make the *bairagis* in the Khak Chauk, whose habits were extremely filthy and where most sickness had occurred, leave the fair. On the 24th, after the *Basant*, arrangements were made for the occupants of the *baras* all leaving their lodgings, and for reducing the numbers in each *akhara* to a small group of the most necessary personages, and the fair may be said to have been virtually broken up: the shopkeepers began to remove their goods, and the attendance on *Puran Mashi*, 3rd February, though the sickness was over, was very thin. All these measures for breaking up the fair, and by which sickness was prevented, were initiated by Mr. Neale, the Officiating Magistrate.

The following is a return of the cholera cases treated by the medical establishment:—

Number.	Place of treatment.	Number of cases admitted.	Deaths.	Discharged.	Remarks.
1	Fair dispensary	100	14	11	75 transfered to Jhúsi.
2	Fair cholera hospital at Jhúsi ...	72	79	68	
	Total ...	172	93	79	
3	City Khurdabad hospital ...	116	70	46	5 returned as "otherwise" out of the 46.
4	Nynee	46	34	12	
5	Arail hospital	20	12	8	
6	Sarai Akil road	6	1	5	
7	Cawnpore road	6	...	6	
8	Jaunpur road	8	1	7	
9	Fyzabad road	12	1	11	
10	Benares road	31	12	19	
11	Bánda road	26	7	19	
	Total ...	443	231	212	

No. 3. The percentage of deaths in cases, 52, is not I believe large for epidemic cholera, nor even, if Nos. 6 to 11, which appear to contain a different class of cases, be excluded, is it very high, only 59 per cent., which does not, I believe, indicate a severe type of the disease. But of course there were numerous cases which never got medical treatment; for instance, the 72 admissions at Jhúsi hospital represent the living cases sent by the Tahsíldár or police who were watching the crowds leaving the fair by Rájghát bridge or camped at Jhúsi, and does not include those who died before they could be got to the hospital. SEP. 23, 1882. No. 67.

According to the police returns there were [in the city circles, with Jhúsi and Gurpur (Nynee) circles] no cases before 21st January: between that day and 31st January, 196 cases and 131 deaths; and between 1st and 11th February, 12 cases and 10 deaths. Since then the sickness directly traceable to the fair has ceased. For the whole district the cholera deaths were in January 284, and in February 89.

That such a vast gathering should have collected and dispersed with so little sickness and death seems to me almost wonderful; and it needs no recondite search for reasons of illness, when the conditions under which these masses assembled are considered,—tired travellers insufficiently and badly provided with food and drink, overcrowded and herding together so as necessarily to cause and communicate contamination.

General health.

33. Besides the cholera cases, the general health of the fair-goers was provided for by the treatment of the following cases at the dispensary:—

Serial number.	Diseases.	Number.	Serial number.	Diseases.	Number.
1	Ulcer	209	25	Fracture, compound	1
2	Primary syphilis	30	26	Inflammation	31
3	Acute rheumatism	109	27	Liver diseases	3
4	Herpis	64	28	Inflammation of the ear ...	33
5	Diarrhœa	104	29	Wound	3
6	Hypertrophy of spleen ...	29	30	Asthma	1
7	Cystitis	1	31	Not diagnosed	9
8	Gum boil	13	32	Opacity Carnea	1
9	Neuralgia	18	33	Fistula in ano	1
10	Bronchitis	228	34	Epilepsy	2
11	Ascites	2	35	Orchitis	1
12	Gonorrhœa	37	36	Skin diseases	56
13	Dysentery	69	37	Abscess	29
14	Hæmorrhoids	24	38	Whitlow	3
15	Dyspepsia	131	39	Ozœna	1
16	Colic	15	40	Hernia	2
17	Constipation	21	41	Diseases of rectum and anus ...	3
18	Ague	12[illegible]	42	Caries	20
19	Hæmoptysis	1	43	Pneumonia	5
20	Burn	3	44	Tumour	4
21	Conjunctivitis	2[illegible]	45	Debility	4
22	Bubos	5	46	Scrofula	3
23	Diabetes	1	47	Spermatorrhœa	1
24	Contusion	1[illegible]		Total	1,472

The total expenditure on medical charges, Rs. 1,323-7-2, may be considered large, but I cannot think that it will be held to have been ill spent.

Public Works.

34. The charges for works are high, amounting to Rs. 9,203-6-6, or, after deducting Rs. 1,590 for the kankar road made across the Fort Esplanade to the embankment, and Rs. 3,028 paid to the Executive Engineer, Military Works, Public Works Department, as compensation for the roads round the Fort which were utterly ruined and ground to dust by the

No. 3. enormously heavy traffic at the time of the fair, to Rs. 4,585-6-6: this is high as compared with 1870, Rs. 1,916-10-6, but includes the charges for constructing all the fair latrines and also for digging filth-pits, which were included in conservancy in 1870. The charges compare with those of 1880 and 1881 thus:— SEP. 23, 1882. No. 67.

	Rs.	a.	p.
1880	2,277	1	6
1881	3,933	7	6
1882	4,585	6	6

and it is to be recollected that everything was provided this year on a large scale, 50 to 150 per cent. larger than ordinary. The materials used comprise—

	Rs.	a.	p.
Bamboos and rafters	1,405	9	9
Thatching grass	239	2	6
Karb	510	5	0
Ready-made thatches	60	0	0
Total	2,215	1	3

against which there is a credit on the receipt side for Rs. 350-8-0 of materials sold.

Esplanade road.

35. The re-metalling of what was once a metalled road across the Fort Esplanade, for a length of nearly half a mile (860 yards), was done under my orders, and proved a great benefit and relief to the large wheeled traffic coming to the fair, besides saving the Esplanade. The six inches of kunkar laid down was not all of the best quality, and the metalling was hurriedly done, and the road was half worn out during the fair, but will be of use to the daily frequenters of *Beni-kinara* for a long time.

Military Works roads.

36. The grant to the Executive Engineer was made with the Magistrate's approval, and was fully justified by the condition to which the roads were reduced by the traffic: a grant on similar grounds might have been made to the municipality had they not benefited so largely in octroi income by the fair.

Miscellaneous: rent of land.

37. Miscellaneous expenses amount to Rs. 1,896-6-0, as compared with Rs. 2,748-12-1 in 1870. Compensation for or rent of land taken up gives the most important items. The strip of land appertaining to cantonments, being a piece 5 *jaribs* (750 feet) wide, running along the Fort and embankment, was taken for Rs. 600, the cultivating rental; but, as already noted, the greater part of it was a high bank above, and not required for the fair site, and this was sub-let for cultivation at Rs. 410-10-0, so that really the expense was small. For the rest of the fair site, being land appertaining to Barahi patti, a Court of Wards estate, rent is paid at Re. 1-2-0 per bigha, whether the land is cultivated or not; and on this account Rs. 394-13-0 was paid. On the authority of an arrangement said to have been concluded between Mr. Colvin, Officiating Magistrate, and Major Hanmer, Cantonment Magistrate in 1870, Rs. 350 are paid annually to the Cantonment Fund. The correspondence on the subject is meagre; but it would appear to have been fixed as compensation to the Cantonment Fund from the Fair Fund, on account of land used for erecting shops along the road from Kydganj to the fair, within the embankment, and therefore on the Fort Esplanade. In the present year there were only a few refreshment stalls on the Esplanade close to the embankment, and for a few days only, and from them no income was derived: nor is there ordinarily any income derived from such shops. In the few years when the Ganges runs close under or near the embankment, the fair shops must necessarily be located along the road across the Esplanade,

SERIAL No. | GENERAL DEPARTMENT. | PROGS. No. AND DATE.

NORTH-WESTERN PROVINCES AND OUDH, OCTOBER, 1882.

No. 3. and this grant appears to have been fixed for such contingency. It is however regularly paid year by year and may be regarded as a consolidated annual compensation for the use of the Fort Esplanade across which the fair road runs. In the present year large numbers of vehicles, bringing pilgrims to the fair, put down their passengers at the foot of the embankment, and waited there for return fares. A proposal was made demi-officially on the part of the cantonment committee to make a charge for such standing, but I opposed it on the ground that no such charge had ever been made, and that the Rs. 350 paid covered the use of the Esplanade, and the matter dropped. The number of vehicles plying for hire was so large, that they undoubtedly did more than occupy the sides of the road, and encroached on the Esplanade: moreover, on the big days travellers camped in numbers on the Esplanade at night with their carts and conveyances: it proved impossible to keep them off. Special latrines were however provided, and all the litter left cleaned away immediately afterwards. The charges thus paid by way of rents or compensation amount to Rs. 1,344-13-0, and constitute the greater portion of the miscellaneous charges. SEP. 23, 1882. No. 67.

Other miscellaneous charges.

38. The remainder is made up of charges for lighting, watering, carriage, &c.: the fair streets are regularly lighted, and on the nights of bathing link boys are kept with torches burning at the bathing ghâts. Luckily no fires occurred, and the hooks attached to long poles, provided for cutting down the straw huts, were not wanted, nor the *gharras*. The seven wells, made at a cost of Rs. 112 at the corners of the streets, as a provision for water that might be required for fires, proved of great use to the pilgrims, who drew their water from them. Comments have been made on the dusty state of the fair, and the funds are so large that there was no reason for not spending money on watering; but it was impracticable to do anything owing to the denseness of the crowd, the scarcity of water, and the rapidity with which watered roads again became dusty.

Surplus.

39. The total receipts being Rs. 49,840-4-3, and expenditure Rs. 20,228-0-7, the surplus is Rs. 29,612-3-8.

I had endeavoured to make the accounts as simple and clear as possible, by making all payments out of cash in the Kotwal's hands, he submitting a daily account to me of his receipts and disbursements, and paying from time to time surplus cash into the Nazúl Fund in the Treasury. His accounts were closed on 13th March, on which date there was at credit of Nazúl Fund on account of collections of this year's Mágh Mela—

	Rs.	a.	p.
Paid on 17th January	10,000	0	0
Ditto 25th January	17,000	0	0
Ditto 13th March	2,723	10	11
Total ...	29,723	10	11

Other bills however came in which had to be paid, amounting in all to Rs. 111-7-3, of which Rs. 15-1-0 was paid in March, and Rs. 96-6-3 in the current financial year, 1882-83. The surplus now in Nazúl Fund is as above, *viz.*, Rs. 29,612-3-8.

Disposal of surplus.

40. A charge of Rs. 84 (Rs. 7 per mensem) has to be provided annually out of the surplus for a safety boat kept at the bathing place all the year round: and if the grant of Rs. 500, suggested in para. 26, be

SERIAL No. | GENERAL DEPARTMENT. | PROGS. No. AND DATE.

NORTH-WESTERN PROVINCES AND OUDH, OCTOBER, 1882.

No. 3. approved, that too will have to be met. The usual grants made from the fair surplus, and which accordingly have been budgetted for this year, are— SEP. 23, 1882. No. 67.

	Rs.
To Alfred Park	3,000
To Library and Museum	3,600
To Colvin Dispensary	2,600
Total ...	9,200
Adding as above	584
Total ...	9,784

The amount of surplus still at the disposal of Government is Rs. 19,828-3-8.

41. The surplus last year was applied to the partial discharge of the debt to Government for the expense of constructing the Mayo Hall. I do not know if I am justified in expressing an opinion, but it seems to me that the Hindu community are entitled to some consideration in the disposal of the surplus which results from the taxation of pilgrims. One proposition suggested in the public prints was the construction of a bathing ghát at Baluaghát on the Jumna, which I should think was a practicable and reasonable suggestion: the place is resorted to daily by the people of the city. Improvements too might be made in the road approach to the embankment; and possibly something done for improving the drainage and communications in Daraganj, the principal homes of the *prágwáls*; or the very desirable proposition of removing and entirely re-building the city hospital (Colvin Dispensary) might be entertained.

42. I trust that what I have said in paras. 10, 12, 15, 16, 17, 18, 20, 23, 24, and 38 will be considered a sufficient report on the matters as to which information has been called for by Government. I have explained the necessity for entrusting the management of this year's fair to the present City Kotwal, who happens to be a Musalman: the question of future management is a wide and open one: a representative committee of Hindus might no doubt assist, with advice and information, the Magistrate managing the fair. I am of opinion that the monopolies should be done away with, and I think more moderate shop-rents might be charged (for the high rents charged this year I am responsible). They no doubt contribute to raise the prices of food, though as I have pointed out there was no monopoly of food, and it was competition for sites that raised the prices paid for particular shops, such as the sweetmeat-sellers, that let for Rs. 1,450.

Under the immense demand for food no doubt much inferior food was sold, and flour mixed with juár and bajra commanded the price of wheaten flour; but this is not "adulteration," as many natives seem to think it is, nor is it cheating, unless the tradesman sells it as wheaten flour: it is simply an inferior article selling at the price of a better one owing to the pressure of high demand. It was inevitable, in providing for such vast multitudes, that the providers should be driven to their last resources, and no doubt take advantage of the necessities of the multitudes to sell off inferior articles. It does not seem to me that this could have been checked by authority, or that prices could have been arbitrarily determined; certainly not at the time when the complaints arose, after the leases had been made and the shops let. For the future, if monopolies of the right to sell wood and the like are granted, then undoubtedly the price at which the monopolist must sell should be fixed beforehand; and it is just possible that the same might be done as regards the supplies sold by the sweetmeat-sellers and grain-dealers; though in their case I think the lowering of rents and the encouragement of larger numbers of such traders coming to the fair would be sufficient. The management of the whole of this branch, *i. e.*, the letting of farms and shops, might be taken out of the hands of the Kotwal, and only the executive arrangements, which he has conducted admirably, be left with him. No doubt the high price of food and necessaries, causing the people to stint themselves, or obliging them to live on inferior food,

RIAL
No.

GENERAL DEPARTMENT.

NORTH-WESTERN PROVINCES AND OUDH, OCTOBER, 1882.

PROGS.
No. and
Date.

o. 3.

is one great factor in the causes of sickness, though I think it is an exaggeration to say, as the Rája of Benares has in a letter to the Commissioner, that "bad food, adulterated food, half-cooked food kills many more persons than any accumulation of filth in the fair."

Sep. 23, 1882.

No. 67.

43. Before submitting this report I have caused it to be laid before Mr. Neale, who was Officiating Magistrate at the time of the fair, and who has appended his remarks separately.

Expenditure statement of Kumbh Mágh Mela Fair, 1882.

Number.	Detail of expenditure.	Amount.	Total.
	POLICE.	Rs. a. p.	Rs. a. p.
1	Pay and allowances	3,346 0 7	
	Police boats	60 0 0	
	Dieting prisoners	117 11 9	
	Whipping charges	4 0 0	
	Belts and badges	39 9 0	3,567 5 4
	CONSERVANCY.		
2	Pay of sweepers, jemadárs, &c.	2,482 14 4	
	Purchase of baskets and *pharuas*	230 8 0	
	Benares sweepers	253 5 9	
	Cawnpore sweepers	106 14 0	
	Tahsíldár's bill	40 12 9	
	Mr. Upton's bill	460 2 9	
	City bullocks	121 0 0	
	Fort latrines	186 0 0	
	Miscellaneous, outside fair	104 12 0	
	Field taken up and crops destroyed	236 1 0	
	Disinfecting powder	15 1 0	4,237 7 7
	MEDICAL.		
3	Fair hospital charges	56 10 9	
	Burning the dead in fair	187 11 0	
	Burying the dead at Arail	15 0 6	
	Kahars	107 6 6	
	Boats	48 0 0	
	Charges at Arail and Nynee	21 0 0	
	Cholera pills	12 5 0	
	Salaries and travelling allowance, as per Civil Surgeon	626 9 2	
	Cholera hospital, as per Civil Surgeon	164 8 6	
	Blankets, price	57 13 0	
	Dieting city cholera hospital	26 6 9	1,323 7 2
	PUBLIC WORKS.		
4	*Labour* on earthwork on roads, making out roads, making enclosures, levelling, making filth-pits, &c.	1,423 10 6	
	Materials and labour used in preparing kotwali and hutting police generally, and on hospitals and latrines in the fair.	2,764 1 0	
	Materials (*jhao* and *karb*) for rendering passable quagmires and quicksands.	376 11 6	
	Kankar road across the Fort Esplanade (2,581′ × 20′ × 6″)	1,590 0 0	
	Miscellaneous building charges	20 15 6	
	Repairs of roads round Fort, given to Executive Engineer, Public Works Department, Military Division.	3,028 0 0	9,203 6 6
	MISCELLANEOUS.		
5	*Gharras* and hooks for fires	48 2 0	
	Well-making	112 0 0	
	Lighting	132 14 0	
	Well-repairing	30 0 0	
	Watering	42 8 0	
	Paper and printing	104 0 0	
	Carriage, &c., hire	14 14 0	
	Rupee bags	2 4 0	
	Telegrams, &c.	21 6 0	
	Barriers at railway station	27 9 0	
	Statistics	16 0 0	
	Rent of cantonment land	600 0 0	
	Rent of Barahi patti	394 13 0	
	Grant to Cantonment Fund	350 0 0	1,896 6 0
	GRAND TOTAL	...	20,228 0 7

T. BENSON,
Joint-Magistrate, in charge Mágh Mela.

सन् 1882 में इलाहाबाद के कुम्भ में पधारे तीर्थ यात्रियों का विवरण

सन् 1882 में आयोजित कुम्भ में पूरे भारत से तीर्थ यात्रियों का आगमन हुआ। प्राप्त आकड़ों से पता चलता है कि लगभग 8 लाख से 10 लाख के बीच तीर्थ यात्री इलाहाबाद में पवित्र स्नान के लिए पधारे जो कि उस समय की इलाहाबाद के आबादी से भी ज्यादा थी। विशिष्ट महानुभावों में बनारस, बेतिया, भरतपुर, विजयनगर, बांसी के राजाओं ने भी कुम्भ मेले में एक माह का प्रवास किया। स्थानीय राजाओं में मांडा, दहिया, बारा के राजाओं के अतिरिक्त अनेक गणमान्य व्यक्ति भी उपस्थित हुए।

सामान्य प्रशासन विभाग-प्रोसीडिंग, सन्-1882

No. 3.

Dated the 28th April, 1882.

From—T. BENSON, ESQ., *Joint-Magistrate, in charge Mágh Mela, Allahabad,*

To—*Commissioner, Allahabad Division.*

SIR,—I have the honor to submit my report on the *Kumbh* Mágh Mela of 1882. Owing to the difficulties which I have experienced in the management and conduct of the fair, from the lack of information in former reports, and partly also by reason of the explanations which have been specially called for as regards the present fair, I propose submitting a much more detailed report than has been hitherto usual.

2. The Mágh Mela is, as you are aware, held annually at the confluence of the Ganges and Jumna, and lasts during the whole of the month of Mágh. The fair is a religious one, pilgrims resorting to it for the purpose of shaving the head and bathing at Tribeni,* the confluence of the Ganges-Jumna and supposed under-ground Saraswati. Every twelfth year, when the planet Jupiter is in Aquarius *(Kumbh)* and the sun in Aries, the fair is known as a *Kumbh*, and owing to its increased sanctity is far more largely attended than usual. It is these *Kumbh* fairs only that are formally attended by the corporate bodies of the various sects of religious ascetics, the *akharas* of *fakirs*. Moreover, the belief that the local existence of the Ganges will cease in 17 years from the present time (making this the last *Kumbh* fair but one), conferred a special character of attraction on this year's *Kumbh*. Thus there was every religious reason for an abnormally large number of

* For an account of a pilgrim's morning at Tribeni, see the *Pioneer*, 1st February.

7

(8)

SERIAL No. — GENERAL DEPARTMENT. — PROGS. No. AND DATE.

NORTH-WESTERN PROVINCES AND OUDH, OCTOBER, 1882.

No. 3. — SEP. 23, 1882. — No. 67.

pilgrims attending the fair. Add to this, the enormously increased facilities of communication, as compared with former *Kumbhs*, afforded by the railways, and the not unfavourable seasons of 1880 and 1881, the most important factor in determining the ability of the majority of the population to attend such gatherings.

3. The fair began with the first day of the month of Mágh, corresponding in the present year with 5th January, and lasted till the full moon of the month on 3rd February. The most strict observers of religious duty keep the whole month as a period of sanctity, bathing daily at Tribeni, fasting by day, and abstaining entirely from cereal food. A few who did not commence this month of religious observance till the first great day, *Sankarant*, on 12th January, kept it up till 11th February. The devotees, who keep the whole month, are called *Kalap-báshi*, or good livers. A large proportion of them consisted of inhabitants of Práyág itself, who, living at their houses, resorted daily to the bathing point : the rest (including the bodies of *fakirs*) constituted the permanent pilgrim population of the fair ; but, owing to the causes to be noticed hereafter, which led to the practical breaking up of the fair about 23rd January, there were very few who stayed out the whole month. The majority of pilgrims came merely for one day's bathing, or at most for a few days, perhaps managing to stay from one great day to another. The first great bathing day is *Sankarant*, on 12th January : the great day of all is *Amawas*, or the new moon, falling this year on 19th January : after this comes *Basant Panchami*, or the fifth day of the light half of the month, this year 24th January, and the full moon on 3rd February. Of less importance are *Achla Satmi*, 27th January, and *Yakadashi*, 31st January ; but owing to the causes already alluded to, there were no great crowds after the *Amawas*.

4. The magnitude of the fair, the large numbers attending it, began to show itself at the very beginning, and the crowd on the *Sankarant* seemed so enormous that it would not be likely to be exceeded ; but the *Amawas* proved how wrong this anticipation was. The fair thinned very much about the 15th, but soon began to rise again, and was at its fullest on the 19th. It is worthy of remark that a very large proportion of the bathers on the *Sankarant* were pilgrims from afar, who came by rail.* The up-country pilgrims mostly bathed on 12th January, and then went on their way ; and so did the southern pilgrims from Jabbalpur and the country beyond : though it is said that this class, who are the chief observers of *Sankarant*, did not attend so largely as they otherwise would, owing to the invisibility of the planet Venus till *Basant Panchami* (24th January). *Per contra*, the bathers on *Amawas* were mainly residents of the districts to east and north of Práyág—the numbers who flocked in on foot by the roads leading to Rájghát and Pháphámau bridges, bringing provisions with them for the day and then returning—was immense.

* See statistics below, para 5.

5. The thickest time in the fair was probably about 9 A.M. on the morning of 19th January (or perhaps earlier, for bathing had been going on from a very early hour, it might be said at night), and the people then began to leave. Native estimates put the numbers present at two to three millions of people (twenty and twenty-two to thirty and thirty-two lakhs), and all seem agreed that so large a concourse has never been seen anywhere. I have endeavoured to procure some trustworthy figures on which to form an estimate of the numbers present. People coming to the fair by rail by the Calcutta and Jabbalpur lines alighted at Naini, and thence came across the Jumna either by the fair ferry at Arail ghát, or by the Jumna bridge (Gaoghát) : those coming by the Delhi line got out at Allahabad city station. The Arail ferry boat and the Jumna bridge would also bring the people from all the country round to the south and foot pilgrims from afar in that direction. Other pilgrims coming by road would enter Allahabad either by the kucha road from Sarai Akil, by the Grand

8

SERIAL No. | GENERAL DEPARTMENT. | PROGS. No. AND DATE.

NORTH-WESTERN PROVINCES AND OUDH, OCTOBER, 1882.

No. 3. Trunk Road from Cawnpore, or by the bridges of boats at Pháphámau and Rájghát. Sep. 23, 1882. No. 67.

From the railway authorities I have obtained certain statistics which show that 185,686 departures were booked from the Allahabad city and Nynee stations during January (including bookings at the temporary Fort Station on 21st January). Some of these of course represent local comings and goings, people who visited Allahabad twice or thrice during the month; but I think that from 150 to 175 thousand may be taken as visitors to the fair brought by rail. The day-by-day returns of Allahabad station alone for January show that of 134,044 arrivals during the month, 77,847 arrived on or before the 12th (*Sankarant*), the 11th and 12th alone bringing 42,283, while the succeeding week brought 42,123 more; and in all 120,070 had arrived at Allahabad city station by the 19th. Similar details have not been procured for Nynee; but out of 50,314 departures booked thence, we may allow in the same scale 45,000 as arrivals before 19th: in all 165,000 by the two stations; and allowing even for the numerous departures after the *Sankarant*, probably 125,000 of these were present on 19th January.

The numbers entering by the Sarai Akil and Grand Trunk Roads I had counted from noon of 17th to 19th, and were roughly 25,000 and 39,000, respectively. The amounts collected in tolls at the bridges show that on the 17th, 18th, and 19th the number coming to the fair must have been—

Rájghát	...	400,000.
Pháphámau	...	100,000.

To these figures must be added the permanent residents of the fair and visitors to Práyág not having arrived by rail, the residents of Práyág (Allahabad) itself attending the fair that day, and the uncounted visitors of the day passing by the less important routes, such as Kuresar and Mausaraiya ferries, Baluaghát, and the non-railway passengers by Arail ferry and Jumna bridge. Thus we have—

Arrivals by rail from 1st to 19th, after allowing for 40,000 departures	125,000
Rájghát bridge	400,000
Pháphámau bridge	100,000
Grand Trunk Road	39,000
Sarai Akil road	25,000
Other roads and routes	50,000
Permanent fair residents and visitors not included in railway accounts, say...	50,000
City residents	50,000
Total ...	839,000

Possibly 800,000 to one million may be a fair estimate of the numbers present at the fair on 19th January: it is certain that with the city population not less than a million souls were in Allahabad and its vicinity on that day.

Constitution of the crowd.

6. All parts of India were represented in the pilgrims attending the fair, from Kashmir to Madras, from Kandahar to Calcutta: the railway returns of tickets booked from Allahabad and Nynee will throw

SERIAL No. | GENERAL DEPARTMENT. | PROGS. No. AND DATE.

NORTH-WESTERN PROVINCES AND OUDH, OCTOBER, 1882.

No. 3. some light on the localities from which travellers principally came. The following are some of the most important figures :— Sep. 23, 1882. No. 67.

EASTERN DISTRICTS.

Howrah (Calcutta)	1,737
Patna and Bankipur	3,052
Arrah	1,171
Mogul Sarai	1,042
Benares	34,821
Mirzapur	19,638
Gaepura	2,230

LOCAL (ALLAHABAD DISTRICT).

Manauri	1,772
Bharwari	1,491
Siráthu	2,296

WESTERN DISTRICTS.

Khaga	1,008
Fatehpur	3,551
Mohar	1,461
Cawnpore...	31,275
Etáwah	1,446
Jaswantnagar	1,773
Agra	7,538
Háthras	1,374
Gháziabad	1,924
Delhi	1,814
Lucknow	1,538
Muttra	1,114

SOUTHERN DISTRICTS.

Manickpur	6,779
Sutna	3,889
Maihar	1,084
Jukehi	1,942
Katni	2,003
Sihora	1,066
Jabbalpur...	24,876

These returns clearly show Benares, Cawnpore, Jabbalpur, and Mirzapur as the chief points to which pilgrims returned from Allahabad: the Benares passengers include a large number of pilgrims from other places, who passed on to that holy city from Práyág; but in the case of the other cities the returning pilgrims may be taken to have also started from those places.

Rájas.

7. Amongst the more distinguished visitors to the fair were those regular attendants, the Rájas of Benares and Bettiah, who stay the whole month, the Rája of Bhartpur, Rája of Vizianagram, and the Rája of Bánsi. The Rája of Jaipur also visited the fair for one day, on 26th January. The local Rájas of Manda, Daiya, and Bára were present, and a number of other persons of rank and distinction from all parts.

इण्डियन यूनियन, साप्ताहिक पत्रिका की प्रतिक्रिया - 22 फरवरी, 1886

कलकत्ता से प्रकाशित साप्ताहिक पत्रिका इण्डियन यूनियन पत्रिका के 22 फरवरी, 1886 के अंक में माघ मेला के सकुशल सम्पन्न हो जाने के सम्बन्ध में लेख प्रकाशित किया गया। इसमें लेफ्टिनेंट गवर्नर द्वारा सन् 1882 में जारी एक संकल्प का सन्दर्भ लेते हुए लिखा गया है कि शासन के उच्च स्तरीय निर्देश के बावजूद सरकारी अधिकारियों द्वारा माघ मेला से निरन्तर भारी आय की जा रही है ऐसा तीर्थ यात्रियों पर मनमाने टैक्स लगाकर किया जा रहा है। इस अतिरिक्त आय का उपयोग मेला क्षेत्र में सुविधायें बढ़ाने के स्थान पर अल्फ्रेड पार्क जैसी जगहों का विकास किया जा रहा है। मेला प्रबन्धन में म्युनिसिपल कमेटी की भूमिका को सीमित रखा गया है। यदि शासन के संकल्प के अनुसार म्युनिसिपल कमेटी को मेला प्रबन्धन में अग्रणी भूमिका दी जाये तो निःसन्देह कमेटी कभी भी तीर्थयात्रियें पर इतने भारी टैक्स की सहमति नहीं प्रदान करेगी।

पत्रावली संख्या-20/1887-88-क्षेत्रीय अभिलेखागार, प्रयागराज

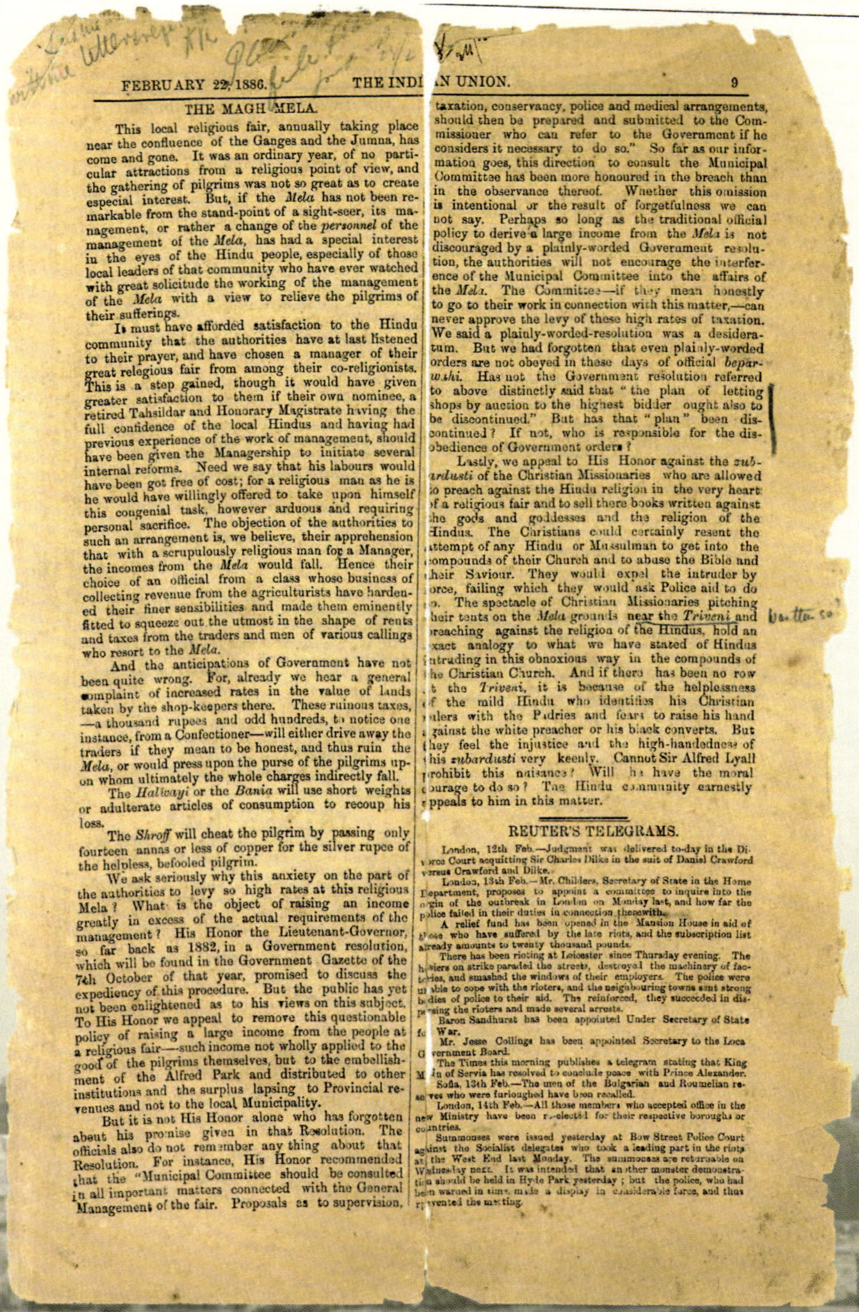

THE MAGH MELA.

This local religious fair, annually taking place near the confluence of the Ganges and the Jumna, has come and gone. It was an ordinary year, of no particular attractions from a religious point of view, and the gathering of pilgrims was not so great as to create especial interest. But, if the *Mela* has not been remarkable from the stand-point of a sight-seer, its management, or rather a change of the *personnel* of the management of the *Mela*, has had a special interest in the eyes of the Hindu people, especially of those local leaders of that community who have ever watched with great solicitude the working of the management of the *Mela* with a view to relieve the pilgrims of their sufferings.

It must have afforded satisfaction to the Hindu community that the authorities have at last listened to their prayer, and have chosen a manager of their great relegious fair from among their co-religionists. This is a step gained, though it would have given greater satisfaction to them if their own nominee, a retired Tahsildar and Honorary Magistrate having the full confidence of the local Hindus and having had previous experience of the work of management, should have been given the Managership to initiate several internal reforms. Need we say that his labours would have been got free of cost; for a religious man as he is he would have willingly offered to take upon himself this congenial task, however arduous and requiring personal sacrifice. The objection of the authorities to such an arrangement is, we believe, their apprehension that with a scrupulously religious man for a Manager, the incomes from the *Mela* would fall. Hence their choice of an official from a class whose business of collecting revenue from the agriculturists have hardened their finer sensibilities and made them eminently fitted to squeeze out the utmost in the shape of rents and taxes from the traders and men of various callings who resort to the *Mela*.

And the anticipations of Government have not been quite wrong. For, already we hear a general complaint of increased rates in the value of lands taken by the shop-keepers there. These ruinous taxes, —a thousand rupees and odd hundreds, to notice one instance, from a Confectioner—will either drive away the traders if they mean to be honest, and thus ruin the *Mela*, or would press upon the purse of the pilgrims upon whom ultimately the whole charges indirectly fall.

The *Halwayi* or the *Bania* will use short weights or adulterate articles of consumption to recoup his loss.

The *Shroff* will cheat the pilgrim by passing only fourteen annas or less of copper for the silver rupee of the helpless, befooled pilgrim.

We ask seriously why this anxiety on the part of the authorities to levy so high rates at this religious Mela? What is the object of raising an income greatly in excess of the actual requirements of the management? His Honor the Lieutenant-Governor, so far back as 1882, in a Government resolution, which will be found in the Government Gazette of the 7th October of that year, promised to discuss the expediency of this procedure. But the public has yet not been enlightened as to his views on this subject. To His Honor we appeal to remove this questionable policy of raising a large income from the people at a religious fair—such income not wholly applied to the good of the pilgrims themselves, but to the embellishment of the Alfred Park and distributed to other institutions and the surplus lapsing to Provincial revenues and not to the local Municipality.

But it is not His Honor alone who has forgotten about his promise given in that Resolution. The officials also do not remember any thing about that Resolution. For instance, His Honor recommended that the "Municipal Committee should be consulted in all important matters connected with the General Management of the fair. Proposals as to supervision, taxation, conservancy, police and medical arrangements, should then be prepared and submitted to the Commissioner who can refer to the Government if he considers it necessary to do so." So far as our information goes, this direction to consult the Municipal Committee has been more honoured in the breach than in the observance thereof. Whether this omission is intentional or the result of forgetfulness we can not say. Perhaps so long as the traditional official policy to derive a large income from the *Mela* is not discouraged by a plainly-worded Government resolution, the authorities will not encourage the interference of the Municipal Committee into the affairs of the *Mela*. The Committee—if they mean honestly to go to their work in connection with this matter,—can never approve the levy of these high rates of taxation. We said a plainly-worded-resolution was a desideratum. But we had forgotten that even plainly-worded orders are not obeyed in these days of official *beparwahi*. Has not the Government resolution referred to above distinctly said that "the plan of letting shops by auction to the highest bidder ought also to be discontinued." But has that "plan" been discontinued? If not, who is responsible for the disobedience of Government orders?

Lastly, we appeal to His Honor against the *zubardusti* of the Christian Missionaries who are allowed to preach against the Hindu religion in the very heart of a religious fair and to sell there books written against the gods and goddesses and the religion of the Hindus. The Christians could certainly resent the attempt of any Hindu or Mussulman to get into the compounds of their Church and to abuse the Bible and their Saviour. They would expel the intruder by force, failing which they would ask Police aid to do so. The spectacle of Christian Missionaries pitching their tents on the *Mela* grounds near the *Triveni* and preaching against the religion of the Hindus, hold an exact analogy to what we have stated of Hindus intruding in this obnoxious way in the compounds of the Christian Church. And if there has been no row at the *Triveni*, it is because of the helplessness of the mild Hindu who identifies his Christian rulers with the Padries and fears to raise his hand against the white preacher or his black converts. But they feel the injustice and the high-handedness of this *zubardusti* very keenly. Cannot Sir Alfred Lyall prohibit this nuisance? Will he have the moral courage to do so? The Hindu community earnestly appeals to him in this matter.

REUTER'S TELEGRAMS.

London, 12th Feb.—Judgment was delivered to-day in the Divorce Court acquitting Sir Charles Dilke in the suit of Daniel Crawford versus Crawford and Dilke.

London, 13th Feb.—Mr. Childers, Secretary of State in the Home Department, proposes to appoint a committee to inquire into the origin of the outbreak in London on Monday last, and how far the police failed in their duties in connection therewith.

A relief fund has been opened in the Mansion House in aid of those who have suffered by the late riots, and the subscription list already amounts to twenty thousand pounds.

There has been rioting at Leicester since Thursday evening. The hosiers on strike paraded the streets, destroyed the machinery of factories, and smashed the windows of their employers. The police were unable to cope with the rioters, and the neighbouring towns sent strong bodies of police to their aid. The reinforced, they succeeded in dispersing the rioters and made several arrests.

Baron Sandhurst has been appointed Under Secretary of State for War.

Mr. Jesse Collings has been appointed Secretary to the Local Government Board.

The Times this morning publishes a telegram stating that King Milan of Servia has resolved to conclude peace with Prince Alexander.

Sofia, 13th Feb.—The men of the Bulgarian and Roumelian reserves who were furloughed have been recalled.

London, 14th Feb.—All those members who accepted office in the new Ministry have been re-elected for their respective boroughs or countries.

Summonses were issued yesterday at Bow Street Police Court against the Socialist delegates who took a leading part in the riots at the West End last Monday. The summonses are returnable on Wednesday next. It was intended that another monster demonstration should be held in Hyde Park yesterday; but the police, who had been warned in time, made a display in considerable force, and thus prevented the meeting.

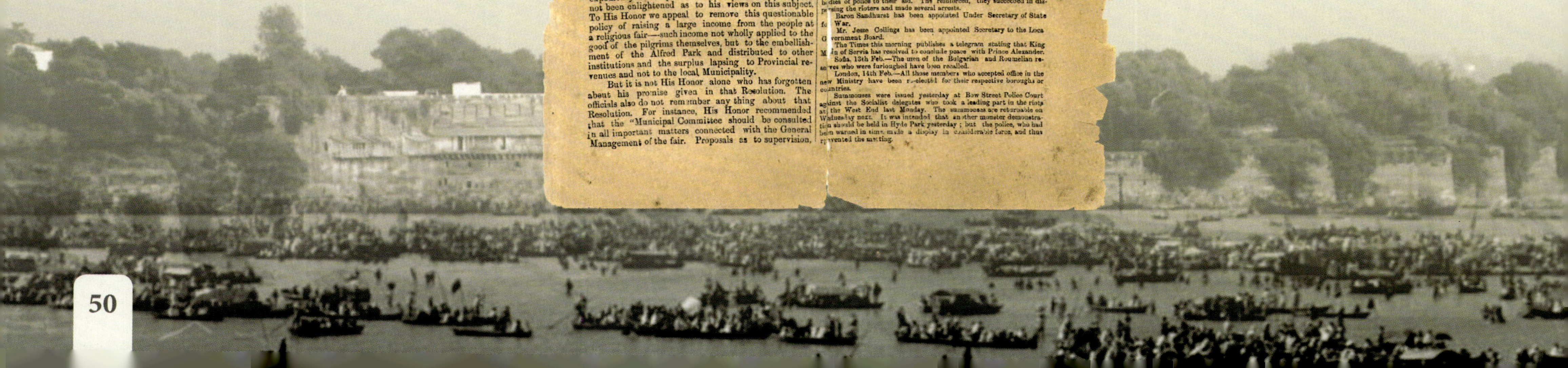

अर्द्ध कुम्भ मेला - सन् 1887

उत्तर पश्चिम प्रान्त एवं अवध के सचिव द्वारा आयुक्त, इलाहाबाद को प्रेषित पत्र 09 जुलाई, 1888 से ज्ञात होता है कि वर्ष 1887 के अर्द्ध कुम्भ मेला में लगभग 5 लाख तीर्थ यात्री आये थे। मेला में स्वच्छता एवं पुलिस की उत्कृष्ट व्यवस्था थी। इस अर्द्ध कुम्भ मेला से सरकार को रू0 37,252/- की आय हुई थी जबकि व्यवस्थाओं पर रू0 17,209/- मात्र का व्यय हुआ था। बचत की धनराशि रू0 22,043/- का व्यय इलाहाबाद नगर में विभिन्न संस्थानों के विकास पर किया गया था।

पत्रावली संख्या-20/1887-88 - क्षेत्रीय अभिलेखागार, प्रयागराज

No. $\frac{813}{\text{XII—372-11}}$ of 1888.

From

The SECRETARY to GOVERNMENT,

N.-W. Provinces and Oudh,

To

The COMMISSIONER, ALLAHABAD DIVISION.

Dated Naini Tal, the 9th July, 1888.

Sir,

(Genl.) Dept. I am directed to acknowledge the receipt of your letter No. $\frac{2876}{20}$, dated 3rd May, 1888, submitting a report on the Magh Mela held at Allahabad on 15th December, 1887, and following days.

2. The fair was an "Adh Kumbh Mela," and as such attracted larger crowds than usually assemble in ordinary years. It is estimated that close on half a million souls were present. Notwithstanding this vast assemblage of pilgrims it is satisfactory to note that the occasion was marked by the almost entire absence of sickness or crime of a serious kind, and that no accidents occurred.

3. The general management of the fair was very successful, and the conservancy arrangements seem to have been excellent. The police worked well. With regard to paragraph 6 of your letter regarding the processions of naked fakirs, I am to say that as the procession only takes place during the Kumbh and Adh Kumbh Melas, the decision of the question may be left to the Government of the day when it practically again arises on the approach of the next Kumbh Mela. A reference should then be made in sufficient time to allow orders to issue before the fair takes place.

4. The income, expenditure, and surplus of the fair were as under:—

Income.	*Expenditure.*	*Surplus.*
Rs.	Rs.	Rs.
37,252	17,209	22,043

From the surplus the following grants, which are annually made from this source, are sanctioned:—

	Rs.
(1) Alfred Park	3,000
(2) Allahabad Public Library	3,600
(3) Colvin Dispensary	2,600
(4) Boatmen and sweepers	168
(5) Fort Garden	200
(6) Eye Hospital	500
Total ...	10,068

The grant of an honorarium of Rs. 250 to Thákur Sitla Bakhsh Singh, Tahsíldár in charge of the fair, recommended by you, is also sanctioned; and, further, a sum of Rs. 3,000 in connection with the Khushru Bágh water-supply scheme.

(2)

5. The balance of the surplus, after deducting the above grants, amounts to Rs. 8,725, which will be credited to Provincial revenues. I am to say that the proposal to allot this amount for additions and alterations to the Colvin Dispensary cannot at present be entertained; but that the project should be submitted to you by the District Board in the ordinary routine for administrative sanction. If the Board cannot provide the amount necessary from their normal budget allotment for this or next year, the case may be represented by you to Government for consideration. The Board should, however, first consider what portion of the cash balance, which is believed to be considerable, of the Allahabad Dispensary Fund can be made available for the work.

6. In conclusion, I am to acknowledge the services of Messrs. Porter and Gray, and of the officers who helped them to bring this important fair to a successful close. The map submitted with your letter is returned.

I have the honor to be,

Sir,

Your most obedient servant,

T. W. HOLDERNESS,

Secy. to Govt., N.-W. P. and Oudh.

No. $\frac{814}{\text{XII—372-12}}$.

Extract, paragraphs 1 and 4 and first sentence of paragraph 5, forwarded to the Accountant-General, North-Western Provinces and Oudh, for information.

By order, &c.,

W. R. PARTRIDGE,

Under-Secy. to Govt., N.-W. P. and Oudh.

अर्द्ध कुम्भ मेला - सन् 1887

इलाहाबाद माघ मेला सन् 1888 में 400 नागा फकीरों के जुलूस को एक अंग्रेज अधिकारी द्वारा स्नान के स्थान (संगम) तक ले जाने पर मख़जान-ए-मसीही नामक अखबार की प्रतिक्रिया- 1888

पत्रावली संख्या-20/1887-88 - क्षेत्रीय अभिलेखागार, प्रयागराज

PROGS. No. 1. SERIAL No. 1.

openly countenance idolatry. Again, the action of the Government in this matter is bad policy, for the natives do not look upon such as favours, but openly boast that *fear* induces Government to do such things. The editor of the *Makhzan* also asks "Would it not be better to send a Hindu to represent Government . . . . ?" This course would be quite as harmful and dishonoring to Christianity; the Government of India is a Christian Government, at least in name, and is in no way called upon to countenance idolatry: the very most that even the most liberal politician can ask is, that Government refrain from taking any active part in Mission work. The editor of the *Makhzan*, in a subsequent paper, remarks that the officer sent on this occasion has himself remonstrated, and that the Christian community, both European and Native, feel the desire no less.

Being informed that you are a Christian gentleman and take an interest in Indian affairs, I, as Chairman of the "Christian Brotherhood," venture to send you these papers for your perusal and consideration. I think in the interest of Christianity which is identical with the best interests of India, and for the honor of the British nation, Parliament ought to take up this matter. If the Government of India is to be neutral in religious matters, let it be a complete neutrality. The action of the Government in this case was a direct insult to Her Imperial Majesty and to Christian Britain; for it is said with truth that Her Majesty approves such exhibitions being present by proxy, *i.e.*, through Her representative. This is how the Native looks upon such courtesy. I may add that this procession is one of the most indecent exhibitions one could imagine. Picture to yourself a procession of 400 men completely naked, smeared with dust and ashes, and escorted by an English officer holding the rank of a Joint-Magistrate: it is not only indecent, it is devilish. Can you, dear sir, do nothing in this matter? For the glory of God and the honor of Christianity, I beg of you to take up the matter and use your best endeavours to induce Parliament to prohibit our Queen-Empress from being represented at such exhibitions for the future.

May God direct you how to act, and bless any efforts you may make: may He crown them with success. You will have the prayers of thousands of Christians here in India.

Extract from the "Makhzan-i-Masihi."

"During the mela at the junction of the Ganges and Jumna this year about 400 fakírs, entirely naked, marched on two different occasions in procession to the bathing-place. Thousands of Hindus, men and women, lined the road to see them; some to worship them. An English officer on an elephant preceded the procession to clear the road and keep order. It was a sad and disgraceful sight. The Government is surely strong enough to put an end to such indecency, even though it call itself Hinduism. By sending a European officer of the rank of Joint-Magistrate to accompany such a procession, the Government upholds that which it punishes as a penal offence elsewhere. It is to countenance that which educated Hindus are ashamed to recognize as a part of their religion.

"The presence of an English officer heading the procession gives an importance and *éclat* to these naked fakírs they would not otherwise have. At any rate, would it not be better to send a Hindu to represent the Government on such an occasion, rather than force an Englishman and a Christian to head the indecents?"

No. 2188, Home Department (Public), dated Simla, the 16th August, 1888.

COPY forwarded to the Government of the North-Western Provinces and Oudh for the favour of an early report as to the facts of the case referred to.

By order,

J. P. HEWETT,

Under-Secretary to the Government of India.

PROGS. No. 2. SERIAL No. 2.

No. $\frac{1111}{\text{III—384A-2}}$.

GENERAL DEPARTMENT.

Dated Naini Tal, the 27th August, 1888.

COPY of Serial No. 1 forwarded to the Collector of Allahabad for report as to what has been the custom in previous years, and precisely what occurred at the last procession.

W. C. BENETT,

Secy. to Govt., N.-W. P. and Oudh.

No. 3. No. 3.

No. $\frac{463}{\text{XXII—97}}$, dated Allahabad, the 21st October, 1888.

From—H. C. CONYBEARE, ESQ., *Offg. Magistrate of Allahabad,*

To—Chief Secretary to Government, N.-W. Provinces and Oudh.

SIR,—I have the honor to answer your No. $\frac{1111}{\text{III—384A-2}}$, dated 27th August, 1888, and to apologize for the delay in answering it. The officers who were Magistrate and Joint-Magistrate of Allahabad at the time of the Mágh Mela are not in India; and the officer who was District Superintendent of Police has been transferred. I was myself not in India at the time.

2. Every twelfth year the great bathing fairs at Hardwár, Allahabad, and other places on the Ganges are called *Kumbh Melas*, that is, fairs of the sign Aquarius; and the fairs which take place half-way between the Kumbh fairs, that is, in the sixth year after a Kumbh fair, are called *Adh-Kumbhs*, that is, half Kumbh fairs. Both the Kumbh and the Adh-Kumbh gatherings are considered much more sacred, and are much more numerously attended, than the bathing assemblages of ordinary years. This year's Mágh Mela was an Adh-Kumbh fair.

3. At the Kumbh and Adh-Kumbh Melas of Allahabad it has always been the custom for different sects of religious mendicants to march down in procession through the fair to bathe at the confluence of the Ganges and the Jumna. Several of these sects belong to a class called Nágas, and the Nágas deem it a religious duty to walk down to the confluence naked. Here as at other places where men bathe naked, such as "Parson's Pleasure" on the Cherwell at Oxford, no one need look at them who prefers not to do so. The custom is not regarded by Hindus at large as an improper custom. The view of these unsophisticated people probably is that the indecency, if any, resides less in the spectacle itself than in the mind of the beholder.

4. In order to prevent quarrels for precedence amongst the various sects of mendicants, and to maintain peace amongst them, it has always been the custom for a Magistrate to accompany the processions to the bathing-place. At the Kumbh and Adh-Kumbh fairs of recent years, if not ever since the introduction of British rule, this Magistrate has been an European. This year the procession, which included three different sects of Nágas, was escorted by the Joint-Magistrate.

5. It is possible that a Native Magistrate—a Muhammadan for preference—would succeed in keeping excellent order; but it is just as well to be on the safe side, and the European officer undoubtedly carries the greater weight. On this point I will venture to refer to what took place under native rule at the great Kumbh Mela of Hardwár in 1760. "An affray," writes Elphinstone, "or rather a battle, took place between the Nágas of Siva and those of Vishnu, in which it was stated on the spot that 18,000 persons were left dead on the field. The amount must doubtless have been greatly exaggerated; but it serves to give an idea of the numbers engaged."

PROGS. No. 4. No. $\frac{1816}{\text{III—384A-5}}$, dated Allahabad the 14th November, 1888. SERIAL No. 5.

From—Secretary to Government, N.-W. Provinces and Oudh,

To—Secretary to the Government of India, Home Dept.

SIR,—I am directed to acknowledge the receipt of your No. 2188 of the 16th August last, forwarding for report a despatch from Her Majesty's Secretary of State for India, and its enclosures, on the subject of the procession of fakírs of the Nága sect at the Mágh Mela or fair held at Allahabad.

2. In reply, I am to state for the information of His Excellency the Governor-General in Council, that the *Kumbh* and *Adh-Kumbh* fairs occur once every twelfth and sixth year, respectively, and that on those occasions it has been customary in Allahabad, and it is believed in other places, to hold the procession referred to. The procession takes place far from the town, on the banks of the river, in the very early morning. It is not forced on the attention of any persons, and can, in truth, be witnessed only by those who actually go at that hour to the confluence of the Ganges and Jumna rivers, far from the city, to see it. There is no indecent action or gesturing of any kind whatever. The men are naked and smeared with earth and ashes; but being considered holy devotees, their nakedness carries with it nothing which shocks the native mind, or suggests to it any idea of indecency. The *Makhzan-i-Masihi*, apparently a Christian paper, does not in this matter reflect the native way of looking at this matter.

3. The Joint-Magistrate or other subordinate English officer attends the fair at Allahabad to keep order between the several rival sects of fakírs and their adherents, among whom much rivalry exists. The cause of his presence is well understood by the natives who frequent the fair and witness the procession.

4. The policy of religious neutrality maintained by the Government of India may, as Mr. Foy in the correspondence forwarded considers, be absurd; so long as it lasts, however, the Lieutenant-Governor and Chief Commissioner sees on the whole no sufficient ground for interfering with a ceremony to which great importance is attached by the Hindu devotees, who in enormous numbers crowd to the Allahabad and other fairs, which is carried out in a place, at an hour, and on an occasion when none but devotees of the Hindu religion need attend, and which the sanctity of the individuals concerned, in the eyes of those of their co-religionists who witness it, robs of all association whatever with anything unbecoming or indecent. I am to add that the matter was referred to the consideration of His Honor the Lieutenant-Governor in March last by a Missionary gentleman resident in Allahabad. He was informed that as the procession takes place once only in six years, and the next occasion will be 1894, any representation which those opposed to the procession might have to make would be more conveniently laid before the Government of that day.

T. W. HOLDERNESS,
Secretary.

Dated Cawnpore, the 11th April, 1888.

From—Arthur Foy, Esq., *Chairman*, "*Christian Brotherhood*,"

To—Samuel Smith, Esq., M.P., *Liverpool*.

Sir,—I send you by to-day's mail three copies each of the *Makhzan-i-Masihi* of the 1st February, and the *Kaukab-i-Hind* or *Star of India* of the 17th February last, and beg to call your kind attention to an article which appears on page 52 of the former, and which is reproduced on page 188 of the latter. The article refers to the fact of an European officer, a Joint-Magistrate, having been deputed by Government to act as an escort to a procession of *naked* fakírs at the "mela" or fair, which took place at Allahabad lately at the junction of the Ganges and Jumna rivers. The editor of the *Makhzan-i-Masihi* very justly remarks that Government in doing this openly supports a part of Hindu religion which educated Hindus themselves are ashamed of. In the opinion, however, of every right-minded Christian, European and Native, in India, the action of the Government in this matter has a wider significance; it officially recognises and supports not a part, but the whole of Hinduism. It is very sad to know that a professedly Christian Government should act in this manner, and that, too, in direct opposition to its own laws—laws framed with a view of putting a stop to such indecent exhibitions. Surely, if the Government of India, following (what I, in common with hundreds of others, cannot but consider absurd) a policy of religious neutrality, cannot actively engage in the work of evangelization, or openly favour even Mission work, it is not called upon to

अर्द्ध कुम्भ मेला 1888 में राजस्व की प्राप्ति तथा व्यय की अर्द्ध कुम्भ मेला 1876 में प्राप्ति एवं व्यय से तुलना

पत्रावली संख्या-20/1887-88-क्षेत्रीय अभिलेखागार, प्रयागराज

Statement No: II

Disbursements from Adh Kumbh Magh Mela for 1887-88 as compared with 1886-87 and also 1875-76.

Serial Number	Heads of charges	1887-88 year under report	1886-87 Last year	1875-76 Last Adh Kumbh	Against 1886-87 Last year: Increase	Against 1886-87 Last year: Decrease	Against 1875-76 Last Adh Kumbh: Increase	Against 1875-76 Last Adh Kumbh: Decrease	Remarks
1	Collection Estt: &c:	1,399 2 1	840 . 8	1,773 . 7	559 1 5	. . .	. . .	373 14 6	
2	Police	3,295 10 10	995 2 .	212 . .	2,300 8 10	. . .	3,083 10 10	. . .	
3	Medical	117 7 3	142 12 6	183 1 3	. . .	25 5 3	. . .	65 10 .	
4	Conservancy	2,227 14 6	1,128 1 7	1,329 6 .	1,099 12 11	. . .	898 8 6	. . .	
5	Public Works	8,995 15 11	3,529 1 3	3,480 9 9	5,466 14 8	. . .	5,515 6 2	. . .	
6	Rent of Land	1,069 9 6	1,351 2 4	2,294 . .	. . .	281 8 10	. . .	1,224 6 6	
7	Miscellaneous	103 8 6	95 3 3	96 12 6	8 5 3	. . .	6 12 .	. . .	
	Total	17,209 4 7	8,081 7 7	9,368 14 1	9,434 11 1	306 14 1	9,504 5 6	1,663 15 .	
			Net		9,127 13 .		7,840 6 6		

Allahabad
The 6th April 1888

[signature]
Magistrate.

Statement No: I.

Receipts from Adh Kumbh Magh Mela for 1887-88 as compared with 1886-87 and also 1875-76.

Serial Number	Description of Receipt	1887-88 year under report	1886-87 Last year	1875-76 Last Adh Kumbh	Against 1886-87 Last year: Increase	Against 1886-87 Last year: Decrease	Against 1875-76 Last Adh Kumbh: Increase	Against 1875-76 Last Adh Kumbh: Decrease	Remarks
1	a Ground Rents	6,208 15 6	4,133 7 -	4,358 11 -	2,075 8 6		1,850 4 6		
	b Shop Rents	17,166 3 9	9,927 15 .	19,065 . .	7,238 4 9			1,898 12 3	
		23,375 3 3	14,061 6 .	23,423 11 .	9,313 13 3		1850 4 6	1,898 12 3	
				Net	9,313 13 3		Net	48 7 9	
2	Search for Money (Divers)	1,092 . .	1,016 8 .		75 8 .		1,092 . .		
						Net	1,092		
3	**License Fees**								
	a Bathing Boats	1,607 . .	1,178 . .		429 . .		1,607 . .		
	b Flower sellers	1,176 . .	1,106 . .		70 . .		1,176 . .		
	c Milk sellers	660 . .	618 . .		42 . .		660 . .		
	d Cow sellers	72 . .	68 . .		4 . .		72 . .		
	e Calf sellers	408 . .	266 . .		142 . .		408 . .		
	f Barbers	7,416 . .	7,592 . .	7,062 14 6		176 . .	353 1 6		
	g Petty Hawkers	741 . .	428 . .		313 . .		741 . .		
		12,080 . .	11,256 . .	7,062 14 6	1,000 . .	176 . .	5,017 1 6		
				Net	824 . .		5,017 1 6		
4	**Miscellaneous**								
	a Beni Dan fees	752 . .	691 8 .		60 8 .		752 . .		
	b Mundan fees	854 4 .	582 4 .		272 . .		854 4 .		
	c Kanat fees	490 . .	370 . .		120 . .		490 . .		
	d Sale of Materials	502 7 .	326 11 6	154 8 .	175 11 6		347 15 .		
	e Sundry receipts	105 15 6	57 2 9	240 . .	48 12 9			134 . 6	
		2,704 10 6	2,027 10 3	394 8 .	677 . 3		2,444 3 .	134 . 6	
						Net	2,310 2 6		
	Grand Total	39,251 13 9	28,361 8 3	30,381 1 6	11,066 5 6	176 . .	10,403 9 .	2,032 12 9	
				Net	10,890 5 6		8,370 12 3		

कुम्भ मेला सन् 1894 में राजस्व की प्राप्ति तथा व्यय की माघ मेला-1895 एवं माघ मेला-1896 की प्राप्ति एवं व्यय से तुलना

पत्रावली संख्या-96/1895-96-क्षेत्रीय अभिलेखागार, प्रयागराज

Statement No. I

Statement showing the receipts from Magh Mela for 1895-96 as compared with that of 1893 and 1894-95. 65

No.	Discription of receipt.	Income for 1895-96	Income for 1894-95	Income for 1893-94 Kumbh	Increase against 1894-95	Increase against 1893-94 Kumbh	Decrease against 1894-95	Decrease against 1893-94 Kumbh	Remarks
1	2	3	4	5	6	7	8	9	10
1	a Ground rent	3090 - 3	2938 3 -	9686 9 9	151 13 3	- - -	- - -	6596 9 6	
	b Shop rent	6103 13 6	5551 8 -	24876 8 -	552 5 6	- - -	- - -	18772 10 6	
		9193 13 9	8489 11 -	34563 1 9	704 2 9	- - -	- - -	25369 4 -	
2	a Divers	704 - -	682 8 -	1874 - -	21 8 -	- - -	- - -	1170 - -	
3	Fees								
	a Boats	1047 - -	826 - -	3311 - -	221 - -	- - -	- - -	2264 - -	
	b Flower Seller	749 - -	840 - -	1600 - -	- - -	- - -	91 - -	851 - -	
	c. Milk "	504 - -	546 - -	1064 - -	- - -	- - -	42 - -	560 - -	
	d Cow "	32 - -	24 - -	176 - -	8 - -	- - -	- - -	144 - -	
	e Calf "	324 - -	370 - -	976 - -	- - -	- - -	46 - -	652 - -	
	f Barbers.	3396 - -	3376 - -	11825 8 -	20 - -	- - -	- - -	8429 8 -	
	g Hawkers	459 - -	454 - -	1440 - -	5 - -	- - -	- - -	981 - -	
		6511 - -	6436 - -	20,392 8 -	254 - -	- - -	179 - -	13881 8 -	
4	Miscellaneous								
	a Beni Dan	921 - -	520 8 -	844 - -	400 8 -	77 - -	- - -	- - -	
	b Mundan	344 - -	373 12 -	1332 8 -	- - -	- - -	29 12 -	988 8 -	
	c. Canat.	300 - -	390 - -	510 - -	- - -	- - -	90 - -	210 - -	
	d Sale of materials	419 4 -	478 10 -	1423 14 -	- - -	- - -	59 6 -	1004 10 -	
	e Sundry receipts	32 2 -	26 1 6	26 11 6	6 - 6	5 6 6	- - -	- - -	
		2016 6 -	1718 15 6	4137 1 6	406 8 6	82 6 6	109 2 -	2203 2 -	
	Grand Total	18425 3 9	17327 2 6	60966 11 3	1386 3 3	82 6 6	288 2 -	42623 14 -	

TRUE COPY
[signature]
Head Assistant.

* [illegible] not yet been included in this account

Sd/ H. M. Bird
Magistrate.

Statement No. II 67

Statement showing disbursements from Magh Mela for 1895-96 as compared with that of 1893-94 & 1894-95.

No.	Heads of charges	Charges for 1895-96	Charges for 1894-95	Charges for 1893-94 Kumbh	Increase against 1894-95	Increase against 1893-94	Decrease against 1894-95	Decrease against 1893-94	Remarks
1	2	3	4	5	6	7	8	9	10
1.	Collection Estb:	933 6 -	849 3 2	2271 7 4	84 2 10	- - -	- - -	1338 1 4	
2	Police.	1517 12 4	1215 13 7	6132 11 9	301 14 9	- - -	- - -	4614 15 5	
3.	Medical.	185 9 3	220 9 8	1225 7 8	- - -	- - -	35 - -	1039 14 5	
4	Conservancy.	1561 - 4	1685 2 10	19286 8 1	- - -	- - -	124 2 6	17725 7 9	
5	Public Works.	6631 7 5	6002 6 6	25604 8 -	629 0 11	- - -	- - -	18973 - 7	
6	Rent of land	729 2 -	1875 5 1	3898 2 3	- - -	- - -	1146 3 1	3169 - 3	
7	Miscellaneous.	55 - -	228 13 2	1008 8 8	- - -	- - -	173 13 2	953 8 8	
	Total	11613 5 4	12077 6 -	59427 5 9	1015 2 6	- - -	1479 3 2	47814 - 5	

TRUE COPY
[signature]
Head Assistant.

Sd/ H. M. Bird
Magistrate.

इलाहाबाद में आयोजित कुम्भ मेला सम्बन्धी सैनिटरी रिपोर्ट सन् 1894

सन् 1894 में इलाहाबाद में आयोजित कुम्भ मेले को स्वच्छता की दृष्टि से सात हिस्सों में विभाजित किया गया, प्रत्येक भाग में एक इंस्पेक्टर, एक सब इंस्पेक्टर, एक हेड कांस्टेबल, चार कांस्टेबल, 20 चैकीदार की व्यवस्था की गयी तथा चिकित्सा उपचार के लिए एक असिस्टेंट सर्जन, चार स्ट्रेचर सहित कहार को नियुक्त किया गया। इन अधिकारियों, कर्मचारियों के निम्न कर्तव्य निर्धारित किये गये:-

1. मेला क्षेत्र के प्रत्येक हिस्से में भ्रमण करना। 2. भीड़ रोकना। 3. उत्पात सम्बन्धी सूचना देना एवं इसे रोकना।

4. अपराधियों के सम्बन्ध में सूचना देना। 5. रोग के बारे में पता लगाना एवं इसकी सूचना देना।

6. बीमार एवं चोटिल व्यक्तियों को सावधानीपूर्वक एवं शीघ्रता से नियत स्थान पर ले जाना।

प्रोसीडिंग, सन् 1894 -वाल्यूम-119 सामान्य प्रशासन विभाग

SERIAL No. 57.

PROGS. No. 1(*b*).

A.—Distribution of the Sanitary staff.

1. The sanitary, medical and police sections of the fair correspond.

2. There are seven sanitary sections :

A, B, C, D, E } On general site.

F, G } On the akhára site.

3. The headquarters of each sanitary and medical section is the thána.

4. Each section is consituted as follows :—

(*a*) *Sanitary*—

(1) One Inspector of Police, Sub-inspector, Head Constable.

(2) Four constables.

(3) Twenty chaukidárs.

(*b*) *Medical*—

(1) Assistant Surgeon or Hospital Assistant.

(2) Four kahárs with stretchers.

5. The above establishment will form the sanitary patrol, each subordinate having an assigned beat. All the police of whatever rank will also perform sanitary duty.

6. The duties are :—

(1) To perambulate every portion of the fair.

(2) To prevent overcrowding.

(3) To report and prevent nuisances.

(4) To report offenders.

(5) To detect, and at once report, sickness.

(6) To remove promptly and carefully those sick and injured.

B.—Sanitary patrol and inspection.

1. The Deputy Sanitary Commissioner will inspect each section at least once a day.

2. The sanitary staff, as detailed, will patrol the fair at all hours of the day and night.

3. The subordinate in charge of each sanitary section will report direct to the Deputy Sanitary Commissioner, and will accompany him in his daily rounds.

4. All special occurrences between visits and general inspections will be reported at once.

5. It will be the especial duty of the sanitary patrol staff under the Inspector, &c., in charge of sections to promptly report sickness and see to the careful removal to the special hospital of persons suffering from diarrhœa and infections or disease of a suspicious nature.

6. All persons suffering from chronic disease or injury should be removed to the Colvin Dispensary, the nearest medical subordinate available tending the injured before removal.

C.—Water-supply and food staff.

1. A piped water-supply will be laid on from the municipal mains, and there will thus be an abundance of pure potable water available at different points on the site of the fair.

4

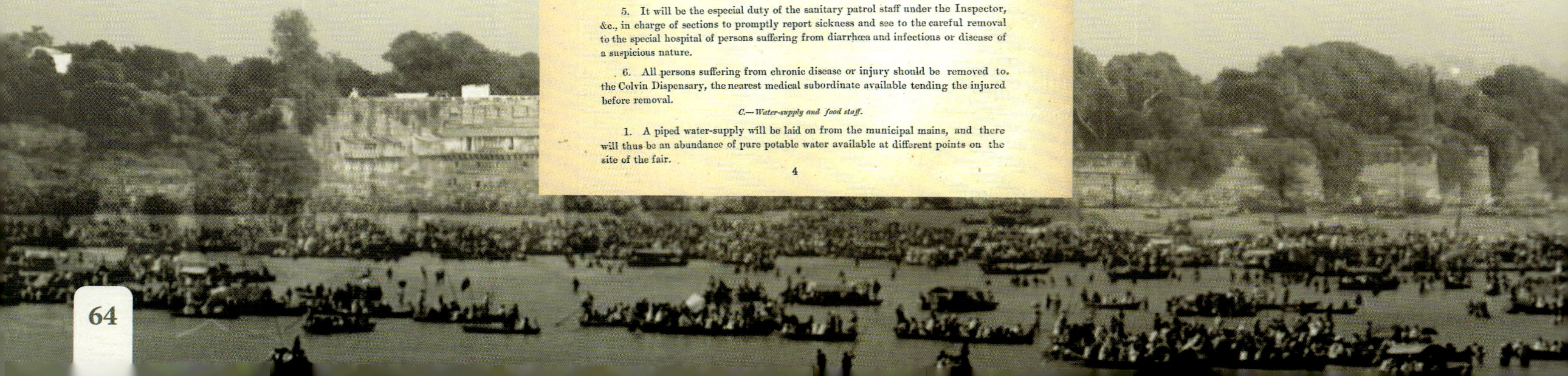

इलाहाबाद में आयोजित कुम्भ मेले से सम्बन्धित एच0 डब्लू0 पाईक, ज्वाइंट मजिस्ट्रेट प्रभारी, माघ मेला द्वारा 16 मार्च, 1894 को जारी मेमोरेण्डम में कहा गया कि इस वर्ष गंगा की धारा झूंसी से बदलकर किले की तरफ हो गयी है इसलिए साधुओं को संगम तक पहुँचने हेतु एक नया नावों का पुल रू0 9500/- की लागत से बनाया गया। गंगा का प्रवाह बदलने के कारण रू0 15700/- का व्यय अतिरिक्त किया गया।

प्रोसीडिंग वाल्यूम- सन् 1894

प्रोसीडिंग वाल्यूम- सन् 1894- सामान्य प्रशासन विभाग

PROGS. No. 2(c).

SERIAL No. 60.

Memo. by H. W. PIKE, Joint-Magistrate, in charge of Magh Mela, Allahabad, dated 16th March 1894.

A KUMBH Melá occurs at Allahabad, acccording to the report on the last Kumbh fair, when the planet Jupiter is in Aquarius and the sun in Aries. This takes place once in 12 years; and the fair is on these occasions of peculiar sanctity and resorted to by enormous crowds of pilgrims.

2. The general management of the fair this year was in the hands of the Tahsíldár, Thakur Sitla Bakhsh Singh, who acted under the direct orders of the Magistrate of the district. My own province, as officer in general charge of the fair, was to see that these orders were carried out, and to arrange for the disposal of minor points of detail as they arose, in communication with the Deputy Sanitary Commissioner, the District Superintendent of Police and the Tahsíldár. For this purpose a meeting was held every day at the Tahsíli at 10 A.M., and the necessary orders were issued.

Surgeon-Major Giles, the Deputy Sanitary Commissioner, was in charge of the sanitary arrangements of the fair, under the orders of the Sanitary Commissioner, who himself paid constant visits to the site.

Mr. Bernard Johnstone was deputed to supervise the police arrangements of the fair, which he did with the assistance of Inspector Kalian Singh, the Kotwal, and Ram Kishen Singh, Sub.-Inspector. The medical arrangements were in the charge of the Civil Surgeon. From about the 10th January to 11th February 1894, the District Superintendent of Police, the Deputy Sanitary Commissioner and myself were encamped at Alopi Bágh, close to the fair, in order to be ready to deal with any emergency.

Thakur Sitla Bakhsh has now held charge of the Mágh Melá for 8 years, and his experience was invaluable. His onerous and arduous duties could not have been performed more efficiently, and the readiness and accuracy with which he met the constant demands of the various departments was admirable. He was also very successful in dealing with that troublesome body, the Bairagis. Munshi Nawal Kishore proved an able assistant, and was assiduous and punctual in the discharge of his duties.

3. The arrangements of this fair are liable to great modifications according to the course taken by the river Ganges. If, as was the case at the last Kumbh, the main stream flows under the cliffs of Jhunsi, there is little difficulty and expense in carrying on the fair. This year the main stream was towards the Fort side, and caused great inconvenience, though, from a sanitary point of view, the division of inhabited sites thus rendered necessary was desirable. Thus the space for bathing at the *Sangam* or confluence of the rivers was confined to about 10 feet from the shore instead of there being a large area of shallow water. The precipitous bank there was some 30 feet high, and was constantly being cut away by the river, entailing great expenditure on coolies employed in cutting it, so as to cause it to shelve more or less gradually to the water's edge. It was necessary to erect a bridge of boats at a cost of Rs. 9,500, to enable the Fakírs located across the main stream to communicate with the *Sangam*. There was some difficulty in marshalling the processions of Fakirs. Finally the river rose considerably just before the two largest bathing days, and rendered communication across the bridge difficult at those points where the road crossed sand which became submerged by the flood. The extra expense may be roughly estimated as follows :—

	Rs.	
(1)	2,200	compensation for Cantonment lands, which it would have been unnecessary to occupy if the river had taken an easterly course. The sum paid on this account at the last Kumbh was Rs. 600, which has been deducted from the sum actually spent this year to give the extra expense.
(2)	9,500	for the bridge.
(3)	4,000	for earth-work. This figure is arrived at from a comparison of the amount paid for labour this year, Rs. 6,800, with that paid at last Kumbh, Rs. 1,400, allowing for the fact that there were more kutcha roads to be made on the present occasion.
	15,700	

The total extra expenditure is thus 27 per cent. of the whole (Rs. 57,199).

1

(104)

MIS. (GENERAL) DEPT.] [AUGUST 1894

PROGS. No. 2(e).

SERIAL No. 60

7. I will now briefly notice the work done by the Police during the Melá—

Reports of crime	...	152
Investigated	...	144
Cases convicted	...	111
Acquitted	...	8
Pending	...	9
Undetected	...	23
Persons arrested	...	250
Convicted	...	225
Acquitted	...	8
Pending	...	17
Stolen	...	Rs. 2,111-13-6 } Property.
Recovered	...	Rs. 597-11-6 } Property.

These figures I venture to think are excellent. No really serious cases of any kind occurred, and the *budmashes* who visited the fair from every district in India were so promptly dealt with, that they really found no opportunity for mischief. Bearing in mind that this was the Kumbh Melá, and that the gathering was, say, five times as large as an ordinary gathering, the Police surveillance may be fairly described as excellent. During the fair a gang of Bauriáhs camped on the outskirt; intelligence was brought to Inspector Kalian Singh and a party of constables disguised as fakirs, sent out, and eight of the gang were arrested and subsequently punished under section 109, C. P. C.

In connection with surveillance of bad characters and general good work during the fair, I beg to recommend the following officers to favorable notice :—

Inspector Kalian Singh, a host in himself.
,, K. Muhammad Husain, sound and good work.
Sub-Inspector Hamid Husain, ,, ,,
,, Baldeo Singh, ,, ,,
,, Pancham Singh, ,, ,,

Officiating Inspector Ram Kishun Singh, who, in conservancy and other duties, worked exceptionally hard, never sparing himself.

Sub-Inspector Manni Lal was posted at the bridge: he performed his duties conscientiously and with much tact.

Head-Constable Girwar Singh of Daraganj police-station did good work in seeing that Pragwals kept their houses clean.

Sub-Inspector Mahabir Singh looked after the Bairagis in particular and conservancy in general. These duties he performed most satisfactorily.

8. On the bathing days, when the multitude might without exaggeration be estimated at over a million, the following officers rendered most valuable assistance :—

Messrs. E. Lawson, Assistant Superintendent of Police.
R. Kinloch, ditto ditto.
A. Ashdown, ditto ditto.
W. Martin, ditto ditto.
Inspector E. Mayho.
Sergeant F. Down.
Sub-Inspector of Mounted Police, Chandan Singh.

9. *Conservancy.*—The Conservancy staff of sweepers, numbering roughly 1,500, was under the orders of Surgeon-Major Giles, but the station officers exercised control over the sweepers of their respective circles. I also detailed Sub-Inspector Mahair Singh, one head constable, and 20 constables, for Conservancy duties.

10. Two fires broke out, clearing in each instance about an acre of huts. The fires were got out by pulling down surrounding houses. Water I found practically useless; a brush wood hut burns like touch-paper, and the only thing to do is to r the space around and let it burn out.

PROCS. No. 2(*e*). SERIAL No. 60.

11. At each end of the bridge communicating with the island on which the bodies of Ascetics were encamped, a party of police under a Sub-Inspector was posted. Head-constables were at first tried, but as the duty was one requiring both influence and discretion, I found it necessary to place officers of higher rank at these posts.

12. Each thána kept its own register of births and deaths, which were received in Daraganj police-station and sent from that thána to the head-quarter's office.

13. Lost children were taken to the thána in the precincts of which they were discovered, and in all cases were recovered by their friends.

B. JOHNSTON,
Assistant District Superintendent of Police.

सन् 1906 में कुम्भ मेला इलाहाबाद पर सैनिटरी रिपोर्ट

इस रिपोर्ट में 10 जनवरी, 1906 से 12 फरवरी, 1906 तक इलाहाबाद में आयोजित किये गये कुम्भ मेले में की गयी स्वच्छता व्यवस्था के बारे में बताया गया है साथ ही विभिन्न विभागों द्वारा की गयी व्यवस्था के बारे में जानकारी दी गयी है। रिपोर्ट में विशेष पर्वों पर कुल स्नान करने वाले श्रद्धालुओं का संख्या वार विवरण प्रस्तुत किया गया है। मेडिकल और स्वच्छता हेतु कुल मेला प्रांगण (Ground) को दो भागों में बाटा गया था। प्रथम भाग में संगम, बाजार, नाईबारा तथा तीर्थ यात्रियों हेतु कैंपिंग ग्राउण्ड को सम्मिलित किया गया जबकि दूसरे भाग में साधुओं तथा अखाड़ों के निवास हेतु व्यवस्था की गई थी। कैप्टन पियरसन को प्रथम भाग का इंचार्ज बनाया गया तथा उनके अंडर में 1 असिस्टेंट सर्जन, 5 हॉस्पिटल असिस्टेंट, 1 महिला हॉस्पिटल असिस्टेंट तथा कम्पाउंडर के साथ 27 वैक्सीनेटरों को रखा गया। डा0 ओहडीदार को द्वितीय भाग का इंचार्ज बनाया गया तथा उनके अंडर में 1 असिस्टेंट सर्जन, 1 यूरोपियन सेनीटरी इंस्पेक्टर, 1 हॉस्पिटल असिस्टेंट, 1 महिला हॉस्पिटल असिस्टेंट तथा 3 कम्पाउंडरों के साथ ही 21 वैक्सीनेटरों को भी रखा गया।

सन्-1906 - मिस्लेनियस विभाग प्रोसीडिंग

Sanitary Report on the Kumbh Magh Mela at Allahabad in 1906.

I.—DURATION AND ATTENDANCE.

FROM a religious point of view the *mela* commenced on January 10th, and continued till February 12th—the last of the special bathing days—but it had been anticipated that there would be a considerable population of Sadhus and others on the *mela* ground by January 1st. Till January 6th, however, with the exception of a few hundred Bairagis, practically no pilgrims had arrived, and the population consisted almost solely of shopkeepers, Pragwalas and their servants, and others connected with the general preparation for the arrival of pilgrims. After that date, the *mela* really started, and the population went up quickly. The following table gives the dates of the chief bathing days and the estimated population on each, but the latter can only be considered as a fair approximation :—

Date.	*Name.*	*Population (approximate).*
10th January 1906 ...	Puranmashi	200,000
14th " " ...	Shankrant	1,000,000
24th " " ...	Amawas	2,500,000
29th " " ...	Basant Panchmi ...	500,000
31st " " ...	Achala Satami	200,000
5th February " ...	Ekadashi	100,000
9th " " ...	Puranmashi	150,000
12th " " ...	Shankrant	100,000

The numbers given above do not represent the actual number of people supposed to be resident at any one time within the *mela* grounds, but the full number who visited the *mela* for bathing on each particular day. This point is especially important from a sanitary point of view, as it makes a very obvious difference both in the amount and distribution of the sanitary accommodation required. I have, therefore, attempted to give in the following table an estimate of the numbers actually resident in the *mela* grounds, as distinguished from residents of the city, pilgrims living in houses in the city and other daily visitors :—

Date.	*Population (approximate).*
December 15th to 31st	1,000 to 6,000
January 1st to 10th	6,000 " 100,000
" 11th and 12th	100,000 " 150,000
" 13th " 14th	150,000 ...
" 15th to 20th	100,000 ...
" 21st and 22nd	100,000 to 500,000
" 23rd " 24th	500,000 " 1,500,000
" 25th	700,000 ...
" 26th to 31st	600,000 to 100,000
February 1st to 12th	100,000 " 25,000

After February 12th the *mela* dispersed rapidly.

As in the case of the first table, these figures must be taken as a rough approximation only, as there was no means of actually counting the people. It will be seen, however, that the population is a very fluctuating one, and that the vast majority of the people come in for a few days only, and then go off to their homes, while the number of true Kalpbashis is very small indeed.

II.—SITE AND DISPOSITION OF CAMPS.

In my preliminary report forwarded early in December, the general disposition of the camps was fully described, and later no alterations were made except in minor details to meet special circumstances. Both the Ganges and the Jamna fell much in volume, and while this was of great benefit in that a much better approach to the *sangam* than had been expected was provided, it increased the

danger of pollution of the water-supply enormously. The general area of the *mela* was also much larger than was at first anticipated, especially on the far side of the Ganges along the bank of the river, at Arail, and to the north and west on this side of the *bandh*. In the first of these areas a long line of small encampments extended for about 1½ miles from the *sangam*.

The *sota* near the Bairagi encampment became much smaller as the Ganges and the Jamna fell, and it was enclosed completely with a barbed wire fencing strengthened by thorns.

The *achaibat* in the fort has always been one of the chief plots in the sanitary conduct of the *Magh mela*. The temple, which is underground, was approached by a single narrow stair and a long narrow underground passage, and the only means of natural lighting and ventilation was an isolated small grated opening in the roof of this passage. The temple itself, even at mid-day, was in complete darkness, but for the scanty light given by a large number of *chirags* on the walls of the passage and shrine and in front of the different idols. On a big bathing day, when crowds of pilgrims visited the shrine, the condition of the air was intolerable to any one but a devotee, and the fear of crime was so great that many Hindus refused to allow their women to visit the shrine. This has all been changed, and the temple is now well lighted and ventilated by a sufficiency of openings in its roof, and a new stair has been provided for the exit of pilgrims. I understand that it is contemplated making coverings for these new-sky lights to protect the temple from rain, but the greatest care should be taken that, if made, nothing should be allowed which will in any way interfere with the lighting and ventilation and so lessen the improvement which has been gained.

III.—GENERAL PREPARATIONS.

Arrangements for the sanitation of the *mela* were begun early in November, and were carried out on the lines indicated in my preliminary report and as sanctioned by you. I visited Allahabad three times during November and December.

IV.—MEDICAL AND SANITARY STAFF.

From 15th December 1905 the following staff was present :—

Assistant Surgeon	1
Hospital Assistants	4
European Sanitary Inspector	1

The Naib Tahsildar had been working for some time previously. Captain Pearson, I.M.S., arrived on 27th December 1905, and took charge till my arrival on 9th January.

From 1st January the staff was increased by the following :—

Assistant Surgeons...	2
Hospital Assistants	10
Female Hospital Assistants	2
Compounders	2
Vaccinators	14

and, again, on the outbreak of cholera, the following additional staff was posted for duty :—

Dr. Ohdedar.	
Hospital Assistants	2
Compounders	4
Vaccinators	50

For sanitary and medical purposes the whole *mela* ground was divided into two sections. Of these, section I included the area on this side of the Ganges and also Arail, and section II was the area beyond the Ganges. Section I thus comprised the pilgrims general camping-ground, the *bazar* and *naibara*, the approach to the *sangam*, the ferry to Arail and the *sangam* itself, while section II was almost

wholly occupied with the different sects of Sadhus either as *akharas* or individuals. As occasion demanded, changes were made in the disposition of the staff, but the general distribution was as follows :—

Captain Pearson, I.M.S., was in charge of section I, and had under him :—

Assistant Surgeon	1
Hospital Assistants	5
Female Hospital Assistant	1
Compounders	3
Vaccinators	27

Dr. Ohdedar was in charge of section II with following staff :—

Assistant Surgeon	1
European Sanitary Inspector	1
Hospital Assistants	7
Female Hospital Assistant	1
Compounders	3
Vaccinators	21

One Assistant Surgeon was in charge of the sanitation and lodging-house inspection in Daraganj and Kydganj with a staff as follows :—

Hospital Assistants	2
Vaccinators	8

One Hospital Assistant and four vaccinators were on railway inspection duty at Naini and Allahabad railway stations respectively. The Naib Tahsildar was my assistant for general executive work, pay of sweepers, coolies, beldars, &c.

V.—FOOD.

All shops selling food were inspected regularly, and any supplies found unfit for human consumption were condemned and destroyed with the consent of the owner. The chief complaints were against the Halwais for bad cooking, and this in the majority of cases was more the result of inability to meet the demand than of carelessness. In two cases only were prosecutions resorted to and, in each case, it was only after repeated warnings had been given.

VI.—WATER.

In section I (this side of the *bandh*) filtered water from the Municipal supply was laid on in pipes to standposts placed at regular intervals over the whole area, and all the wells were disinfected and closed down with the exception of three. Of these latter, two were regularly disinfected, but the third, which was used only for supplying water to pour on the shrines at Hanuman's temple, had to be left undisinfected owing to the objection raised by the owners.

In previous years much difficulty has been met in preventing the formation of quagmires round each standpost, as the pilgrims constantly leave the taps running. To prevent this, as far as possible, a circular area round each standpost was hollowed out and laid with kankar, and to one side of this a large pit was dug to catch as much of the spilled water as possible. At each standpost one kahar and two sweepers had to be stationed—the former to close the tap when left running, and the sweepers for emptying the waste water *hauz*. Self-closing taps had been ordered, and it had been hoped that they would allay the nuisance considerably. Unfortunately there was a delay in their delivery, but after they did arrive, they were found very useful.

In section II the population consisted almost wholly of Sadhus who will not use pipe-water, and it was, therefore, decided to allow them to have wells. Altogether forty-one wells were sunk, of which fourteen were made by the *mela* authorities and twenty-seven others were made by private individuals. All were of one pattern, and were provided with galvanized iron cylinders. On the outbreak of cholera the question arose as to whether it would not be possible to close all these

wells and lay on a supply of pipe-water, but it was decided for the following reasons that the wells would have to be kept open if possible :—

(*a*) The only pipes available could not be obtained and laid in less than a fortnight, *i.e.* till after the 24th, which was the chief bathing day—a date too late to be of much practical use.

(*b*) The pipes when laid would not have been able to deliver a full supply of water and only a partial solution of the difficulty would be obtained.

(*c*) The difficulty of closing some wells and not others. Measures had, therefore, to be taken to protect the wells from pollution as far as possible, and for this two kahars with *doles* and ropes were placed at each of the public wells to draw water for any pilgrims requiring it; and, after the danger from pollution had been fully explained to them, the owners of the private wells were asked to make the same arrangements. Two chaukidars were stationed at each well to help the kahars, but it was soon obvious that these were useless and, even when constables had been placed, the Sadhus still persisted in using their own *lotas*. It was then decided that all the Government wells should be closed at once, with the exception of four which had to be left for watering roads. This was done on the 18th January, and it was explained to private owners that their wells also would have to be shut. Much opposition was at first met, but by persuasion all the wells were gradually closed down. The Bairagis, however, gave much trouble by continually digging small shallow excavations in the lower lying areas of sand, and one Hospital Assistant and two vaccinators had to be told off to search for these and have them closed as soon as found.

At Arail the Jamna and the Ganges were the only source of water-supply, and everything was done to keep the edges of these rivers, there, and also throughout the *mela* area, as free from pollution as possible.

For wells outside the *mela* area and in Daraganj it was arranged that the Health Officer of Allahabad should see to their disinfection regularly, and should station two Brahmans at each with ropes and *doles* for the supply of water. This arrangement continued till the 23rd when, owing to the very large influx of people, it was found that two men could not possibly draw all the water required, and the arrangement had to be temporarily suspended in the case of one or two wells.

In the city the general water-supply is the filtered supply laid on in pipes.

VII.—HOSPITAL AND MEDICAL RELIEF.

(*a*) There were two main dispensaries—one in each section. These were centrally situated, and each was supplied with the necessary drugs and instruments for the treatment of ordinary diseases and injuries. At the dispensary in section I was kept the complete stock, from which the other dispensary and hospitals were supplied.

In section II was the cholera hospital for the whole *mela*, and here all cases from both sections were taken for treatment. Originally of 8 huts, it had to be enlarged to 14. To this hospital were also taken such cases as occured in Daraganj, Kydganj and Jhusi.

When cholera broke out at Arail a small hospital was started there, as it was found impossible to convey cholera cases by boat across the river without serious risk. Towards the end of the *mela* a separate leper asylum was built in section II, but this was never occupied as the lepers preferred to leave the *mela* rather than be segregated.

(*b*) All cases of sickness applying for relief were attended to. Cholera cases were sent to the cholera hospital, and other cases were either treated in their own

huts as out-door patients, or sent to the Colvin Hospital in the city : 281 cases were sent to the cholera hospital and observation huts. Of these, 4 cases turned out to be suffering from other diseases and were discharged. Of the remainder 207 died, and 70 were cured. The percentage of deaths seems high, but was not really so when it is remembered that cases were usually received after they had spent the first night of sickness lying in the sand in the open air, and that the majority of the patients were old people.

Of general diseases there were 1,609 cases treated as out-door patients, and of these 1,321 attended the main dispensary in section I, and 288 the smaller dispensary in section II. The diseases which were so treated were either less serious ones, or the patients were unwilling to go to hospital.

An abstract of the cases is given below :—

Disease	Cases
Local injury	40
Toothache	76
Sinus	1
Ulcers	189
Parapphimosis	1
Eye diseases	39
Ear diseases	37
Foreign body	1
Burns	5
Abscess	18
Dysentery	122
Diarrhœa	65
Stomatatis	3
Round worm	1
Other digestive diseases	163
Malaria	208
Nervous diseases	48
Debility	12
Skin diseases	201
Erysipelas	2
Pneumonia	3
Other respiratory diseases	288
Throat	16
Rheumatism	32
Syphilis	11
Gonorrhœa	8
Glands	14
Urethritis	5
Orchitis	1
Soft chancre	5
Heart disease	1
Circulatory diseases	38
Piles	7
Epilepsy	4

Twenty-three cases were sent to hospital in the city for treatment, and these were as follows :—

Disease	Cases
Pneumonia	3
Dysentery	2
Debility	1
Diarrhœa	1
Ulcer	4
Injuries	12

VIII.—GENERAL HEALTH.

Unfortunately cholera broke out early in January and continued practically to the end of the *mela*, but if this is omitted the general health on the whole was good. There were 167 non-cholera deaths in the *mela*, and this, calculated on an average population of 200,000 for one month, gives a death-rate of only 10 per mille per annum, and if the 267 deaths from cholera be added (excluding cholera deaths amongst cases brought into the cholera hospital from outside for treatment) the full death-rate per mille per annum becomes 26, which compares very favourably with the average death for cities in these provinces—45·11.

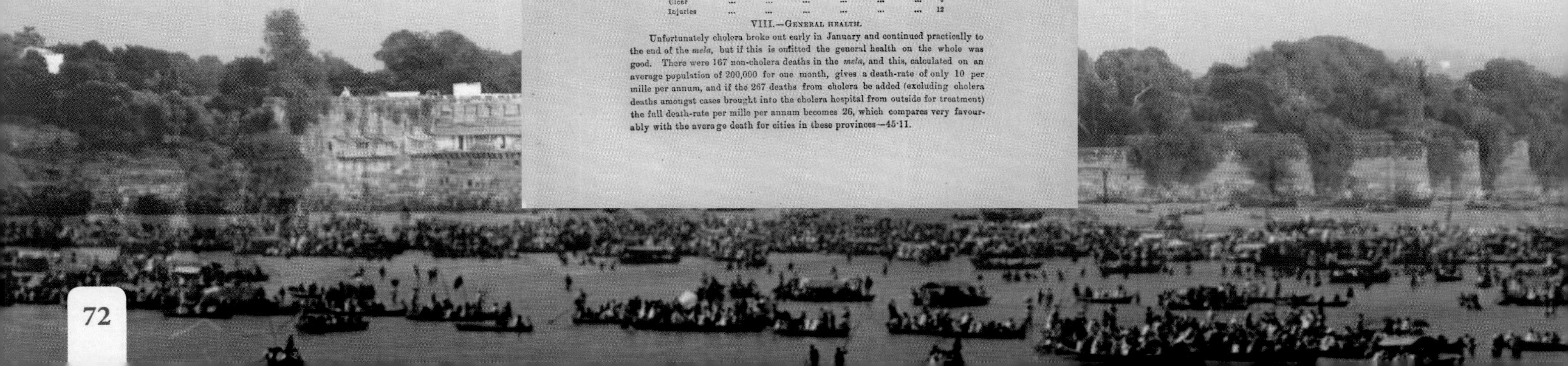

सन् 1906 में कुम्भ मेला इलाहाबाद की पुलिस व्यवस्था की रिपोर्ट

सन् 1906 के कुम्भ मेला की पुलिस व्यवस्था के सम्बन्ध में पुलिस अधीक्षक, इलाहाबाद मिस्टर डगलस स्टेग्ट द्वारा पुलिस व्यवस्था के सम्बन्ध में प्रस्तुत मेमोरेन्डम में अवगत कराया गया कि 10 जनवरी से 12 फरवरी के मध्य आयोजित कुम्भ में भीड़ नियंत्रित करने एवं कानून व्यवस्था बनाये रखने के लिए सामान्य पुलिस बल के अतिरिक्त 400 पुलिस बल की व्यवस्था की गयी, तीन सिग्नल स्टेशन स्थापित किए गये। इनको नियंत्रित करने के लिए यूरोपीय और देशी सिग्नलर्स को नियुक्त किया गया जो मिलिट्री के थे। 24 जनवरी मौनी अमावस्या के दिन संगम पर 25 लाख लोगों की भीड़ नियंत्रित करने के लिए भी पुलिस व्यवस्था की गयी। पुलिस को सहायता के लिए 50 इन्फेन्ट्री को भी लगाया गया। जिलाधिकारी के आदेश से कोतवाली पर फायर स्टेशन स्थापित किया गया जिसमें किसी भी स्थिति से निपटने के लिए एक दल का भी गठन किया गया।

पत्रावली संख्या-153/1906 - सामान्य प्रशासन विभाग

PROCEEDINGS

OF THE

Government of the United Provinces

IN THE

MISCELLANEOUS DEPARTMENT

FOR THE MONTH OF

JULY 1906.

PROGS. NOS. 1 TO 6. File no. 153/1906.] SERIAL NOS. 1 TO 6.

No. 1. No. 1018/II—848-1905, dated the 29th March 1906. No. 1.

From—R. H. BRERETON, ESQ., *Inspector-General of Police, United Provinces,*

To—Secretary to Government, United Provinces.

SIR,—I have the honour to forward, for the information of Government, a memorandum by Mr. D. M. Straight, superintendent of police, Allahabad, on the police arrangements made in connection with the Kumbh Mela of 1906. The memorandum is valuable, as it contains full details of the disposition of the police and of the various incidents which occurred, and which will have to be guarded against on future similar occasions. Although the extra force of police deputed to Allahabad was a very large one the accident which occurred on the 24th January and the fact that it was found necessary to call on the military for assistance are clear indications that it was scarcely sufficient. The number of visitors was, however, quite abnormal and it is unlikely that it will ever be exceeded. In any case it appears certain that there should always be on the spot a small squadron of cavalry to assist the police in emergencies such as those described. The force of police employed on this occasion may therefore be considered to be the maximum required on future occasions. The unfortunate outbreak of cholera spread to the police on duty and by the death of sub-inspector Ramadhin the department has lost an exceptionally good officer. Mr. Straight's proposal made in paragraph 9 that all members of the force should be supplied with water bottles of the pattern used in the Native Army is scarcely feasible. The expense would be considerable and complications would arise owing to resignations, discharges and other casualties. Moreover, it is only on a few particular occasions that water bottles would be necessary and they would probably not be kept by the men properly clean. Mr. Straight points out that on the 2nd and 3rd bathing days he arranged to have supplies of drinking water at various places along the route of the processions, the result being that the disease practically disappeared and the same precautions should be taken on future occasions.

I agree with Mr. Straight in his commendation of the officers and men mentioned by him in paragraph 10. In the case of inspector Lachmi Das his recommendation contravenes the orders of Government laid down at page 52, department IV, volume I of the Manual of Government Orders. Suitable rewards will presumably be given to deserving officers and men from the fair fund.

PROGS. NO. 1(*a*). *Memorandum by* MR. DOUGLAS STRAIGHT, *District Superintendent of Police, on the police arrangements made in connection with the* Kumbh Mela *of* 1906. SERIAL NO. 1.

THE Kumbh Mela of 1906 commenced approximately on the 10th January and terminated on the 12th February, on the occasion of the second day of the Sankrant. Arrangements had been made for an additional police force of 400 men with a complement of officers to control the crowds and maintain order generally throughout the fair, and according to the original programme these were to have been supplemented on the big bathing days, namely, the 14th January (Sankrant), the 24th (Moni Amawas) and the 29th (Basant Panchimi), by reinforcements of native cavalry and infantry, who had been requisitioned to assist the police. Unfortunately the arrangements were somewhat dislocated, owing to an outbreak of cholera in the fair, and it was considered undesirable to employ native troops. Arrangements were accordingly made by the Inspector-General of Police for a second contingent of additional police and sawars. These arrived on the 9th and 10th January. I have given in Appendix A the strength of the additional police force as it stood on the 12th January 1906, and have shown in Appendix B the disposition of the force. I have also drawn up a rough sketch map showing the sites of the various *akharas*, and the positions of police stations, outposts, &c.

2. From this it will be seen that the principal *akharas* were located on the far side of the Ganges in the sandy bed of the river. On the big bathing days, the *akharas* marched in procession according to order of precedence, across the Ramghat bridge on to the esplanade below the Fort, proceeding thence *viâ* the *Sangam* to the *Tribeni* and returning to the encampment *viâ* the *Sangam* bridge-of-boats. The general idea was that no *akhara* was to be allowed on to the *Sangam* until the preceding *akhara* had recrossed the *Sangam* bridge-of-boats; and in order to prevent any possibility of rival *akharas* clashing, a strong force of police mounted and foot was detailed for duty with each procession, special precautions being taken in respect to the three factions of Bairagis. I have shown in Appendix B the strength and disposition of the reserve police detailed for duty on the principal bathing days, and have also attached a copy of my orders regulating the general police arrangements.

3. The first contingent of additional police was accommodated in thatched huts to the north of the pakka road leading to the bandh. The second contingent was accommodated in 160lb tents, very kindly lent us by the Ordnance Department, and was encamped to the south of this road; and the mounted police was accommodated in tents, also lent us by the Ordnance Department, in a grove known as Lalkothi.

4. Signalling stations were established at—

(1) No. 6 Battery in the Southern Bastion of the Fort.
(2) The Ramghat bridgehead.
(3) The Bairagi encampment.

These signalling stations were controlled by European and Native signallers lent us by the Military Department, and orders to start the processions, &c., were heliographed from the Fort Station to the bridgehead. This arrangement enabled the authorities to keep in constant touch, and was, in fact, the means of averting a serious riot on the third big bathing day.

5. *14th January (Sankrant).*—The first big day of the bathing passed off quietly. The arrangements were completely satisfactory and everything went without a hitch.

24th January (Moni Amawas).—On this occasion the crowd of pilgrims had swelled considerably, and was estimated at 25 lakhs, and even in the early part of the day it was found impossible to keep the main approaches clear for the *akharas*. All went well until the *akharas* of Nirbanis had actually reached the *Sangam*. I had personally conducted this *Akhara* to the *Sangam*. On reaching the top of the slope, I noticed an ugly crush on the inside of the barricade, *i.e.* on the slope below

PROGS. NO. 1(*a*). SERIAL NO. 1.

the Fort walls leading to the *Sangam*. At this point a European inspector, one Sergeant and about a dozen constables were available for duty. Here a surging mass of eager pilgrims were bustling to and from the *Tribeni*. The barricade showed signs of giving way, and there were indications of a catastrophe. Mr Sherring and myself with a handful of mounted police did our best to stem the rush, and I eventually made my way to the Beni Phatak and there wrote for the assistance of 50 infantry from the Fort to assist the police in establishing cordons In the meantime an unfortunate accident had occurred: ten persons being trampled to death (mostly old women) and 18 injured. Subsequently half a squadron of cavalry was requisitioned, and with the assistance of the Military, we were able to cope with the vast multitude of pilgrims without further accidents.

29th January (Basant Panchimi).—On the occasion of the Basant Panchimi, precautionary measures were taken to avoid a possible repetition of the accident on the 24th, half a squadron of native cavalry being requisitioned to assist the police. All went well until the Bairagi procession was about to start. This would be at about 12 midday. At that time I received a heliograph message from Mr. Fawkes, Assistant District Superintendent of Police, intimating that trouble between rival factions of Bairagis might be expected on the *Sangam*. I may here mention that, by agreement, the *akhara* of Nirbanis was to lead the procession in order of precedence, followed by the Digambars, the Nirmohis bringing up the rear. On the return journey, the order was to be reversed, the Nirmohis leading, and the Nirbanis following the Digambars; the three *akharas* following each other in close order.

On receipt of Mr. Fawkes' message I hastened to inform the District Magistrate. By that time a second half squadron of cavalry had arrived in relief of the two troops on duty from the early morning. With the sanction of the Magistrate both half squadrons were detained. After the Nirbanis had passed on to the *Sangam*, Lieutenant Pearse formed his half squadron up in rear of the *akhara*. I formed a troop of mounted police up in rear of the Digambars, and Lieutenant Harenc formed his half squadron up in rear of the Nirmohis. This disposition of troops and police was of course in addition to the force already detailed for duty with each *akhara*. The Nirbanis hurriedly made their way along the *Sangam*, and rapidly performed their ablutions, their object being, obviously, to steal a march on the Nirmohis, and return first in the order of the procession. As they were returning from the *Tribeni*, they passed the Digambars, who were by that time about half way down the *Sangam*. I was then with the Digambars, and noticed that they were excited and truculent, and within a few seconds, numbers of *lathis* were "in evidence." Anticipating trouble, I formed the mounted police up in line of single file on the right of the standards, thus enfilading them. After the two lines of standards had passed each other there was much shouting in both *akharas*, and I heard two or three Digambars calling out that the Nirbanis had thrown a shoe into their *akhara*. There was a rush on both sides, which was stopped with admirable promptitude by the police and native cavalry, and the two *akharas* passed without any blows being exchanged on either side. After this the Digambars bathed quietly, and by making a wide detour, we got them back from the *Tribeni* without any further trouble. Further difficulties, however, arose on our return to the Bairagi encampment. By this time the Nirbanis had planted their standards, and as the Digambars were about to do the same, the Nirbanis flung a *lathi* into their *akhara*. There was again an uproar, this time of a somewhat serious nature, but on the mounted police and cavalry drawing swords and showing that they meant business, the would-be rioters dispersed within a very short time and returned quietly to their encampments. Nine arrests were effected, and subsequently some two or three hundred *lathis* were collected and confiscated by the police. An object lesson has been learnt by the disturbance, namely, that no two *akharas* of Bairagis should be allowed upon the *Sangam* at the same time, and there should be an interval of not less than 1,000 yards between each *akhara*.

PROGS. NO. 1(*a*). SERIAL NO. 1.

This was not the only instance of misbehaviour on the part of the Bairagis. On the 18th January, what promised to be a serious riot was suppressed owing to the promptitude of Sub-Inspector Makand Singh of P. S. Khakchauk, and the prompt arrival of a strong reinforcement of reserve police under Mr. Kemp, Assistant District Superintendent of Police. The origin of this riot was a party quarrel between the Jogis themselves. Again, on the 22nd January, there was a great tumult at Alopi Bagh, where a philanthropic Mahant had invited several thousand Bairagis to a meal which lasted the greater part of the day. At one time there was a danger of the place being rushed, and it required a strong force of police to maintain order. Apart from these disturbances there was no serious trouble or breach of the peace, and the behaviour of the pilgrims generally was exemplary. It is satisfactory to note that the nine Bairagis who were prosecuted for rioting were sentenced to three months' rigorous imprisonment each.

6. ***Fires.***—Under the orders of the District Magistrate a fire station was established at kotwali headquarters, and a fatigue party detailed for emergent duties.

The first fire broke out on the 15th January in the Kotwali circle, in which a woman was unfortunately burnt to death. A second fire of no importance broke out on the same date in police circle Tal, which was promptly extinguished by the police. On the 21st January a third fire broke out also in the Kotwali Circle, a bania's shop being burnt to the ground. Owing to the exertions of the police the fire was prevented from spreading.

The last fire occurred on the 27th January in police circle Nirmullah, one hut being destroyed. Considering the inflammatory nature of the surroundings, it is astonishing there was not more damage, and much credit is due to the police in preventing these fires from spreading.

Conservancy.—Mr. Scott O'Connor, Assistant District Superintendent of Police, was detailed for duty in connection with conservancy arrangements, also a permanent staff of two head constables and 20 constables, but apart from this two constables were told off for duty over each well, and from 5 A.M. to 9 A.M. and from 5 P.M. to 7 P.M. one sub-inspector, one head constable and 50 constables were told off for duty in order to prevent people from easing themselves in unauthorized places.

8. *Crime.*—The total number of cognizable offences reported was 69 as against 152 reported in the previous Kumbh. There were for disposal 68 cases, 54 of these were investigated, 34 were detected and brought to trial, 26 were convicted, two were acquitted and six were pending trial at the close of the mela. Of the 54 persons arrested, 35 were convicted, four were acquitted, and the cases of 15 persons were pending trial at the close of the mela. The percentage of cases convicted to cases disposed of is 93·0 and of persons convicted to persons whose cases were disposed of 90·0. There were two cases of some importance. In one, a murder, a Sadhu, acting under the hallucination that the goddess Debi required him to offer up a human sacrifice, seized a child by the legs and battered its brains out on some stones. The man was promptly arrested and has been committed for trial under section 302, Indian Penal Code. There was also an important case of coining. A gang of seven persons, all professionals, were arrested, with no less than 189 counterfeit rupees in their possession. Four of these persons have been traced by the Central Bureau having been previously convicted of coining. These seven accused also have been committed to Sessions. Another smart piece of work by a member of the Punjab police force was the capture of an absconded offender wanted in the Hoshiarpur district for a brutal murder.

The total amount of property stolen was Rs. 2,805-2-4 and recoveries amounted to Rs. 451-15-6.

PROGS. NO. 1(*a*). SERIAL NO. 1.

9. *Health of the Force.*—Unfortunately cholera broke out among the police on the 9th January, when a head constable of the Sultanpur district was attacked and died. This was followed by further cases on the 15th idem, *i.e.* the day following the first big bathing day, and among the fatal cases I regret to say that my late reader, Sub-Inspector Ramadhin, a most experienced and trustworthy officer, was attacked, after accompanying me round the fair, and succumbed the following day. The total number of seizures from cholera was—1 sub-inspector, 2 head constables and 12 constables; and of these only 4 constables recovered. Apart from these casualties, 3 constables, a sowar of the Agra troop, and a chaukidar died from natural causes. The medical authorities are unanimous in tracing the origin of this epidemic to the fact that the men on duty were without food and proper drinking water for several hours at a stretch. This to a great extent is borne out by the fact that on the 2nd and 3rd of the big bathing days the men were supplied with rations, and I arranged to have supplies of drinking water at various places along the route of the processions; the result being that the disease practically disappeared. It has been suggested to me that all members of the force should, on joining the department, be supplied with water-bottles of the pattern used in the native army. I would strongly urge the Inspector-General of Police to take this suggestion into consideration, as it seems to me that if good water is supplied to men on duty at a long stretch, in a contaminated atmosphere, it minimizes the risks of cholera.

10. *General.*—As regards the behaviour of both officers and men on duty during the Kumbh Mela, nothing could have been more exemplary. All duties were cheerfully attended to, and all orders quietly and carefully carried into effect. Among the rank and file, especially, I am glad to mention that no violence was used towards the pilgrims, and they were treated with the utmost consideration, and I may say that I heard many gratuitous expressions of satisfaction from Mahants and even ordinary pilgrims. I would specially mention my Assistant District Superintendents of Police Messrs. Fawkes and Mayers, as well as Messrs. Eyre, Kemp and Scott O'Connor, who were sent here on special duty, all of whom worked admirably. Inspector Lachmi Das, who was generally in charge of the police arrangements, deserves special mention. He carried out my orders to the letter and was always ready to turn out, and on the alert. In recognition of his services I am inclined to recommend this officer either for the title of Rai Bahadur or for the much-coveted post of Deputy Superintendent. Inspector Evatt and Sergeant Blunt, who were detailed to control the crowds on the approaches to the *Sangam*, had very responsible duties, and it was greatly owing to their efforts that the catastrophe on the slope to the *Sangam* was not more serious. I would also commend Inspectors Walker, Howard, Nestor, Crozier and Page. Upon Mr. Walker's shoulders has fallen the brunt of the arrangements for the despatch of the additional police returning to their districts, and this he has done with admirable promptitude. In conclusion, I have to thank Mr. Percy Bramley for the loan of his crews of Benares river-police who did most excellent work in saving persons from drowning. Thanks are also due to Lieutenant Yool of the South Stafford Regiment for the very useful work done by his signallers; in fact the Military authorities generally assisted us most loyally throughout, and it was greatly owing to the reinforcements of cavalry that the two concluding days of the Kumbh passed off so satisfactorily.

ALLAHABAD: DOUGLAS M. STRAIGHT,
The 15th February 1906. *District Superintendent of Police.*

PROGS. NO. 1(*a*). SERIAL NO. 1

APPENDIX A.

		Inspectors.		Foot police.			Mounted police.					
	A. D. Ss. Police.	Europeans.	Natives.	Sub-inspectors.	Head constables.	Constables.	Sub-Inspectors.	Daffadars.	Sowars.	River police (boatman) head constable.	Chaukidars.	Remarks.
First contingent arrived 1st January 1906.	...	1	1	13	39	*427	...	...	...	1	235	*Including 10 river police.
Second contingent arrived 10th January 1906.	3	4	2	6	29	310	2	4	60	...	...	
Outside detectives of Foreign Provinces.	...	...	...	...	...	20	...	...	...	...	...	
Of Allahabad district ...	...	...	..	...	...	41	...	2	11	...	...	
Total ...	3	5	3	19	68	798	2	6	71	1	235	

APPENDIX B.

Distribution of officers and men at police stations and outposts.	Inspectors.	Sub-Inspectors.	Head constables.	Constables.	Chaukidars.
Police station A. Kotwali and reserve	8	14	33	475	...
" B. Bazar ...	...	1	2	18	...
" C. Chhauni ...	...	1	2	22	...
" D. Sangam ...	...	2	2	32	...
" E. Nirmala ...	...	1	2	22	...
" F. Khakchauk ...	...	1	2	22	...
" G. Tal	...	1	2	18	...
Outpost A-1. Naka Bandh ...	...	...	1	8	...
" A-2. Guzar Ramghat ...	...	...	1	8	...
" A-3. Murdaghat ...	...	...	1	4	...
" B-1. Jamna patti ...	...	...	1	3	...
" B 2. Shew Charan Das' well.	...	...	1	3	...
" B-3. Naka behind the Fort.	...	...	1	3	...
" C-1 Naka Arya Sabha ...	...	...	1	4	...
" C-2 Naka Lalkothi ...	...	...	1	4	...
" C-8 Naka Kamba Tal ...	...	...	1	4	...
" D-1 Naka Sursati Kund...	...	...	1	8	...
" D-2 Naka Beni Phatak...	...	...	1	4	...
" D-3 Naka Jamna Kanara	...	...	1	4	...
" D-4 Naka Acchaibat ...	...	...	1	4	...
" E-1 Naka Nirbani Niranjani.	...	...	1	3	...
" E-2 Naka Jhusi ...	...	...	1	4	...
" E-3 Naka Murdaghat ...	...	...	1	3	...
" F-1 Rani Parpanah ...	...	...	1	4	...
" F-2 Chatt Naggar ...	...	...	1	4	...
" F-3 Bairagi and Udasi ...	...	...	1	4	...
" F-4 Sota	...	...	...	4	...
" F-5 Jhusi	...	...	1	4	...
" F-6 Sangam bridge ...	...	...	1	3	...
Other outposts and patrols ..	...	...	...	65	...
On sanitation staff	...	...	2	20	...
Railway booking offices	...	...	1	10	...
Total ...	8	21	69	798	...

PROGS. NO. 1(a).

SERIAL NO. 1.

APPENDIX C.

Distribution of force in reserve on days of procession.	Inspectors.	Foot police.			Mounted police.		
		Sub-Inspectors.	Head constables.	Constables.	Sub-Inspectors.	Daffadars.	Sawars.
1st procession with *akhara* of Nirbani	[illegible]	1	3	44	...	1	10
2nd procession with *akhara* of Niranjani and Juna.	...	1	6	64	...	1	10
3rd procession with *akhara* of Bairagis	[illegible]	1	7	70	1	1	20
4th procession with *akhara* of Udasi (Chhota Panchayat).	[illegible]	1	4	44	1	...	10
5th procession with *akhara* of Udasi (Bara) Panchayat.	[illegible]	1	4	40	...	...	..
6th procession with *akkara* of Nirmalla and Brindabani	[illegible]	1	4	44	...	1	10
Holding bridges	...	3	4	30	...	1	10
Clearing roads	[illegible]	1	5	36	...	...	...
At Sangam	...	1	1	20	...	...	...
Lining Bairagi encampment ...	...	1	5	50	...	...	...
Total ...	7	12	43	442	2	5	70

PROGS. NO. 1(a.)

SERIAL. NO. 1.

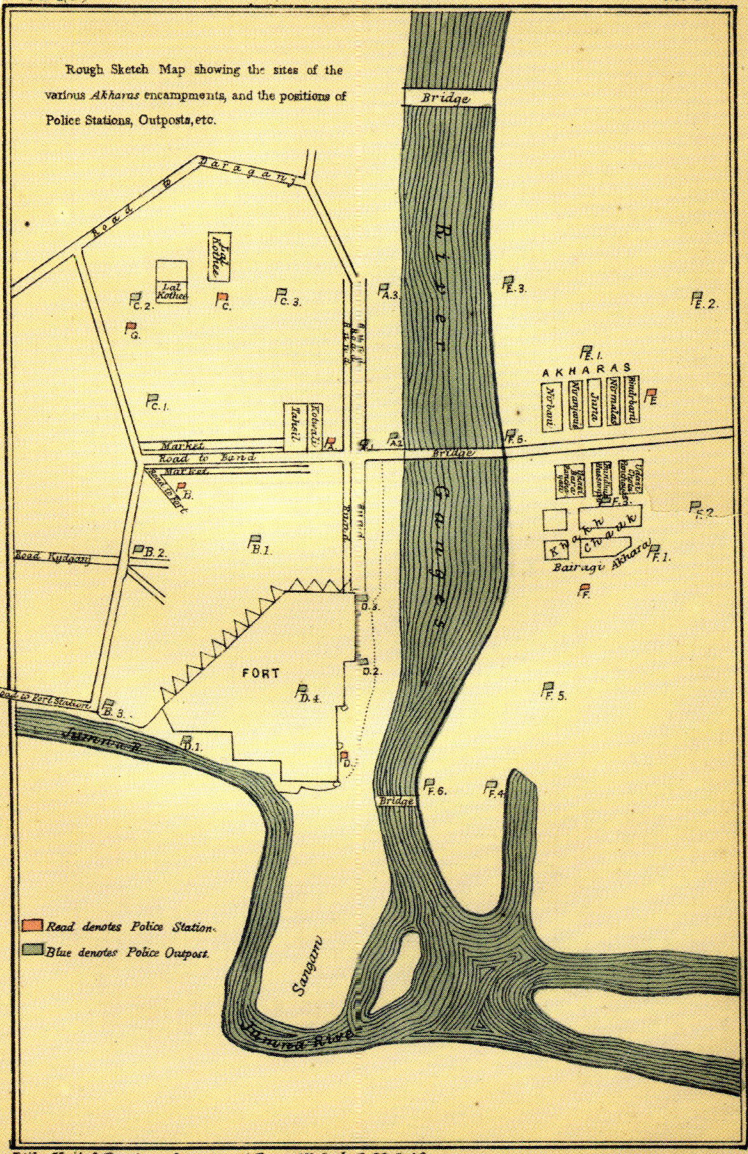

Litho, United Provinces Government Press, Allahabad. 22-5-06.

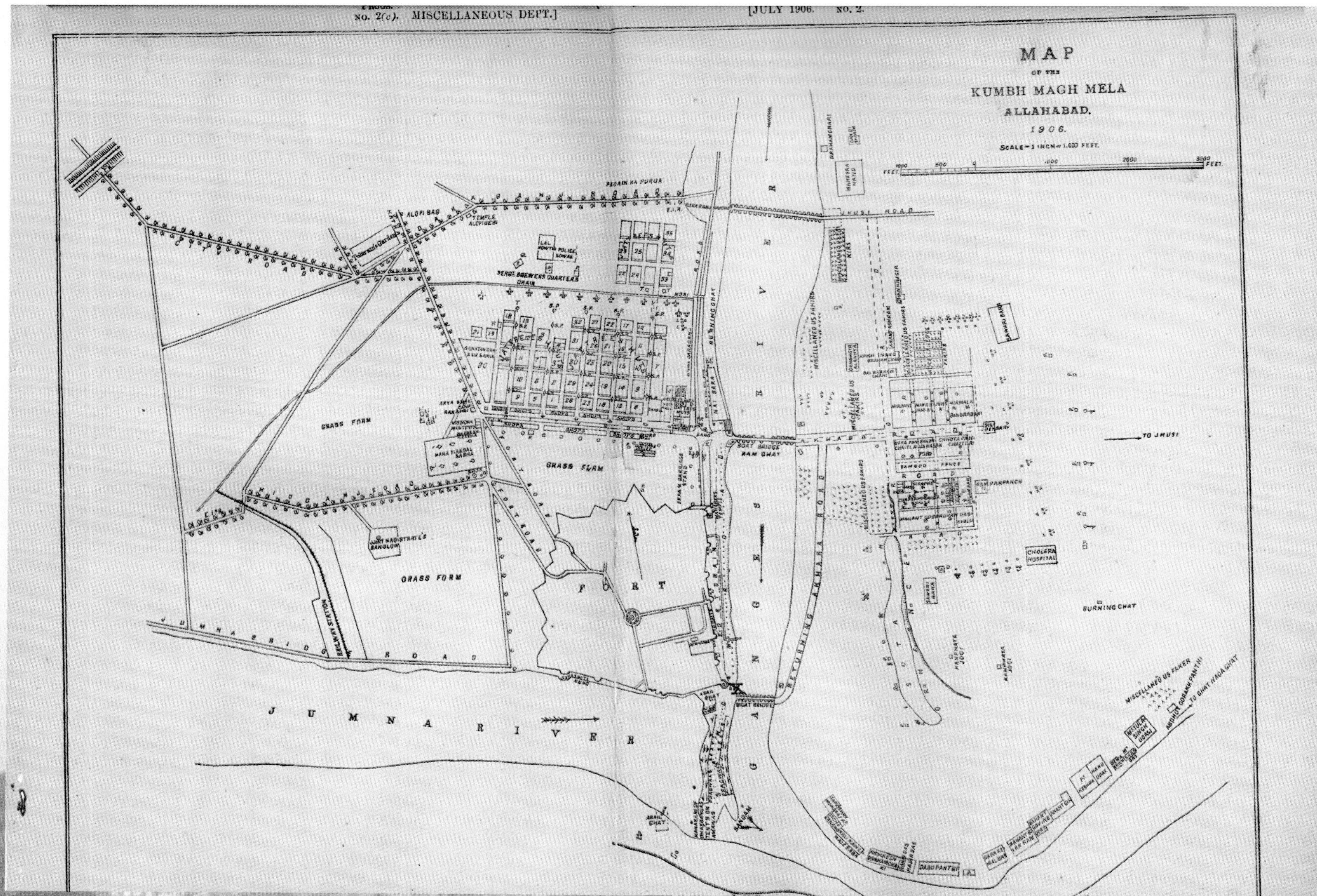

No. 2(c). MISCELLANEOUS DEPT.]
[JULY 1906. No. 2.
MAP
OF THE
KUMBH MAGH MELA
ALLAHABAD.
1906.
JUMNA RIVER
GANGES
FORT
GRASS FORM
GRASS FORM
GRASS FORM
JHUSI ROAD
TO JHUSI
CHOLERA HOSPITAL
BURNING GHAT
BOAT BRIDGE
RETURNING AKHARA ROAD
ALOPI BAG

PROGS. NO. 1(a).

APPENDIX D.

Statement of crime during the Kumbh Magh Mela, 1906.

Crime.	Cases reported.	Expunged.	Balance.	Cases enquired into.	Cases chalaned.	Convicted.	Acquitted.	Pending.	Untraced.	Persons arrested.	Chalaned.	Convicted.	Acquitted.	Pending.	Property stolen.	Property recovered.	Remarks.
															Rs. a. p.	Rs. a. p.	
Section 302, I. P. C. ...	1	...	1	1	1	...	...	1	...	1	1	...	...	1	...	...	
„ 239 „	1	...	1	1	1	...	...	1	...	7	7	...	...	7	...	...	
„ 392 „	1	...	1	1	1	1	...	...	...	1	1	1	...	...	25 0 0	...	
„ 457 „ with loss ...	4	...	4	4	...	...	...	...	4	...	...	...	...	...	1,285 4 0	162 4 0	
„ 457 „ without loss	1	...	1	1	1	...	...	1	...	4	4	...	...	4	...	...	
„ 379 „ above Rs. 10	22	...	22	22	9	8	...	1	13	9	9	8	...	1	1,119 4 7	248 2 3	
„ 379 „ below Rs. 10	23	1	22	10	10	9	1	...	...	13	13	10	3	...	86 11 9	36 3 9	
„ 380 „ above Rs. 10	2	...	2	2	...	...	...	...	2	...	...	...	...	...	287 0 6	...	
„ 380 „ below Rs. 10	1	...	1	...	...	...	...	...	...	...	...	...	...	...	2 3 6	2 3 6	
„ 411 „	1	...	1	1	...	...	...	...	1	...	...	...	...	...	...	3 2 0	This case was enquired into, but the property recovered was disputed. Some information was asked from Hoshiarpur district, but no reply has been received as yet.
„ 448 „	1	...	1	...	...	...	...	...	...	...	...	...	...	...	...	...	
„ 147 „	1	...	1	1	1	1	...	...	...	9	9	9	...	...	...	...	
„ 225B „	1	...	1	1	1	...	...	1	...	1	1	...	...	1	...	...	
„ 363 „	1	...	1	1	1	...	...	1	...	1	1	...	...	1	...	...	This case has been transferred to Sakhar.
„ 279 „	1	...	1	1	1	1	...	...	...	1	1	1	...	...	...	...	
„ 109, C. P. C. ...	7	...	7	7	7	6	1	...	...	7	7	6	1	...	...	...	
Total ...	69	1	68	54	34	26	2	6	20	54	54	35	4	15	2,805 8 4	451 15 6	

SERIAL NO. 1.

सन् 1906 कुम्भ मेला चिकित्सीय सहायता रिपोर्ट

सन् 1906 कुम्भ मेला क्षेत्र में चिकित्सीय सहायता के लिए प्रत्येक भाग हेतु एक प्रमुख औषधालय स्थापित किया गया। इन औषधालयों में आवश्यक दवाइयाँ एवं उपकरण भी रखे गये। दूसरे भाग में पूरे मेला क्षेत्र के लिए कालरा हास्पिटल बनाया गया जिसमें 8 झोपड़ियाँ बनायी गयीं तथा जिनका विस्तार कर 14 बनाया जा सकता था। मेला क्षेत्र के अस्पताल में कुल 1609 लोगों की चिकित्सा की गयी। अरैल क्षेत्र में कालरा का प्रकोप प्रारम्भ होने पर यहाँ पर रोगियों के इलाज हेतु एक छोटा अस्पताल स्थापित किया गया।

पत्रावली संख्या-153/1906 -सामान्य प्रशासन विभाग

VII.—Hospital and Medical relief.

(a) There were two main dispensaries—one in each section. These were centrally situated, and each was supplied with the necessary drugs and instruments for the treatment of ordinary diseases and injuries. At the dispensary in section I was kept the complete stock, from which the other dispensary and hospitals were supplied.

In section II was the cholera hospital for the whole *mela*, and here all cases from both sections were taken for treatment. Originally of 8 huts, it had to be enlarged to 14. To this hospital were also taken such cases as occured in Daraganj, Kydganj and Jhusi.

When cholera broke out at Arail a small hospital was started there, as it was found impossible to convey cholera cases by boat across the river without serious risk. Towards the end of the *mela* a separate leper asylum was built in section

huts as out-door patients, or sent to the Colvin Hospital in the city: 281 cases were sent to the cholera hospital and observation huts. Of these, 4 cases turned out to be suffering from other diseases and were discharged. Of the remainder 207 died, and 70 were cured. The percentage of deaths seems high, but was not really so when it is remembered that cases were usually received after they had spent the first night of sickness lying in the sand in the open air, and that the majority of the patients were old people.

Of general diseases there were 1,609 cases treated as out-door patients, and of these 1,321 attended the main dispensary in section I, and 288 the smaller dispensary in section II. The diseases which were so treated were either less serious ones, or the patients were unwilling to go to hospital.

An abstract of the cases is given below :—

Local injury	40
Toothache	76
Sinus	1
Ulcers...	189
Parapphimosis	1
Eye diseases	39
Ear diseases	37
Foreign body	1
Burns	5
Abscess	18
Dysentery	122
Diarrhœa	65
Stomatatis	3
Round worm	1
Other digestive diseases	163
Malaria	208
Nervous diseases...	48
Debility	12
Skin diseases	201
Erysipelas	2
Pneumonia	3
Other respiratory diseases	288
Throat	16
Rheumatism	32
Syphilis	11
Gonorrhœa	8
Glands	14
Urethritis	5
Orchitis	1
Soft chancre	5
Heart disease	1
Circulatory diseases	38
Piles	7
Epilepsy	4

Twenty-three cases were sent to hospital in the city for treatment, and these were as follows :—

Pneumonia	3
Dysentery	2
Debility	1
Diarrhœa	1
Ulcer	4
Injuries	12

VIII.—General health.

Unfortunately cholera broke out early in January and continued practically to the end of the *mela*, but if this is omitted the general health on the whole was good. There were 167 non-cholera deaths in the *mela*, and this, calculated on an average population of 200,000 for one month, gives a death-rate of only 10 per mille per annum, and if the 267 deaths from cholera be added (excluding cholera deaths amongst cases brought into the cholera hospital from outside for treatment) the full death-rate per mille per annum becomes 26, which compares very favourably with the average death for cities in these provinces—45·11.

जिलाधिकारी इलाहाबाद द्वारा कमिश्नर इलाहाबाद डिवीजन को कुम्भ मेला पर भेजी गई रिपोर्ट-सन् 1906

प्रत्येक बारह साल बाद कुम्भ मेले का आयोजन होता है इस अवसर पर विभिन्न भागों से श्रद्धालु कुम्भ में स्नान करने आते हैं। इलाहाबाद में कुम्भ मेले का आयोजन 10 जनवरी से शुरू होकर 12 फरवरी, 1906 तक चला। इस रिपोर्ट में मेले के आयोजन में स्टाफ, साइट्स (जगह) नावों की व्यवस्था, पुलिस व्यवस्था, मेडिकल व्यवस्था, विद्युत व्यवस्था, प्रमुख स्थानों से सम्बन्धित सूचना के साथ संगम, अरैल क्षेत्र में प्रमुख अखाड़ों के पूर्वी जमीन पर एक कालरा अस्पताल बनाने की बात कही गई है।

यहाँ पर तीन दिवसों में गंगा में स्नान हेतु अखाड़ों का आगमन हुआ जैसे 14 जनवरी मकर संक्रान्ति, 24 जनवरी मौनी अमावस्या तथा 29 जनवरी बसन्त पंचमी। गंगा में स्नान हेतु अखाड़ों का आगमन इस प्रकार से हुआ:-

1. निर्वाणी अखाड़ा

2. निरंजनी एवं जूना अखाड़ा

3.बैरागी-इनका विभाजन तीन भागों में होता है -

I. निर्वाणी

II. दिगम्बरी

III. निर्मोही

4.छोटा पंचायती अखाड़ा

5.बड़ा पंचायती अखाड़ा और बन्धुहसनपुर अखाड़ा

6.निर्मला एवं बिन्द्राबनी अखाड़ा

मि0 एफ0 वी0 शेरिंग जो कि इलाहाबाद के ज्वाइंट मजिस्ट्रेट थे उनको मेले की व्यवस्था तथा मेले का इंचार्ज भी बनाया गया तथा ठाकुर शीतला बक्स सिंह, राय बहादुर को मेले का मैनेजर बनाया गया था साथ ही नायब तहसीलदार बाबू विश्वनाथ प्रसाद को उनके सहायक के पद पर नियुक्त किया गया। पुलिस व्यवस्था हेतु मि0 डगलस स्ट्रेट की नियुक्ति की गई थी।

इस रिपोर्ट में आय-व्यय का पिछले कुम्भ के आय-व्यय से तुलनात्मक विवरण भी प्रस्तुत किया गया है।

पिछले कुम्भ की तुलना में इस बार मेडिकल स्टाफ भी काफी बढ़ा दिया गया। इस बार 2 मेडिकल कमिश्नर तथा डा0 ओहडीदार के साथ ही 3 असिस्टेंट सर्जन, 16 हास्पिटल असिस्टेन्ट, 6 कम्पाउंडर, 2 लेडी डाक्टर तथा 64 वैक्सीनेटरों को लगाया था। पिछले कुम्भ की तुलना में इस बार पुलिस स्टाफ को भी बढ़ाया गया।

सन् 1894 में पुलिस व्यवस्था इस प्रकार थी:-

2 इंस्पेक्टर, 8 सब इंस्पेक्टर, 53 हेड कांस्टेबिल, 325 कांस्टेबिल, 5 सवारों तथा 220 ग्रामीण चैकीदारों की ड्यूटी लगाई गयी थी।

सन् 1906 में पुलिस व्यवस्था इस प्रकार थी:-

5 यूरोपियन तथा 3 नेटिव इंस्पेक्टर, 1 सार्जेंट, 20 सब इंस्पेक्टर, 68 हेड कांस्टेबिल, 801 कांस्टेबिल, 235 ग्रामीण चैकीदार, 2 माउंटेड सब इंस्पेक्टर, 6 दफ्तरी तथा 71 सवारों की ड्यूटी लगाई गयी थी।

साफ-सफाई की व्यवस्था हेतु भी स्टाफ की काफी वृद्धि की गयी जिनमें 1747 सफाई कर्मी, 46 जमादार, 6 मेट तथा 2 इंस्पेक्टरों को लगाया गया।

PROGS. NO. 2(*a*). MISCELLANEOUS DEPT.] (13) [JULY 1906. SERIAL NO. 2.

No. $\frac{1599}{\text{XXIV}-23}$ OF 1906.

FROM

H. V. LOVETT, ESQ., C.S.,

MAGISTRATE, ALLAHABAD,

To

H. Z. DARRAH, ESQ., C.S.,

COMMISSIONER, ALLAHABAD DIVISION.

Dated Allahabad, the 14*th April* 1906.

SIR,

I HAVE the honour to report as follows on the recent *Kumbh mela*.

2. A *Kumbh Magh mela* takes place every 12 years; and the *Magh mela* bathing fair is on these occasions of peculiar sanctity, and thronged with multitudes of worshippers from far and near. The last *Kumbh mela* seriously began on the 10th of January, and continued to the 12th of February.

3. *Staff.*—Mr. F. B. Sherring, Joint Magistrate, held charge throughout, both of the preparations for the Fair and the Fair itself. He took a house close to the spot, and entirely devoted himself to his charge. After the outbreak of cholera, he was assisted by Mr. Charles, C.S., and on the big bathing days, the whole district staff was employed on fair duty from morning till night under my own supervision. I was in constant communication with Mr. Sherring throughout the *mela*.

Babu Budh Sain, Manager of Government Estates, was deputed as Manager of the Fair until the arrival of Thakur Sitla Baksh Singh, Rai Bahadur, on November the 22nd. The last-named officer has had a unique experience of *Magh melas* acquired during some twenty years. His knowledge and experience were invaluable, and he spared no efforts to make all the arrangements a success. His assistant was Babu Bishwanath Parshad, Naib Tahsildar, who did very good work in managing the large number of coolies and sweepers, and keeping the accounts and stock of materials. He was ably assisted by Babu Chatarpat Rai.

The police arrangements were under the careful and painstaking supervision of Mr. Douglas Straight, who was assisted by Assistant District Superintendents of Police Messrs. Fawkes and Mayers of the Allahabad district, and Messrs. Eyre, Kemp and Scott O'Connor sent on special duty after the outbreak of cholera.

The conservancy arrangements were under Captain Robertson, I.M.S., Deputy Sanitary Commissioner. He had under him Captain Pearson, I.M.S., and Dr. Ohdedar. The Sanitary Commissioner, Major Chaytor-White, was himself present at the Fair supervising health arrangements for some days.

4. *Description of site.*—The accompanying map will give a clear idea of the general arrangement of the Fair. The site is divided into two parts by the Ganges. On the east side was an enormous sandy plain on which were located the *akharas* of fakirs, both those who were allowed to go in procession on the great days of the Fair, and those who were not. Before Thakur Sitla Baksh Singh arrived, it was maintained by the fakirs and many influential Hindus that these *akharas* could not be located on the east bank, unless there was at least a small channel of flowing water to the far east of the sandy plain, so that they might be considered to be living within the confluence of the Ganges and Jamna. This theory was put forward so positively that it was universally accepted until Thakur Sitla Baksh Singh arrived. He, however, promptly demolished it, and, without any serious opposition, planted all the *akharas* across the river, where they contentedly

PROGS. NO. 2(*a*). MISCELLANEOUS DEPT.] (14) [JULY 1906. SERIAL NO. 2.

remained throughout. This is an important feature in this year's proceedings, which may be useful for future guidance. In view of the subsequent outbreak of cholera, it is difficult to estimate what Allahabad owes to this measure, or how things would have gone had the *akharas* of 60,000 fakirs been located in immediate proximity to the city. The fakirs allowed to go in procession numbered about 30,000, and those who did not enjoy this privilege were equally numerous.

5. The Ganges was spanned by two bridges of boats specially constructed for the occasion. On its west bank, the land west and north of the bund road was occupied by the huts built by *Pragwals* for pilgrims. On each side of this road were shops, and at the east end of the road were the *tahsili*, *kotwali* and principal hospital. Below the bund north of the Ramghat bridge was placed the *naibarah* or enclosure set apart for barbers to shave pilgrims in. South of this was the road to the *Sangam*. This road to the *Sangam*, bisected for part of its length by the open drain from the Fort, was one of the great difficulties of the Fair. At the last *Kumbh mela* the distance between the Fort and the Ganges was 400 to 500 yards: this year the distance was nowhere more than 250 feet, and, at the narrowest part between the south-east bastion of the Fort and the river where there is a steep slope and a turn, the distance is only 100 feet. In October and November the Ganges was cutting away the bank next to the Fort at the rate of several feet a day, and the water was very deep below the bank. The matter was put into the hands of the District Engineer, who succeeded in eventually stopping the cutting by the construction of short spurs into the river every 40 feet from the burning ghat down to nearly the end of the *Sangam*, a distance of about three quarters of a mile. Even thus preserved, however, the approach to the *Sangam* was a constant source of anxiety, as can well be understood when it is remembered that on the day of *Amawas* some $2\frac{1}{2}$ millions of people, including various long drawn processions, had to pass along it.

6. The *Sangam* itself was situated at the end of a long strip of land about 1,000 yards south of the Fort, and within 50 yards of the south Jamna bank. There was an abundance of shallow water in which pilgrims could bathe, but the position was safeguarded by River Police, borrowed with their boats from Benares by Mr. Straight, who prevented all drowning and saved four lives on the *Amawas* day.

7. Across the Jamna at Arail it was eventually found necessary to open a cholera hospital and burning ghat. The regular cholera hospital was situated on the land east of the main *akharas*.

8. *Arrival of cholera.*—Cholera broke out early in January; and as at first it seemed likely to spread, not only was every precaution taken on the spot, but every effort was made by the despatch of telegrams and notices as well as by communications to the newspapers to deter intending visitors. Owing, however, very largely to the splendid work done by Captain Robertson, Mr. Sherring, and their assistants, the disease never assumed an epidemic form, and the number of pilgrims kept away by it must have been infinitesimal. The total number of deaths from cholera was only 267, of whom 103 were cases found dead.

9. *Principal bathing days and arrangements for passage of processions.*—The principal bathing days during the fair were as follows:—

Puranmashi	January 10th.
Shankrant	" 14th.
Ekadashi	" 21st.
Amawas	" 24th.
Basant Panchmi	" 29th.
Achala Satami	" 31st.
Ekadashi	February 5th.
Puranmashi	" 9th.
Shankrant	" 12th.

There are three days on which processions of fakirs go to the Ganges to bathe; they are *Shankrant*, January 14th; *Amawas*, January 24th; and *Basant Panchmi*,

January 29th. The order in which the fakirs' *akharas* go in procession is as follows :—

(1) Nirbanis,
(2) Niranjains and Junas,
(3) Bairagis, of whom there are three bodies—Nirbanis, Digambars and Nirmohis,
(4) Chhota Panchaiti Akhara,
(5) Bara Panchaiti Akhara and Bandhua Hasanpur Akhara,
(6) Nirmalas and Bindrabani Akhara.

The *Junas* do their best to make themselves into a distinct procession, but otherwise none of the *akharas* give trouble except *Bairagis*. The *Nirbani Bairagis* and the *Digambar Bairagis* are extremely jealous of each other, and the *Nirmohis* side with the *Digambars*. There is no clear or settled order of precedence between these three sects, except that the *Digambars* always seem to occupy the middle position. Experience has taught us one lesson, that it is practically impossible to carry out the idea described in the report of the last *Kumbh*, viz., that the three *Bairagis'* sections should go down to bathe in the order (1), (2) and (3), and, after bathing, return in the order (3), (2), and (1). It might be possible to work this with a very wide space at the *Sangam* and with a very strong body of troops to keep order; but otherwise it is almost certain to lead to a riot, as the first sect will always bathe quickly and start on the return journey before the last sect has had time to come up. At the present *Kumbh* each procession was formed up on the east of the Ramghat bridge, where it waited until a signal was heliographed from the south-east bastion of the Fort to the signalling station at the east end of the Ramghat bridge. It may be noted here that besides these two signalling stations, there was another half way across the sandy stretch between the second bridge and the *Bairagis'* encampment. Signallers were provided by the South Staffords and the Bhopal Light Infantry. These signalling stations were of the greatest utility.

10. On receipt of a message to start, each procession crossed the Ramghat bridge. On the west side of the river they joined their elephants on which they placed their "*Nishans*." They then proceeded down the *Sangam* road. At the second bridge the elephants were stopped and sent back, their "*Nishans*" being taken off. In the meanwhile the procession went on to the *Sangam*, bathed and returned to the lower bridge, over which they carried their "*Nishans*," and then continued their way back to their *akharas*.

11. The ordinary procession was allowed to begin crossing the Ramghat bridge as soon as the procession before it had passed the south-east corner of the Fort on the way to the *Sangam*. No difficulty was experienced in stopping any procession, and making it wait a reasonable time in case the way was not clear. Indeed the difficulty was generally to get them on. The *Bairagis*, however, were not allowed to start until the procession before them had got clear across the lower bridge after bathing. A strong force of police, at least one Magistrate and one Police Officer, accompanied each procession.

12. Mr. Sherring was stationed permanently to watch the arrangements between the Fort and the *Sangam*, while Mr. Straight and I moved about from place to place as occasion arose.

13. *The events of the three great bathing days.*—The first procession day—January 14th—passed off without a hitch of any sort. It was relieved from monotony, however, by the escape of two elephants, who got rid of their mahants and charged down towards the *Sangam*. One was caught very soon; the other was fortunately turned by prompt action on the part of Mr. Sherring, and bolted into the Jamna where it remained for some hours. Neither of these animals injured any one or anything.

14. The crowds on the *Amawas* day were tremendous, and the ground was covered with persons camping out for the night. Bathing began at midnight, and continued throughout the day till late in the evening. Thus when the first procession arrived at the narrow part of the road below the south-east bastion of the Fort, Mr. Straight and Mr. Sherring who accompanied it found that the crowds at this early hour were already so great that the barriers, set up to keep them apart from the route for the procession, were showing signs of giving way. Mr. Straight remained on this spot, while the procession was taken on by Mr. Sherring to the *Sangam*. Finding the police near him were unable to cope with the enormous throng, Mr. Straight went off to the nearest gate of the Fort to obtain the aid of troops. This was promptly furnished, and cavalry was requisitioned from Cantonments, but before the position could be adequately strengthened, a catastrophe had occurred. One or two unfortunates had come down in the press* at the bottom of the slope, and over their prostrate bodies others too had fallen. The lower end of the barrier had burst, and the crowd had naturally streamed on down the slope and added to the calamity. It must be remembered that the width of the road at this point was only 100 feet.

* Point X on the map.

15. Inspector Evatt and Sergeant Blunt, with the few police at their command, did all that men could do to stem the tide; and some non-officials, among whom I may mention the Honourable Pandit Madan Mohan Malaviya and Rai Jagat Narain, exerted themselves in the same cause; but before the situation could be restored, lives had been lost and injuries had been received. All available police were hurried to the spot; "breakwaters" of mounted men were arranged at intervals along the road to the *Sangam*, and, with the assistance of the Military, the crowds were in time brought under effective control. In all eight women had lost their lives, six of whom were old and feeble; two men were killed, while 18 persons were more or less injured—none fatally. The catastrophe above described was mainly accountable for these figures, but they include two or three isolated cases of persons falling on the *Sangam* road and perishing under the feet of the throng.

16. I was myself busy in another part of the field when the accident took place; but, on hearing of its occurrence, I hurried to the spot. I had the greatest difficulty in making my way over part of the route owing to the density of the press, and as you were there yourself and gave us your utmost assistance, your observations will confirm mine. In fact the narrowness of the *Sangam* road, the slope at its lower end, and the enormous crowds were indeed difficult to cope with, and we may be thankful that the calamity stopped where it did. Before leaving this sad subject, I would strongly emphasize the priceless value of mounted men on such occasions. While the foot-police were lost among the crowd, confused by the din and pressure and therefore largely useless, the mounted police and cavalry sowars under considerate and intelligent leadership did splendid service. It may be asked why was not all this foreseen, and aid from the military procured beforehand? The answer is—*(a)* that we had originally asked for military and cavalry assistance for each of the big bathing days, but that I had cancelled my request on account of the cholera and had instead received a strong extra force of police; *(b)* that the police at our disposal had effectively dealt with all difficulties on the first bathing day "*Shankrant*," and that although we gave most careful consideration to the arrangements for the *Amawas*, we did not sufficiently realize how greatly the crowds that day, some two and a half millions, would exceed our previous experiences. (Perhaps unconsciously our minds were over-concentrated on the "processions" and the prevention of riots among the *Bairagi* sects.) We did our best to safeguard the situation, although we were to learn by sad experience its full difficulties. The scene of the accident was by no means the only dangerous spot: as a matter of fact a similar catastrophe on a smaller scale was only averted in another part of the field by prompt and sufficient action.

17. No further incident of importance occurred on the *Amawas*. On the *Basant Panchmi*, January 29, a half squadron had been sent by the 4th Cavalry

to help the police to manage the crowds. The latter were, however, far from as numerous as those of the *Amawas*, and no accident took place. The *Bairagis* on this day gave much trouble. Before their procession started it was seen that they had made up their minds to fight, the cause of quarrel being the order of precedence between the three sects. Just about this time the first half squadron of cavalry under Lieutenant Pearse was relieved by a second half squadron under Lieutenant Harenc. Both half squadrons were retained until after the *Bairagis'* processions had ended. These were headed by the *Nirbani* sect, the *Digambars* coming next, and the *Nirmohis* last. The arrangement which had previously received the concurrence of all three sects was that this order was to be reversed on the return journey after bathing. The *Nirbanis*, however, bathed quickly, and it was at once seen that it would be impossible to keep them standing at the *Sangam* until the *Digambars* and *Nirmohis* had finished their ablutions. The *Nirbanis* started back immediately after bathing, and in this way had to pass the on-coming *Digambar* and *Nirmohi* processions. It was only the presence of the police and cavalry sowars, who were lined up between the two processions, that prevented a fight at the *Sangam*. Once the *Nirbanis* had passed, the trouble was over for the time, as the *Nirmohis* and *Digambars* are on good terms. When, however, the three *Bairagi* sects had got back to their encampment, a fight began; but the Joint Magistrate, the District Superintendent of Police, the two Military Officers, and myself were present, swords were drawn by the cavalry, and the opposing forces of *Bairagis* rapidly retreated to their quarters, nine of the ringleaders being arrested who were subsequently tried and punished for rioting. On this day, too, the far superior value of cavalry and mounted men was effectively demonstrated.

18. On January 1st there were two fires in the fair, some 20 or 30 *chhappars* being burnt in each. In the first an unfortunate woman, who went back four times for her property, was eventually caught by the flames, and, though at once attended by Captain Robertson who was present at the time, she died the same day. In the second fire Babu Charu Chander Mittra, Municipal Member, greatly distinguished himself by his efforts. He was one of the first on the spot, and immediately organized arrangements for pulling down the neighbouring *chhappars*, leading the way into the hottest places himself. On January 21st the promptness of the police stopped a fire in a big Halwai's shop in the bazar, which might have caused enormous damage if not at once checked. A further fire broke out in the cook-house of the *Nirbani Akhara* on January 26th, but the timely occurrence of a thunderstorm soon put it out and little damage was done.

19. * *Crime and Police.*—"The total number of cognizable offences reported was 69 as against 152 reported in the previous *Kumbh*. There were for disposal 68 cases, 54 of these were investigated. Thirty-four were detected and brought to trial, 26 were convicted, 2 were acquitted, and 6 were pending trial at the close of the *mela*. Of the 54 persons arrested, 35 were convicted, 4 were acquitted, and the cases of 15 persons were pending trial at the close of the *mela*. The percentage of cases convicted to cases disposed of is 93, and of persons convicted to persons whose cases were disposed of 90. There were two cases of some importance. In one, a murder, a *Sadhu*, acting under the hallucination that the goddess Debi required him to offer up a human sacrifice, seized a child by the legs and battered its brains out on some stones. The man was promptly arrested, and has been committed for trial under section 302, Indian Penal Code. There was also an important case of coining. A gang of seven persons, all professionals, were arrested, with no less than 189 counterfeit rupees in their possession. Four of these persons have been traced by the central *bureau*, having been previously convicted of coining. These seven accused also have been committed to Sessions. Another smart piece of work by a member of the Punjab Police Force was the capture of an absconded offender, wanted in the Hoshiarpur district for a brutal murder.

* This is extracted from Mr. Straight's memorandum.

The total amount of property stolen was Rs. 2,805-2-4, and recoveries amounted to Rs. 451-15-6."

The police worked well, too, in other matters. On January the 18th they suppressed a party quarrel among the *Bairagis*, and altogether they were excellently officered and handled. The only part of their duties that lagged behind the rest was their sanitary work. The remarks in the 11th paragraph of Captain Robertson's report are worthy of perusal in this connection. I would advise that at future *Kumbh melas* a strong force of police be specially provided for sanitary duty *alone*.

20. *The Achaibat Temple.*—A pilgrim to the *Kumbh Magh mela* has not carried out the essentials of his pilgrimage until he has been shaved, bathed at the *Sangam*, and visited the three temples of the *Achaibat* in the Fort, *Beni Madho* in Daraganj, and *Bharatdwaj* in Colonelganj. Of these three temples the most important is the *Achaibat* temple in the Fort, the famous shrine of the undying tree. It is under-ground, and was till January last approached by a single narrow staircase and a long narrow dark passage which served for ingress and egress. No ray of daylight had for centuries pierced the murky blackness of the temple, and the passage was lighted and ventilated by a solitary small skylight. Visitors and pilgrims were left in entire dependance on such scanty illumination as the priests chose on payment to allow them; and on a big bathing day when the whole place was thronged with a surging crowd, the condition of the air was intolerable to all but devotees, while the fear of outrage and robbery was so great that many respectable persons refused to allow their womenkind to visit the temple. Early in January I received, through Mr. Sherring, a memorial from some of the most influential Hindus in Allahabad asking that this unsatisfactory state of things might be remedied. Mr. Sherring strongly supported the memorial. The priests of the shrine of course protested, but, after careful investigation, the matter was vigorously taken up; His Honour the Lieutenant Governor visited the spot, and by the first great bathing day the temple was, in the words of the Deputy Sanitary Commissioner, "well lighted and ventilated by a sufficiency of openings in its roofs while a new stair had been provided for the *exit* of pilgrims."

His Honour the Lieutenant Governor too, has prohibited the exaction of entrance fees by the priests of the temple. These reforms have been greatly and widely appreciated by those whom it was intended to benefit, and their good effect will last long after the *Kumbh* of 1906 has been forgotten. The temple is now a shrine which even the weakest and most helpless can visit with comfort and without fear.

21. *Medical and Conservancy.*—Captain Robertson has kindly sent me a copy of his report to the Sanitary Commissioner. As it is not clear that you will see it, I forward a copy for your information. It is of great interest, and shows all the difficulties which he had to overcome. In my opinion it is impossible to speak too highly of his work.

A noteworthy feature of the present *Kumbh* is the fact that the area supervised by the *mela* authorities was so great. It included not only the grounds of the *mela* proper, but also parts of the Municipality such as Daraganj and Kydganj. Disinfection and conservancy were carried out in Jhusi and Arail, and medical officers from the *mela* helped the Railway authorities at Naini and Allahabad stations. The inspection of lodging-houses was also part of the work undertaken by the fair management. The ordinary conservancy arrangements of the Municipality are not enough to cope with the extra work entailed by the fair, and this fact should be thoroughly well understood. Places like Daraganj and Kydganj, where most of the pilgrims congregate, should always be under special management at such times. This special management should be financed by the Fair fund. The Municipality makes very little out of the *mela*, which, as a matter of fact, subjects our citizens to considerable risk of epidemics; and it is hardly fair to compel them to incur large expenditure on account of outside visitors who pay no

taxes. It is indeed creditable to Captain Robertson and his staff, among whom I should like to mention Dr. Ohdedar, that the large and populous area shown in the annexed map was kept as clean as it was, and that, notwithstanding the early import of cholera, sickness was so scant.

22. *Financial.*—The statement given at the end of this report gives the receipts and expenses of the Fair, compared with the receipts and expenses of the last *Kumbh.*

It is satisfactory to note that the accounts were closed on March the 27th. At the last *Kumbh* they were closed on April 20th, on which date Rs 7,161-4-0 were still unrecovered. Out of that sum only Rs. 400 were subsequently realized after tedious litigation in the Civil Court, leaving an unrecovered balance of Rs. 6,761-4-0.

The total receipts this year come to very much the same as the receipts of the last *Kumbh.* There is no doubt that the shops this year would have let at far higher figures, and we would have had more fees from barbers and hawkers if it had not been for the cholera which appeared just at the time that licenses were being issued. Many persons then feared that the Fair would be broken up, or would, at any rate, be greatly restricted. Consequently competition for shops and licenses was by no means what it would otherwise have been.

23. The receipts from sale of old articles this year are satisfactory. Special care was taken to find purchasers for the different things sold, and good prices were paid for good material.

24. When we come to the expenditure side the difference between this and the last *Kumbh* is at once apparent. This year we built two bridges, instead of the one built at the last *Kumbh.* The Rs. 16,296 includes a contract for a road through the *Akharas'* camps, and for cutting the bank down to the Ramghat bridge on the Fort side.

Rupees 1,080 were paid to the Municipality by Government order for repair of roads.

Compensation for land was given as follows ;—

(a) Between Fort road and the Bund—Rs. 224-4-9 were paid to the Grass Farm at Re. 1 per bigha. The Grass Farm cut and carried off all grass before the fair began.

(b) West of Fort road—Rs. 20 were paid to a grass contractor holding from the Cantonment Committee some 12 bighas of land.

(c) Across the river—Rs. 568-5-6 were paid to Musammat Gumti Bibi for some 505 bighas at Re. 1-2-0 per bigha, and Rs. 72-9-6 were paid to her for compensation of tenants for occupation of 36 bighas cultivated by them.

The Cantonment Magistrate agreed to claim no compensation for land below the Bund.

25. The medical expenses were necessarily heavier than those of the last *Kumbh* owing to the great increase in staff. At the last *Kumbh* there were seven Hospital Assistants and two compounders. This year, in addition to two Sanitary Commissioners and Dr. Ohdedar, there were—

3 Assistant Surgeons,	6 Compounders,
16 Hospital Assistants,	2 Lady Doctors,

64 Vaccinators.

Even this very much increased staff was extremely hard worked.

26. Tahsil expenses were much higher this year than at the last *Kumbh.* Then only Rs. 393 were paid towards the Manager's salary. This year the fair funds defrayed his whole salary, Rs. 1,618, although he left us on February the 28th

instead of March the 26th, the date of his giving over charge in 1894. It should be noted that there were then 13 clerks who cost Rs. 206 a month. This year there were an Assistant Manager, an Accountant and an Ahlmad who all together cost Rs. 190 a month. In Mr. Sherring's opinion it is far better to have a few really good men than a crowd of second-rate officials.

27. The police were far more numerous this year than at the last *Kumbh.*

In 1894 there were—

2 Inspectors,	325 Constables,
8 Sub-inspectors,	5 Sawars,
53 Head Constables,	220 Village chaukidars.

* In 1906 there were—

5 Europeans and 3 Native Inspectors,	801 Constables,
	235 Village chaukidars,
1 Sergeant,	2 Mounted Sub-Inspectors,
20 Sub-Inspectors,	6 Daffadars,
68 Head Constables,	71 Sawars.

* Mr. Straight's elaborate memorandum gives interesting details (for which I have no space) regarding the disposition of this large force. Should you wish to see it, I can send you a copy.

Expenses in connection with all these were necessarily greater than the expenses of the last *Kumbh.*

Conservancy again was more costly this year as we had 1,747 sweepers, 46 jamadars, 6 mates and 2 inspectors, as compared with the 1,456 sweepers, 3 jamadars, 5 mates and 2 inspectors of the last *Kumbh.*

Under "*chhaoni*" are included all expenses incurred in building huts and putting up barricades, latrines, &c. The expenses this year are double what they were at the last *Kumbh*, because of the great increase in the medical, police and conservancy staff, and also because of the larger number of latrines and cholera huts provided.

The Cantonment Magistrate is paid Rs. 186 for a latrine kept up by him.

The Municipal Engineer's bill is larger than at the last *Kumbh*, as the water-supply had to be extended over a larger area and the Fort drain had to be arranged by him.

28. Moreover, the last three items of expenditure find no counterpart at all in the last *Kumbh* accounts.

29. In addition to the details of expenditure given above, sanction of Government has been asked to the payment of two further items, *viz.* Rs. 1,074-13-0 due to the Municipality for interest on the *Magh mela* loans and sinking fund, and Rs. 500 due to the Cantonment Committee for their conservancy establishment maintained during the 10 months that no Fair is taking place.

30. After carefully reviewing all the above financial details, I have no hesitation in stating that what increase of expenditure took place was unavoidable, and that Mr. Sherring's management was as economical and careful as it could possibly be.

31. *Services of officials and others.*—Mr. Sherring's* work was all that could be desired—careful, thorough, judicious. He never spared himself, and deserves great credit. So does Mr. Straight, who was unremitting in his attention to his duties. His management and handling of his large force of police were carefully thought out, and he did his utmost to get the best work he could out of them. His assistants—Messrs. Fawkes, Mayers, Eyre, Kemp, and O'Connor—worked splendidly. Messrs. Lambert, Charles and Dobbs, Joint and Assistant Magistrates, did good service on the chief bathing days.

* I am indebted to him for parts of this draft.

I have already expressed appreciation of the work done by Captain Robertson and his subordinates.

PROGS. No. 2(*a*). MISCELLANEOUS DEPT.] (21) [JULY 1906. SERIAL NO. 2.

Mr. Sherring recommends for notice and reward Thakur Sitla Baksh Singh, Tahsildar in special charge; Babu Bishwanath Parshad, Naib Tahsildar; and Babu Chatarpat Rai (see my paragraph 3 above). I recommend that the first of these should receive a reward of Rs. 500, that Babu Bishwanath Parshad should receive Rs. 100, and that Babu Chatarpat Rai should get Rs. 50.

Mr. Straight has recommended his Assistant Superintendents to the favourable notice of the Inspector-General of Police; also Inspector Lachmi Dass who was in charge of the subordinate police, Inspectors Walker, Howard, Nestor, Crozier, Evatt, Page, and Sergeant Blunt. Of all these I would especially select Sergeant Blunt and Inspectors Evatt and Walker for particular and honourable mention, and would urge that they be all three given some reward for their services, not only throughout the Fair but on the *Amawas* day. I was at some pains to obtain evidence as to all that then took place, and a Military Officer of considerable standing, who saw the accident from the Fort, has informed me that Inspector Evatt's conduct was deserving of "the greatest credit." Other testimony is to the same effect, and from it, as well as from my own observation, I am able to say much the same of Sergeant Blunt and Inspector Walker.

32. In paragraphs 15 and 18, I have noticed special services of non-official gentlemen. I must add that Rae Jagat Narain, who is an Honorary Magistrate, disposed of all petty cases within the Fair area, and, though an old man and far from strong, exerted himself to give all possible assistance. Babu Jai Gopal, Municipal Member, also did what he could to be useful. Babu Lachmi Narain Agarwala, Municipal Member, was a prominent member of a society formed for the relief of waifs and strays and the distribution of blankets. My Judicial Assistant, Pandit Lalji Sahai Awasti, should receive a reward of Rs. 30 for the heavy work entailed on him by the Fair. He has done it well.

33. I must acknowledge the prompt and valuable assistance we have received from the General Officer Commanding at Allahabad, and from the Officers Commanding the South Staffordshire and 4th Cavalry Regiments.

34. Finally I must apologize for the length of this report, but had I confined it to the prescribed 10 pages of manuscript, I must have omitted much that will be useful for future guidance.

I have the honour to be,

SIR,

Your most obedient servant,

H. V. LOVETT,

Magistrate.

18 जनवरी, 1906 को समाचार पत्र 'इण्डियन पीपुल' में प्रकाशित समाचार द्वारा अवगत कराया गया है कि कुम्भ मेला से प्राप्त राजस्व से तीर्थ यात्रियों, साधुओं के लिए सुविधाएं मुहैया करायी जानी चाहिए परन्तु नगर पालिका व्यवस्था असंतोषजनक है जबकि माघ मेला कमेटी के पास आवश्यक सुविधाएं उपलब्ध कराने हेतु पर्याप्त धनराशि उपलब्ध है। अतः मेला कमेटी को स्वच्छता हेतु, सड़कों पर पानी के छिड़काव हेतु, प्रकाश व्यवस्था हेतु तथा बीमारियों की रोकथाम हेतु आवश्यक प्रयास करना चाहिए।

वर्नाक्युलर न्यूज पेपर -सन् - 1906

(30)

NASIM-I-HIND,
15th January, 1906.

Complaint regarding the butchers cleansing hides in an inhabited part of the town at Fatehpur.

8. The *Nasím-i-Hind* (Fatehpur), of the 15th January, says that butchers collect hides in a house in muhalla Panni at Fatehpur, and cleanse them there. This is calculated to endanger the health of the people, and the Municipal Secretary should see that the cleansing of hides is done outside the municipal limits.

INDIAN PEOPLE,
18th January, 1906.

Need for better lighting and watering the pilgrims' camps and the streets at the Kumbh Mela, Allahabad.

9. The *Indian People* (Allahabad), of the 18th January, says:—During the annual *Mágh Mela* a considerable revenue is derived from the pilgrims, the boatmen, the boat bridge at Daraganj and other sources. On the occasion of the *Kumbh* this revenue is much larger, and it is supposed to be spent in providing comforts for the pilgrims and the Sádhus, and giving them medical and other help. The municipal arrangements, however, are extremely unsatisfactory. We do not know whether the matter drew the attention of His Honour the Lieutenant-Governor the day he inspected the camp on the eastern side of the Ganges as well as the huts on the western side. There are a few scattered lights on the roadside, but there is absolutely no arrangement for lights in the various camps where Sádhus and pilgrims are located. The fires lighted by the former, and the *chirágs* afford a dim, uncertain light in the huts, but for the rest the whole encampment, covering an area of several square miles, is in intense darkness immediately after nightfall, and it is difficult to pick one's way from one hut to another. There are no lamp-posts and no lamps anywhere in the camps. We are not aware whether the *chaukidárs* placed in charge of the camps at night are provided with lanterns, or whether any special precautions are taken to prevent thefts on dark nights. There are no arrangements, again, for watering the streets. The dust is in some measure unavoidable, on account of the sandy nature of the soil, the breeze that blows during the day and the tramp of many millions of feet over the roads and the sands. But it seems rather invidious that only a small length of the street in front of the principal police officer's quarters should be watered, while all the main streets leading to the riverside from the city, Colonelganj and Katra, are never watered, and the dust is allowed to lie ankle-deep in most places. We think there are ample funds at the disposal of the *Mágh Mela* Committee to permit of both better lighting and better watering the streets. Even from a sanitary point of view, measures should be taken to lay the dust as far as practicable, for the thick and fine dust is calculated to produce irritation of the throat and lungs, and it is disquieting to learn that several cases of pneumonia are reported from the city. The precautions that have been taken for the proper management of the fair should have included measures for the better watering and lighting of the streets.

28 जनवरी, 1906 को समाचार पत्र 'इण्डियन पीपुल' में प्रकाशित समाचार द्वारा अवगत कराया गया है कि सिविल एवं पुलिस अधिकारियों ने कुम्भ में दुर्घटना रोकने हेतु अथक प्रयास किया परन्तु अमावस्या के दिन कुम्भ मेला क्षेत्र इलाहाबाद में दुर्घटना हुयी जिसमें जन-धन की हानि हुयी है। इस दुर्घटना के लिए सिविल एवं पुलिस अधिकारियों में किसी को जिम्मेदार नहीं ठहराया गया है।

वर्नाक्युलर न्यूज पेपर -सन् - 1906

INDIAN PEOPLE,
28th January,
1906.

Casualties at the *Kumbh mela* at Allahabad.

12. The *Indian People* (Allahabad), of the 28th January, says:—The civil and police officers present exerted their utmost to prevent accidents, and no blame attaches to them for the lamentable loss of life and the injuries that did happen on the *Amawasya* day. These are to be ascribed to an error of judgment. The error lay in treating the *Kumbh* day in the same manner as the *Sankranti* day. As a matter of fact, there is an immense difference between the two. It was a topic of common conversation that some deaths would inveitably take place on the *Kumbh* day. The authorities were fully aware that the number of bathers on the Kumbh day would be much larger than on the Sankranti day. Consequently, it should have been anticipated that the arrangements and the police assistance that were found sufficient on the Sankranti day might prove inadequate on the Kumbh day. That was what actually happened. The help of the military authorities should have been obtained before, and not after the terrible accidents. The barriers should have been shifted and the passage should have been kept uniformly wide from the second to the third bridge of boats. Part of the passage reserved for the *Sádhus* might have been fenced off for the pilgrims, whose number was much larger. If three or four cordons had been established along the route the rush would not have been so great, and the crowd would have been under better control. Part of the crowd could have been halted on the top of the *bund*, part below and then again at the temple of *Hanuman* and near the south bastion of the fort. If there had been a steady, regulated flow of traffic backwards and forwards the day might have passed without accidents. Similarly, at the second bridge of boats a cordon should have been established on the top, in continuation of the fencing of the enclosure of the space reserved for the shaving of heads. This would have prevented people from tumbling down in heaps at the head of the bridge of boats. Crowds of these proportions do not come often together, and the error of judgment may be well ascribed to want of experience, but it will be well to put together the lessons learnt by this Kumbh gathering, so that similar gatherings in future may be better and more successfully controlled, and loss of life and injury to limb may be avoided.

AL BASHIR,
30th January,
1906.

Suggestion for effecting union between Shias and Sunnis for the purposes of promoting their common well-being.

13. A Muhammadan correspondent of *Al Bashír* (Etáwah), of the 30th January, in a long article, endeavouring to show that union is impossible between the Hindus and Musalmans, because the former are hypocrites, urges that the Muhammadans, instead of seeking to cultivate amity and good-will for Hindus, would do well, on the principle of charity begins at home, to direct their efforts to uniting the Shias and Sunnis into one body co-operating for their common well-being. Both the sects believe in the same God, and follow the same gospel; and if their respective *ulamas*, or learned men, be moved in the matter, they still enjoy sufficient influence among their people and will easily be able to effect a union of hearts between the two sects.

HINDOSTHAN,
31st January,
1906.

Suggestion for suppression of begging nuisance in large towns.

14. The English *Hindosthán* (Kalakankar), of the 31st January, says:—The begging nuisance in all large cities in India, Calcutta, Madras, Bombay and Allahabad, etc., has reached such a degree of reproach on Government that it is high time some drastic measures were adopted to suppress the nuisance. Begging on public roads and streets as years roll by seems to increase. Some of these beggars, whose very appearance is shockingly disgusting, are seen running after not only pedestrians, but also after the occupants of carriages and tram-cars, letting the motor-cars seriously alone from their inability to keep pace with them. Many of these beggars, who have no claim to be so called, being strong in body, mind and limb, venture even so far as to touch the body of the passers-by until either they are pleased with a pice or well thrashed aside with a cane. The Chief Presidency Magistrate, Bombay, Mr. N. W. Kemp, had half a dozen of these gentry before him, charged with soliciting alms in public places, and convicted and sentenced all to periods varying from fifteen days to one month's rigorous imprisonment. Such leniency in the case of vagabonds who are perfectly able, but too lazy to work, is quite a ridiculous method of dealing with the ever-increasing nuisance. In most cities and large towns on the Continent they deal effectively with the begging nuisance and the Contagious Diseases Act. With regard to the first, every offender detected in soliciting alms, who is capable of doing a day's

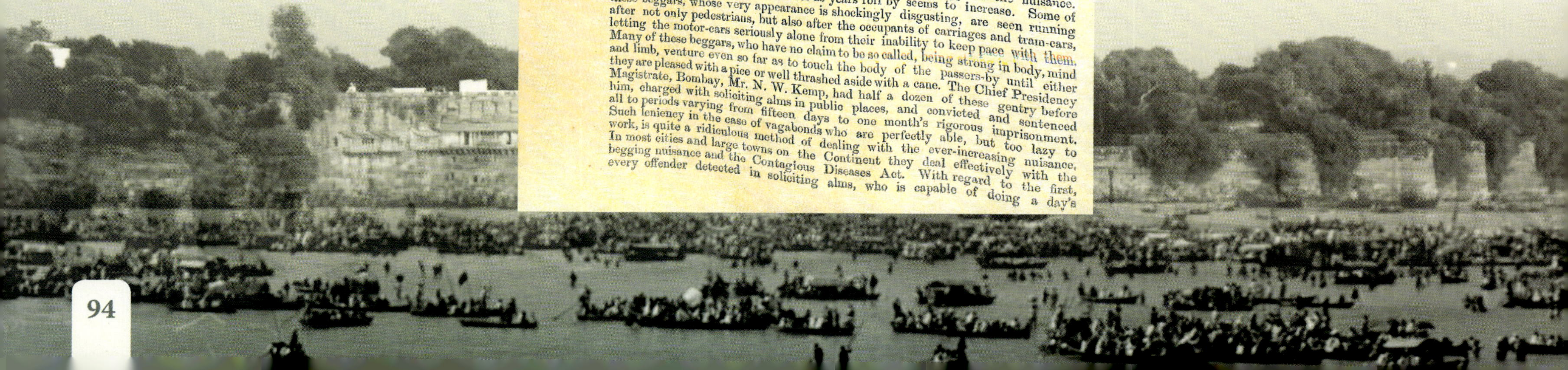

‘इंडियन पीपुल’ समाचार पत्र इलाहाबाद में 28 जनवरी, 1906 को प्रकाशित समाचार के अनुसार इलाहाबाद किले में स्थित ‘अक्षय वट’ वृक्ष के दर्शन हेतु दर्शनार्थियों से फीस लेने के लिए तैनात यूरोपियन सिपाहियों का विरोध किया गया क्योंकि उनका मानना था कि सिपाहियों से स्पर्श होने के कारण वे अपवित्र हो जाते हैं।

वर्नाक्युलर न्यूज पेपर -सन् - 1906

INDIAN PEOPLE,
28th January,
1906.

Objection taken to British soldiers being employed to collect a fee from pilgrims and admit them to the sacred tree inside the Fort at Allahabad during the *Magh Mela*.

6. The *Indian People* (Allahabad), of the 28th January, says :—Pilgrims to the *Tribeni* and the *Magh Mela* usually go to see the *Akshay Bat*, or perennial Bo-tree, inside the fort. A small fee is demanded from each visitor. We do not profess to know to what fund the collections are credited. It seems rather unfortunate that the *Akshay Bat* should be inside the fort, but the Government is not responsible for what was done by the Emperor Akbar. What seems to us, however, open to objection is the placing of European soldiers at the entrance to the passage and their employment on the collection of fees. Since the tree is inside the fort the military authorities may be its proper custodians, but there is religious objection to the employment of European soldiers on duty connected with the admission of pilgrims. They do not go to see the fort but the *Akshay Bat* alone, which is to them a sacred object. Complaints have reached us that men and women, who go to see the *Akshay Bat* after they have bathed in the *Tribeni*, have religious scruple to touch the hands of Europeans, which is unvoidable so long as the soldiers are on duty and collect the fees from the pilgrims. We have no right to go behind the sentiment, or to discuss a question of religious faith. The pilgrims may be told to stay away if they dislike the present arrangement, but they may just as well be forbidden to bathe at the *Tribeni*. The best thing would be to make over the *Akshay Bat* to the civil authorities. If that is impracticable, only high caste Hindu sepoys assisted by some Brahmins should be employed to admit the pilgrims and collect the fees ; or, a self-registering turnstile like that used in the Calcutta Zoological gardens might be employed, and the fees could be collected by any one without the slightest chance of fraud or peculation. The exercise of a little discretion would remove all cause of complaint, and the Local Government would earn the gratitude of the Hindu community and the pilgrims who come annually to see the sacred tree in the fort.

ADVOCATE,
1st February, 1906.

(e).—Education.

The Government of India insisting on the Bombay Government to prescribe an age-limit for the Matriculation examination.

7. The *Advocate* (Lucknow), of the 1st February, says :—Individuals die but a nation lives. In the same way rulers come and go but policy endures. Such has been the idea that struck us when we learnt how the Government of India have, presumably under Lord Minto's *régime*, written to the Bombay Government to prescribe a limit as to the age at which candidates should be allowed to appear at the Matriculation examination. We are at a loss to make out why, in spite of popular and reasonable opposition, the Government should insist on an age-limit at all, what to say of putting it at sixteen. That the Allahabad University has done it is no reason why others should follow suit. The fact that a very small percentage of pupils go up for the examination at a very early age, say at from twelve to fourteen, should be enough to make Government less uneasy about the matter. And the anxiety of the State about the health and development of

अवध और रोहिल खण्ड रेलवे तथा ईस्ट इंडियन रेलवे द्वारा माघ मेले में विशेष रेलगाड़ियों की व्यवस्था - सन् 1908

पत्रावली संख्या - 299/1908 -सामान्य प्रशासन विभाग

(3)

SERIAL NO. 13. THE Commissioner, Allahabad division, replies to serial no. 8.

Please see notes on page 2. For orders. Commissioner of Meerut has not replied to serial no. 8. The Hardwar fair is held next month after which he will doubtless report.

23-3-1908. J. M.

23-3-1908. C. H. C.

CHIEF SECRETARY—

It is not necessary. J. P. HEWETT.

If it is intended to refer to resolution XII we have now all the information. It appears that the defects in the arrangements for conveyance of pilgrims to and from the *Magh mela* were principally—

(*a*) want of lighting in wagons,

(*b*) failure to ensure a proper distribution of pilgrims between the wagons.

The railway companies might be addressed in connection with these points.

23-3-1908. S. P. O'DONNELL.

HIS HONOUR—

The question of referring to this matter in Council is one that I will speak of when I come to His Honour next.

But meantime the question is whether any orders are needed upon this report of the railway arrangements at the last *Magh mela*.

I fear so, though, I personally do not like it. J. P. HEWETT.

These three defects should be strongly condemned by us. J. P. HEWETT.

So long as the one railway (Oudh and Rohilkhand Railway) has to send in ninety-three special trains to one *mela* (as it did in 1907 to Allahabad) the fact that goods wagons must be used seems to be established. Granting that for the present it is clear from Mr. Moore's report that on the East Indian Railway the rule that each wagon used for a night journey should be lighted was not followed, that in some cases on the same line coal wagons, uncleaned, were used, and that on both the Oudh and Rohilkhand Railway and the East Indian Railway there was overcrowding. It is said this cannot be avoided without additional staff. (But it was not often that the overcrowding caused discomfort); if that is the case the staff ought to be provided and some definite responsibility laid on one or more officials at each place to enforce the prohibition against overcrowding.

Most certainly. J. P. HEWETT.

Yes: we must address them politely but firmly. J. P. HEWETT.

This might be said to the two railways concerned, and they might be asked to take further precautions in future *melas*.

I do not think the suggestion as to issue of tickets after 7 p.m. at Prayag is one that can be taken up without further enquiry. Probably the railway management does not wish to start trains from Prayag all night—it is in the middle of the old civil station of Allahabad—and no doubt by this time the pilgrims know that tickets are not sold.

I think we should do so. J. P. HEWETT.

If His Honour thinks it should be taken up, we should ask Collector for the whole case to be fully stated.

24-3-1908. J. W. HOSE.

SEE above.

28-3-1908. J. P. HEWETT.

THE above orders were carried out in serial nos. 15 to 17.

SERIAL NO. 14. THE Commissioner, Allahabad division, requests that the word "fort" may be substituted for "Naini" in paragraph 2 of Mr. Moore's report on *Magh mela* fair.

The necessary correction has been made. For information. Record?

14-4-1908. J. M.

15-4-1908. C. H. C.

16-4-1908. S. P. O'DONNELL.

SERIAL NO. 1 OF FILE NO. $\frac{299}{1908}$. THE Commissioner, Allahabad division, forwards a copy of a letter from the Magistrate of Allahabad stating that no orders were issued by the railway

जिलाधिकारी इलाहाबाद की कुम्भ मेला विषयक रिपोर्ट

डब्ल्यू0 गैसकेल, जिलाधिकारी, इलाहाबाद ने सन् 1918 में मण्डलायुक्त, इलाहाबाद को प्रेषित अपनी रिपोर्ट में कुम्भ मेले के सम्बन्ध में विस्तार से जानकारी दी है। रिपोर्ट में श्रद्धालुओं के आवागमन, साधुओं के अखाड़ों एवं उनके जुलूस, अक्षयवट मंदिर, संगम स्थल, मेला स्थल का आवंटन, संगम में स्नान की व्यवस्था, पुलिस व्यवस्था, अग्निशमन व्यवस्था, पुल एवं घाटों की व्यवस्था, प्रकाश व्यवस्था, जल आपूर्ति व्यवस्था, चिकित्सा व्यवस्था, लेखा इत्यादि के सम्बन्ध में विस्तार से चर्चा की है।

पत्रावली संख्या-401/1917 -सामान्य प्रशासन विभाग

PROGS. NO. 20. deserves special commendation—among his assistants the Magistrate specially mentions Mr. Pilditch. On the medical side, the Magistrate records that the very sanitary condition of the mela site is a tribute to the tireless exertions of Dr. A. Sousa, Deputy Sanitary Commissioner. Altogether this fair has been a bright spot in a rather gloomy period. SERIAL NO. 65.

4. I concur with Mr. Gaskell's remark that officers in charge of Adhkumbhs and Kumbhs should, as was the case this year, be in charge of the ordinary Magh mela fair for at least one previous year.

No. 21. No. 772, dated the 20th May, 1918. No. 66.

From—W. GASKELL, ESQ., District Magistrate, Allahabad,

To—Commissioner, Allahabad division.

SIR,—I have the honour to submit a report on the recent Kumbh mela. The main portion of the report was drafted by Mr. Wallace before he left the district.

2. The origin of the Kumbh mela and the sanctity of the Tribeni have been discussed in previous reports and are well known, so that I need not deal with the question here. The recent Kumbh was of a peculiar sanctity in that the Amawas, being a Somwati and Mauni Amawas, was extremely propitious and provided opportunities for the devout which had not occurred for 36 years.

3. *Attendance.*—It was anticipated originally that pilgrims would come to Allahabad in unusually large numbers, especially as the tendency in recent years had been towards a marked increase in the visitors at the ordinary Magh mela. But as the time for the mela approached the pressure on the railways for the carriage of goods and material required for war purposes increased, and it became clear that the usual facilities could not be provided for pilgrim traffic. The East Indian Railway was thus compelled early in October to publish a notification that special trains would not be run in connection with the mela. Subsequently the Government of India, in a notification issued on the 21st December, 1917, prohibited the booking of pilgrims to Allahabad or any station within a certain distance from it between 3rd January and 25th February. The restriction, however, was relaxed on 8th to 11th February. Speculation was rife as to the effect of the prohibition on travelling, but the people largely solved the difficulty by travelling by road and to some extent by river. The attendance on the Shankrant (14th January) was normal for a Kumbh mela and at the Amawas was probably larger than on any previous occasion. Thereafter the crowds rapidly disappeared, the people going by road or by such trains (including special trains) as the railway companies were able to provide. It is always a matter of difficulty to judge the numbers in an assembly like that at the Kumbh mela on an important festival and in the current year the estimates of different people have varied widely owing to prepossessed ideas on account of the railway restrictions. The area covered by the mela was also unusually large. The official estimate of the people present on the great bathing days (when the akharas went in procession) is as follows:—

Shankrant—14th January	700,000
Amawas—10th and 11th February	between 2,000,000 and 3,000,000
Basant Panchmi—15th February	300,000

3A. *The site of the mela.*—The site of the mela was more favourable than at the last Kumbh in 1906. Then the main stream of the Ganges ran close to the fort walls. The fair was held on the high land by the fort belonging to the Military Grass Farm and on the Jhusi bank of the Ganges, requiring the bridging of the river. No such elaborate arrangements were necessary this year. But at first a certain amount of doubt existed as to whether history would not repeat itself; for owing to late rains and the flooding of the Ganges the river flowed in two streams, one below the fort and the other about a mile away to the east. This was the position so late as the end of October, when the work of preparation for the fair was set on foot. By

PROGS. NO. 21. the middle of November the stream below the fort had separated from the main river and resolved itself into a long narrow stretch of dead water. It was then apparent that the Sangam would be far to the east of the fort and that an area would be found more than sufficient for the needs of the fair. The map was prepared; and it will be seen on comparison that the general arrangement of the fair resembles that of the Adhkumbh in 1912. SERIAL NO. 66.

4. A portion of the fair was located on the Grass Farm above the bund on both sides of Tribeni road. The police officers' camp was pitched on the fort glacis. On the Daraganj side sites were allotted to the police force, recruiters for the Indian Army, missionaries, and a Hindi society. Large camps of pandits and sadhus were also formed on the Jhusi bank of the Ganges.

Considerable difficulties were met in preparing the main site. Owing to the vagaries of the Ganges, work did not commence till the middle of November; and railway construction work at neighbouring stations created a serious deficiency of labour by taking all available workmen in the locality. After considerable exertion 1,200 labourers and 100 mules were secured from the district. Dead water was removed by daglas and pools were filled in. A large depression too deep to be filled in by hand was perforce left fenced with bamboos.

5. Roads are of primary importance in order that traffic may be dealt with adequately. They were laid out on a large scale. The main road from the bund to the Sangam was a mile and a half long and 320 feet wide, and was so constructed as to run equidistant from the Ganges and Jumna for the greater part of its length, finally sweeping round in a curve towards the Sangam. The labour entailed in preparing it may be estimated by the fact that it passed through two streams and two pools over 300 feet long and three feet deep. The middle part of the road, measuring 24 feet across, was roped off and specially prepared for traffic and the passage of the processions on the big days. Care and labour in the construction of this traffic road were well expended; for its surface remained excellent up to the very last day of the fair and was level enough for cycling. Elephants and motor cars failed to damage it; and undoubtedly some measure of the success of the fair was due to the comfort and facility afforded by this thoroughfare to pedestrians and wheeled traffic alike. Two other big roads were made, chiefly with a view to facilitating the return of the *akharas* from bathing on the processions days. One was specially set apart for the Bairagis, who lived in a separate encampment in Ganga Patti. The other was used for the remaining *akharas*, taking them along the Jumna bank to their enclosures towards the bund. The usual branch roads were made separating each block of the bazar and the different enclosures of the ascetics. A road was also constructed towards the fort for the use of pilgrims visiting the temples of Mahabir and Achaibat, the latter of which lies inside the fort.

6. The current of the Ganges gave much anxiety and required to be carefully watched. After the first of the great festivals (14th January) the river suddenly changed its course to the west and bit into the main land considerably in rear of the Sangam. The road intended for the return of the Bairagis was washed away as well as part of the main road. Just enough space was left for the passage of the processions on 11th February; and the Sangam became situated at the end of a narrow spit about 300 feet wide. These changes are marked on the map.

7. *The Sangam.*—On the Shankrant the bathing place was in front of Someshwar Nath Mahadeo; and for the rest of the fair it remained in very nearly the same place. The water was shallow except in the Jumna direction and for the purpose of bathing was ideal. A barrier of boats lashed together and a fence of timber posts connected by ropes encircled the Sangam and rendered it safe. Ten boats were placed at the disposal of the police as necessarily a good deal of bathing went on outside the circle. Four life belts were procured and over 800 people were helped out of difficulties in deep water. The numbers given by the police are 140, but many cases were

not recorded. Beni Pershad and Sheo, boatmen, were specially retained to help pilgrims; and Lal Mohan Banerji, a well known local swimmer, worked strenuously throughout the mela at this point.

8. *Processions.*—A Kumbh mela is attended by many orders of ascetics, the most important of whom go down in procession to the Sangam to bathe. The following *akharas* are those allowed to go in procession and in the order shown :—

1. Nirbanis.
2. Niranjanis and Junas.
3. Bairagis.
4. Chhota Panchayati.
5. Bara Panchayati and Bandhwa Hasanpur.
6. Nirmala and Bindrabani.

The Junas are regarded as a sub-division of the Niranjanis and follow them on the great processions at a distance of 30 paces. But the Junas are increasing in numbers while the Niranjanis are falling off, and on the occasion of the next important festival it will in all probability be necessary to allot a large area for the camp of the Junas. The Bandhwa Hasanpur did not arrive in time for the Shankrant. The Bindrabani *akhara* did not come at all as an *akhara*, but a few of their sadhus attended and joined the Nirmala ascetics. There was a noticeable tendency among the *akharas* towards splitting up; and attempts were made by sub-sects to gain recognition from the authorities in order to have separate processions of their own. There was a quarrel among the Niranjanis. One Mahant seceded and on his request for a separate site being refused he joined the Junas. This quarrel is stated to be of long standing and to have been in evidence at the preceding Kumbh at Hardwar. The Digambar sect of the Bairagis petitioned for the right to take out in procession with torches the disciple of Mahant Ram Papun of Rewah. This was disallowed at the last Adhkumbh and was also refused this year. The disciple and his followers eventually went to the Sangam with the Digambars. On the other hand the Goshains held a maha sabha at which religious differences were settled amicably and in other respects there was also a tendency towards unity in religious matters.

9. Meetings were held before the big days, at which the mahants were present. The order of the *akharas* was fixed after consultation with the Mahants, but except in the case of the sub-divisions of the Bairagis the proceedings were formal, and the Mahants were willing to follow precedent. The three chief sects included in the Bairagis are :—

1. Nirmohi.
2. Digambar.
3. Nirbani.

The Digambars always occupy the second place, but the other two sub-divisions dispute hotly for the first. At the last Kumbh an attempt was made to arrange for each of them to occupy the first place during some part of the procession but owing to a breach of faith the arrangement failed. In 1912, when the Adhkumbh took place, an agreement was reached on the basis of the following table of precedence which varies according to the bathing days :—

On the Shankrant—

1. Nirmohi.
2. Digambar.
3. Nirbani.

On the Amawas and Basant Panchmi—

1. Nirbani.
2. Diagambar.
3. Nirmohi.

The arrangement was successful and, despite a protest of a more or less formal nature, was prescribed again this year. No trouble occurred on this account and the

table of precedence may now be considered as established custom. The Bairagis, however, are by their very nature of a turbulent disposition, and a keen look-out has to be maintained against untoward incidents. On two or three occasions trouble threatened but was fortunately averted.

10. The progress of the processions was controlled from signalling stations, of which three were erected at the Sangam, the kotwali, and below the bund, and by means of telephones which were attached to each police station. The processions lasted from 6·30 a.m. to 4 p.m. on each occasion.

11. The procession of each *akhara* was accompanied by a Magistrate (whose place was filled on several occasions by Goshain Rampuri of Benares, an old friend, whose help I cordially acknowledged), an Assistant Superintendent of Police, and a detachment of police. Most processions were accompanied by elephants carrying the "nishans." The elephants stopped just beyond the kotwali; and thence the "nishans" were carried on foot over the softer and more sandy portion of the road to the Sangam, the elephants crossing to the return road along the Jumna to meet the processions returning from bathing The Nirbanis, the Niranjanis (the destitute of passion) and the Junas contained a large numbers of naked fakirs in their ranks, called Nagas; while the Junas were followed by numbers of female devotees clothed in saffron-coloured garments and hailing chiefly from Nepal. The processions on all three occasions passed off without a hitch; and the mahants and members of the *akharas* expressed themselves in warm terms of approval of the arrangements. As District Magistrate I was present on all the procession days. The officer in charge accompanied the first procession to the Sangam and remained at the bathing place with Mr. Burton, who was in special charge of the police.

12. *Achaibat temple.*—The Achaibat temple which is situated under-ground in the fort is visited by pilgrims after bathing. It contains the "undying banyan tree" and its walls are damp with the moisture of the Saraswati river, which, the superstitious allege, here passes on its way to the Sangam after being lost in the sands near Jhansar in Sarhind some four hundred miles to the north. The road to this temple was made sufficiently broad to dispense with the usual bamboo fencing. No accidents occurred, the police arrangements being all that could be desired.

13. *Police.*—The police force was under the charge of Mr. B. H. Burton, Superintendent of Police, who was placed on special duty. He was assisted by 4 assistant superintendents and 4 deputy superintendents. In addition the force comprised 5 European inspectors, 9 Indian inspectors, 41 sub-inspectors, 130 head constables, 1,151 constables, 150 mounted police, and 265 chaukidars. The total police force of all ranks numbered 1,760, exceeding the numbers detailed for the Kumbh of 1906 by about 550. The statistics of crime at the last Kumbh mela are not available and no comparison is possible. But there was a considerable increase in crime over the returns for the Adhkumbh in 1912. It may however be said that there was less crime than was expected. The remarkable state of cleanliness in which the fair area was maintained and the consequent healthiness resulting from this favourable condition was largely due to the watchfulness of the sanitary police and action taken under section 34 of the Police Act. The greatest transgressors were the Bairagis, who showed a strong tendency to disregard all sanitary rules. They were specially warned by the officer in charge to observe the rules, which were explained to them by the Sanitary department, but they persisted in neglecting them and in a certain number of cases prosecutions were found necessary.

A gang of Barwars hailing from the Eastern districts visited the fair. Chaube Ramji Das, sub-inspector in charge of the kotwali, effected their arrest and a visible decline in the number of thefts was afterwards noticed.

14. *Magisterial.*—The magisterial work was done by Mr. Wallace assisted by a probationary Deputy Collector, Mr. Cartman. Two Honorary Magistrates, Babu Batuk Prasad and Lala Behari Lal, very kindly consented to sit as a bench and

(25)

GENERAL ADMINISTRATION DEPT.] [JULY, 1918.

PROGS. NO. 21. SERIAL NO. 66.

disposed of sanitary offences. Thakur Har Pratap Singh, Special Magistrate, and Rais of Dhokri, held his court at Jhusi and settled petty cases in that area.

15. *Fire*—An important part of the duties of the police consisted in precautions against fire. The structures in the fair being extremely inflammable, preventive action had to be taken on a large though rather primitive scale. Efforts to secure a portable fire engine was not successful and recourse was had to the time-honoured methods of storing water in earthen jars, plastering kitchens and places where the lighting of fire was unavoidable, heaping up sand at accessible spots, warning the inhabitants of the fair by beat of drum, and stationing special persons to act as firemen. In spite of these precautions fifteen fires broke out; they were promptly suppressed and save in two cases the damage was insignificant. Experience has shown that the only effective way of dealing with an outbreak of fire among the thatched huts of the fare is to have in readiness long poles fitted with sickles. By means of these instruments it is possible to demolish the neighbouring huts and tents with great speed by cutting the tent ropes or grass ropes that bind the huts together. Extensive use was made of these sickles.

16. *Bridges and ferries.*—Large encampments arose on the Ganges bank at Jhusi opposite to the main fair. Traffic therefore from Jhusi and along the Grand Trunk road from Benares to the opposite bank became very heavy. The water in places was sufficiently shallow to allow pilgrims to walk across the Ganges, but the vast majority crossed by the Daraganj pontoon bridge and by the Ramghat ferry.

Trouble was experienced at the pontoon bridge on the Amawas (11th February). Owing to the restrictions on railway travel. The numbers who came to the mela by the Grand Trunk road were unprecedentedly large, while pilgrims who had spent a long time in their journey to Allahabad showed no desire to stay there after bathing. The consequence was that a large number of people had not reached the mela when an equally large number who had bathed early in the morning wished to set out on their return journey. The result was that for a few hours the traffic was greater than the bridge could carry. An assistant superintendent of police had already been posted to control the bridge, but the police force originally deputed proved insufficient and had to be strengthened. At the same time the difficulty was increased by a leak in one of the pontoons owing to the strain from the numbers on the bridge and some time was occupied in its repair, during which the crowd naturally increased. It was necessary then to delay a number of people, many of whom were diverted to the Ramghat and to the shallow portion of the river which the people were able to ford without assistance. The contractor of the ghat who was expecting only a small number of pilgrims owing to the restrictions on travel, failed completely, but the arrangements were taken in hand by the officer in charge and Mr. Bishop, Joint Magistrate, and a regular ferry service was arranged.

On the 12th February the crowd endeavouring to cross the pontoon bridge was as great as ever in spite of the relief afforded by the ferry near by. A large police force was working at the bridge under my direct orders and was ably assisted by members of the Ambulance Corps of the Muir Central College and the Ewing Christian College and of the Sewa Samiti. But after several hours of strenuous work it was apparent that they were becoming exhausted in keeping back the struggling crowd and it was necessary to ask for help from the 2nd Lancers. The crowds were rapidly passed over the bridge and by 4 p. m. traffic was normal. It is remarkable that on both the 11th and 12th of February only two persons were injured in the crush at the pontoon bridge in spite of the vastness of the crowd. The police force on duty there deserve credit for their untiring efforts to create order and to regulate the traffic in a situation which might easily have resulted in disaster. If there should be any restrictions on traffic at any future Kumbh mela it will be a matter for consideration whether a second pontoon bridge should not be constructed.

(26)

GENERAL ADMINISTRATION DEPT.] [JULY, 1918.

PROGS. NO. 21. SERIAL NO. 66.

17. *Lighting.*—A scheme for lighting the fair area by means of electric light was entertained but was not feasible owing to the enhanced price of materials due to the war. Use was made of standard lanterns and Kitson lights, lamps being placed on each side of the main road at intervals of 100 feet, and at all public latrines, cross-roads, pilgrim enclosures, public offices and the sangam. The several *akharas*, pragwals, and shop-keepers made their own arrangements.

18. *Water supply.*—A grant of nearly Rs. 60,000 was made by Government for laying water pipes throughout the mela area, the work being in charge of Mr. Platt, Assistant Sanitary Engineer. An assistant engineer was resident in the fair. The water supply came from the Daraganj tube well, and for a reserve supply it was hoped that water would be obtained by tapping the municipal main near the fort. Despite these arrangements the supply practically failed just when it was most needed, viz. on the most important days of the fair, 10th, 11th and 12th February. The pressure did not appear to be great enough to supply both sides of the fair area at once and the deficiency made itself apparent in the Jumna patti. It was also found that nothing was to be gained by tapping the municipal main. With this exception the water supply proved adequate and was of untold advantage as there was a complete absence of any kind of epidemic whatever at the fair itself or after it. There was little or no objection to the use of the water as pilgrims and ascetics alike are now habituated to the use of pipe water. The practice of digging wells along the main route was abandoned by the advice of the Sanitary authorities and the digging of wells elsewhere was discouraged. In two instances only were wells sanctioned, certain ascetics objecting to using any other supply of water for their cooking. Taps of the self-closing type were fitted to each standpost. A good deal of waste was thereby prevented. The standposts were erected on pakka platforms each with its absorption pit. There were no difficulties experienced with them, though the constant disappearance of their brass fittings often created a problem. It would be as well on future occasions, if the amount of water available has not increased, to devise methods by which a reserve supply of pure water would be available for the big bathing days. A number of large tanks or reservoirs, or large canvas receptacles such as are used by the army on field service, containing many thousands of gallons, would seem to be an obvious arrangement in the face of the prohibition of wells.

19. *Medical.*—The sanitary arrangements for the fair were under the control of Dr. A. Sousa, Deputy Sanitary Commissioner, whose staff was made up as follows :—

4 assistant surgeons.	6 health officers.
23 sub-assistant surgeons.	1 chief sanitary inspector.
2 female sub-assistant surgeons.	4 assistant superintendents of vaccination.
11 compounders.	9 sanitary inspectors.
1 female compounder.	60 vaccinators.

2 Ayurvedic practitioners.

The fair area was divided into six sanitary circles in which were included the Alopi Bagh contiguous to the fair area, Arail on the opposite side of the Jumna to the fair and the police camps. In all 17 jamadars and 1,401 sweepers were employed. The sanitary authorities asked for double this number. Every means was employed to get them, but the results were disproportionate, even though Government circularised all district officers. The number of available sweepers in the provinces had decreased for several abnormal reasons such as recruitment for war service and the ravages of plague. The number obtained was, however, found to be just sufficient.

It is gratifying that no epidemic broke out. The cases of cholera and plague (one and two respectively) that came to light were imported. There were five cases resembling cholera. The deaths that took place in the mela area were 126 in number, a small total when it is remembered that the permanent population must have been at least one hundred thousand. The staff on sanitary duty, to the excellent result of whose work reference has already been made, consisted of an assistant superintendent of police, a deputy superintendent of police, two inspectors, 3 sub-inspectors, 9 head

PROGS. NO. 21. SERIAL NO. 6 9

constables and 135 constables and 265 chaukidars. Four boats were retained for removing hair from the barbers' enclosure, taking away dead bodies and patrolling the river.

Under this head may be mentioned the fact that the Pragwals, agitated by a baseless rumour that was circulating to the effect that the lodging house rules would be applied to the mela area, were late in taking up their sites and erecting enclosures for the pilgrims. They had previously been annoyed at certain municipal rules which required them to pay licence fees for lodging houses in the city in advance and also prescribed certain conditions of a sanitary nature.

20. *Voluntary organisations.*—The All-India Hindu Sabha, the Sewa Samiti, and its affiliated societies did voluntary work in the fair. They enrolled over 700 "volunteers" as they are termed, who were utilised chiefly for controlling traffic and tracing lost persons. There were also a number of private dispensaries. The Sewa Samiti equipped one hospital with the help of the medical authorities, 4 ayurvedic dispensaries, and 1 allopathic dispensary. The Ram Krishna Mission arranged for one hospital and 1 allopathic dispensary. The Eitkarini Sabha provided one dispensary. The Muir College and Ewing Christian College Ambulance Corps were present fully equipped, and were stationed at the sangam. A woman's bureau was provided for female pilgrims and many Indian lady workers gave their services. There were four enquiry offices set up by the fair authorities and staffed by volunteer workers. All these voluntary workers rendered most valuable assistance and their help was all the more effective by their willing co-operation with the authorities.

21. *Accounts.*—The accounts will be found in appendices B, C and D, but even now are not absolute in all cases. The figures of the last Kumbh mela are also given for purpose of comparison.

22. *Income-Appendix B.*—In spite of the railway restrictions no reduction was made in fees. Protests were received from the mallahs, which were entirely unjustified as the crowds on the Amawas, when mallahs and shop-keepers expect large profits constituted a record. Much difficulty was experienced in selling the sites for shops at the auction. Mr. Wallace sold the shop sites in person and paid particular attention to this main source of revenue. The warnings published in October by the East Indian Railway had, however, impressed the bidders, and the prices paid for shops fell off. The decrease was Rs. 7,000 on the last Kumbh. By custom the Muttra cloth merchants are favoured in the matter of shop sites and fees. They failed to turn up in any numbers, owing probably to the difficulty of transporting their goods. The total income from all sources was Rs. 53,959. The last Kumbh was productive of more income by Rs. 8,521. It may be noted that the *akharas* receive their sites free of charge.

23. *Expenditure.*—The mela has been an expensive one. A large grant of Rs. 59,943 was needed for the purchase of new pipes, the price of which was enhanced by war conditions. They were also laid over a larger area than before. General expenses were largely increased by the need of higher wages to attract labour, the rise in sweepers' wages, and the heavy cost of transporting them from their districts to Allahabad; in many cases sweepers had to be sought in remote districts like Bulandshahr. There was an all-round rise in the cost of materials, sanitary appliances, and medical necessities. The telephone installation was an additional expense that had not existed at previous fairs. A detailed statement of the expenditure under the various heads together with the corresponding figures for the previous Kumbh will be found in appendix D. The chief increases have been nearly Rs. 52,000 under water supply, nearly Rs. 10,000 for catcha roads, Rs. 8,700 under conservancy, Rs. 1,250 on account of the raising by Government of the conservancy contribution to the cantonment committee, Rs. 1,100 under compensation for land, and Rs. 1,000 for the construction of huts. Apart from the general causes already stated, the rise in the cost of catcha roads was due to greater size of the mela area this year, and the extra compensation is explained by the fact that at the previous Kumbh the land taken up

PROGS. NO. 21. SERIAL NO. 66.

on the Jhusi side was mainly occupied by the sadhus and for this the zamindars desired no payment. The chief savings were Rs. 16,300, the cost of the bridge over the Ganges, which was this year unnecessary as ample room existed for the *akharas* on the fort side, Rs. 8,500 under police, and Rs. 2,500 under tahsil expenses. The two last are simply the result of certain payments to the tahsil and police staff not being debited to the mela funds on this occasion. In connection with the increased expenditure it should be noted that disinfectants and non-perishable sanitary materials to the value of about Rs. 4,000 have been retained for future use.

24. *Staff.*—The mela is generally acknowledged to have been a great success and for this the credit is due entirely to the officers in control of it. Mr. Wallace was the executive officer in charge, and did excellently: he has a fund of common sense and of humour which proved invaluable. He was ably assisted by Babu Pitam Prasad, tahsildar, as manager, who was present at the Adhkumbh mela in 1912 and all succeeding Magh melas and whose experience was of the utmost value. It is essential that the manager of the Kumbh mela should have had previous experience of ordinary melas and it will be advisable in a few years to post to the district an officer who will be the manager designate of the Adhkumbh in 1924.

There were two assistant managers, M. Chhatarpat Rai, who is a repository of all mela lore and tradition, being the only one of the staff who worked at the last Kumbh mela, and whose services were indispensable, and Babu Prem Narain, naib tahsildar, who performed his duties satisfactorily.

The police work was excellent throughout and reflects the greatest credit on Mr. Burton and his assistants, of whom I may be permitted to mention, Mr. Pilditch, a past master in the art of managing a crowd.

Dr. A. Sousa, Deputy Sanitary Commissioner, was in charge of the sanitary arrangements and worked with unflagging industry. The very satisfactory sanitary condition of the mela site is a tribute to his tireless exertions.

The military authorities twice rendered timely help, namely, on the first bathing day of the Shankrant, 14th January, and on 12th February at the pontoon bridge, and my acknowledgements are due to the General Officer Commanding at Allahabad and the Officer Commanding the 2nd Lancers.

APPENDIX A.—*Crime statement for the Kumbh mela*, 1918.

Offences.				Cases.							Accused persons.						Remarks.
	Reports.	Action taken by police.	Balance in which no action taken by the police.	Investigated.	Uninvestigated.	Challaned.	Convicted.	Acquitted or discharged.	Under trial.	Untraced.	Arrested.	Convicted.	Acquitted or discharged.	Under trial.	Value of property stolen.	Value of property recovered.	
Sections 295/147	1	1	...	1	...	1	...	...	1	...	12	...	...	31	...	...	
Section 457, Indian Penal Code ...	3	3	...	3	...	1		...	1	1	1	...	...	1	...	...	
" 332, Indian Penal Code ...	1	1	...	1	...	1	1	...	...	...	1	1	...	...	...	...	
" 379, Indian Penal Code, with theft more than Rs. 10	39	37	2	37	2	31	18	1	12	4	43	18	1	24	...	...	
Section 379, Indian Penal Code, under Rs. 10, with theft.	...	...	...	...	...	...	...	...	...	...	...	...	...	...	...	...	
Section 380, Indian Penal Code, value with theft more than Rs. 10.	4	4	...	4	.	1	...	...	1	3	1	...	...	1	...	...	
Section 380, Indian Penal Code, with theft less than Rs. 10	...	...	...	...	...	...	...	...	...	...	...	...	...	...	...	...	
Section 366, Indian Penal Code ...	1	1	...	1	..	...	...	...	...	...	...	...	...	...	...	...	Under police investigation
" 309, ditto ...	1	1	..	1	.	1	1	...	...	...	1	1	...	...	...	...	
" 406, ditto ...	3	3	...	3	...	1	1	...	...	...	2	1	1	...	...	...	
" 109, ditto ...	1	1	...	1	...	1	1	...	...	...	1	1	...	...	...	...	
Total ...	64	52	2	52	2	38	22	1	15	8	71	22	2	47	...	...	
Section 34, Act V, of Police ...	506	506	...	...	...	506	473	31	...	...	506	475	31	..	...	...	

इलाहाबाद में 1921-22 में आयोजित होने वाले माघ मेला हेतु अस्थायी रूप से इलाहाबाद के परगना अरैल क्षेत्र के 23.38 एकड़ जमीन को सार्वजनिक उद्देश्य हेतु अधिग्रहण किये जाने के सम्बन्ध में घोषणा - 26 जनवरी 1922

पत्रावली संख्या - 610/1921 -सामान्य प्रशासन विभाग

GOVERNMENT, UNITED PROVINCES.

APPROPRIATION OF LAND FOR A PUBLIC PURPOSE.

GENERAL ADMINISTRATION DEPARTMENT.

The 26th January, 1922.

No. **154/III**—610.—The land designated below being required for a public purpose, declaration is made accordingly :—

District.	Pargana.	Mau za.	Approximate area.	For what purpose required.	Remarks.
			Acres		
Allahabad ..	**Arail ..**	**Arail ..**	**28·88**	**Magh Mela ..**	**The plan may be inspected at the office of the Collector of Allahabad.**

2. This declaration is made under section 6, Act I of 1894 (the Land Acquisition Act), and, under section 7 of that Act, the Collector of Allahabad is hereby directed to take order for the acquisition of the land specified above.

कुम्भ मेला सन् 1930 की प्रशासनिक रिपोर्ट

सन् 1930 इलाहाबाद में आयोजित हुए कुम्भ में विभिन्न अखाड़ों ने भाग लिया। इस रिपोर्ट में 14 जनवरी, 1930 संक्रान्ति एवं 29 जनवरी, 1930 अमावस्या के दिनों में अखाड़ों के स्नान के समय का उल्लेख मिलता है।

पत्रावली संख्या-98(4)/1939- सामान्य प्रशासन विभाग

Appendix iv.

ARRANGEMENTS FOR THE PROCESSIONS ON JANUARY 14. 1930 (Shankarant).

S.N.	NAME OF AKHARAS	TIME OF DEPARTURE.	BATHING TIME	RETURN FROM SANGAM	ARRIVAL.
1.	Nirbani	6-00. A.M.	6-30. A.M.	6.50. A.M.	7. 5. A.M.
2.	Niranjani with Juna.	6-30. A.M.	7-30. A.M.	8-00. A.M.	8-20. A.M.
3.	Bairagi Nirmohi.	7-40. A.M.	8-10. A.M.	8-30. A.M.	8-50. A.M.
	Digambar.	8-00. A.M.	8-30. A.M.	9-00. A.M.	9-20. A.M.
	Nirbani.	8-20. A.M.	9-00. A.M.	9-20. A.M.	9-40. A.M.
4.	Chhota Panchaiti.	9-00. A.M.	9-30. A.M.	9-50. A.M.	10-10. A.M.
5.	Bara Panchaiti.	9-30. A.M.	10-00. A.M.	10-20. A.M.	10-30. A.M.
6.	Nirmala.	10-00. A.M.	10-30. A.M.	10-50. A.M.	11-10. A.M.

THESE TIMES WERE BASED ON THE RECORDS OF 1924 AND PROVED TO BE INSUFFICIENT.

True Copy.

6.5.31

I.C.S.,

Officer-in-charge,
Magh Mela, Allahabad.

appendix iv.

ARRANGEMENTS FOR THE PROCESSIONS ON JANUARY 29, 1930 (Amawas)

S.N.	NAME OF AKHARA	TIME OF DEPARTURE.	BATHING TIME.	RETURN FROM SANGAM	ARRIVAL
1.	Nirbani.	6-00 A.M.	6-30. A.M.	7-15. A.M.	7-40. A.M.
2.	Niranjani with Juna.	6-30 A.M.	7-30. A.M.	8-30. A.M.	9-30. A.M.
3.	Bairagi.				
	Nirbani.	8-15 A.M.	8-45. A.M.	9-15. A.M.	9-45. A.M.
	Digambar.	9-00 A.M.	9-30. A.M.	10-00. A.M.	10-30. A.M.
	Nirmohi.	9-45 A.M.	10-15. A.M.	10-45. A.M.	11-15. A.M.
4.	Chhota Panchaiti.	10-15 A.M.	11-00. A.M.	12-00. A.M.	1-00. A.M.
5.	Bara Panchaiti.	11-30 A.M.	12-15. A.M.	1-15. A.M.	2-00. A.M.
6.	Nirmala	12-45.A.M.	1-30. A.M.	2-15. A.M.	3-00; A.M.

Owing to the enormous crowd and the difficulty in keeping the route clear these times could not be adhered to and the last Akhara left the Sangam at 4 P.M. These timings were adhered to on-punctually on the Basant Panchami when the arrangements were as above.

Ture Copy.

I.C.S.,

Officer-in-charge,
Magh Mela, Allahabad.

Extract para 5 part (i) from the administration report of the Kumbh Mela 1930 at Allahabad.

-----

5. Processions.

The chief feature of Kumbh and Adh Kumbh Melas is the processions of Akharas of which there are six main divisions. They are as follows.

1. Nirbani.
2. Niranjani and Juna.
3. Bairagis (Nirbani, Digamber and Nirmohi)
4. Chhota Panchaiti.
5. Bara Panchaiti, (and Bandhwa Hasanpur)
6. Nirmala. (and Brindabani).

The first two Akharas belong to the Naga Sanyasi sect and wear no clothes in procession. The others wear clothes, although the Bairagi's garment is rather scanty, and the Bairagis strongly object to the naked Nagas. The Junas are a very large body containing a considerable number of female devotees mainly from Napal who follow the Niranjanis at a distance of about 50 yards. They are increasing in numbers and it will probably be necessary to give them a larger encampment in the next Adh Kumbh and Kumbh Melas. The Bandhwa Hasanpur have a separte camp but they join with the Bara Panchaiti in processions while the Brindabani have a joint camp with the Nirmala Akhara and they go out in procession together. The system of processions has now been fixed by custom, the only processions allowed being those on the Shankarant, Amawas and Basant Panchimi and when the Akharas enter in state with their Mahants, a practice followed by all except the Bairagis, and although one or two attempts were made to introduce innovations especially by the Char Samparada sect of the Bairagis, they were not pressed and they were forbidden. A list of the order and times of the processions is given in Appendix iv. and it may serve as a guide in future years although the ~~times depend on the~~ times depend on the size of the Akharas and the distance from their camps to the Sangam. Each Akhara must travel some distance down the return road before the following Akhara is allowed to approach the parking ground. The Akharas always adopt the order given on page 5 with the exception of the Bairagis who go out in the order Nirmohi Digambar, Nirbani on the Shankrant and Nirbani, Digambar, Nirmohi on the Amawas and Basant Panchami.

True Extract.

I.C.S.,
Officer-in-charge,
Magh Mela, Allahabad.

इलाहाबाद में आयोजित हुए कुम्भ मेला में आग दुर्घटना की रिपोर्ट सन् 1930

सन् 1930 इलाहाबाद में आयोजित हुए कुम्भ में आग लग गई जिसमें रू0 575/- की सरकारी सम्पत्ति की क्षति हुई।

इस रिपोर्ट में रू0 287/- क्षतिपूर्ति करने का भी उल्लेख मिलता है।

सामान्य प्रशासन विभाग -प्रोसीडिंग, सन्-1882

Provl. Form 56. E—0185 Provl.—1929

1930.

All Communications to this Office should give the No., Date and Subject of any previous correspondence, and should note the department quoted.

FROM S. H. Thompson, Esquire, I.C.S.
District Magistrate,
Allahabad. UNITED PROVINCES.

To The Commissioner,
Allahabad Division,
Allahabad.

DEPARTMENT.

No. 1009, Date April 19..1930

Received

SUBJECT.

Sir,

I have the honour to report that at about midday on February 13th 1930 a fire broke out in the Peon's lines at the Kumbh Mela. As far as has been ascertained the fire was caused accidentally by a woman cooking food and in the absence of most of the staff on duty and fanned by a strong wind which was blowing at the time, the fire spread rapidly and the following articles belonging to Government were totally destroyed.

Articles	Estimated value
1. 18 shouldaries at 20/ each	Rs 360/-
2. 18 Blankets, 3.12 each	Rs ~~[illegible]~~ Rs. 67-8-0.
3. Leather strap one	Rs 2.2.0
4. Cycle Lamp one	Rs 1.8.0
5. Cycle Pump one	Rs 1.8.0
6. Dusters, three, at /4/-	Rs 0.12.0
7. Beds, superior, 2 at 6/- each	Rs 12. 0.0
8. Beds, ordinary, 2 at 1.8.0	Rs 3. 0.0
Total	Rs ~~412. 6.0~~ 448.6.0.

Apart from this considerable loss was caused to some nineteen peons whose property

2.

was destroyed in their absence on duty. The loss to these men is estimated at Rs 575/-

With regard to the Government property I would request that sanction be given to write off the loss, ie. Rs 412.6.0.

As regards the personal loss suffered by the peons, I would ask whether Government would be disposed to consider giving them some compensation from the Mela Funds. Admittedly the fire was caused in the first instance by the carelessness on the part of some person or persons, but the great majroity were not to blame, as they were away on Governmeyt duty, and the loss suffered by them has been considerable. If Government approve of granting them any compensation I would recommend that they be given half the estimated amount, that is Rs 287-8.0. the amount to be met from the Mela Funds.

I have the honour to be,
Sir,
Your most obedient servant,

For Magistrate
18/4/30

NOTES AND ORDERS.

DEPARTMENT.

FILE No.________

Name of peons.	Loss sustained. G.C.Notes and cash	Loss sustained. Belonging worth.	Estimated amount.	Amount of compensation recommended.
1. Ram Autar Singh peon.	40/-	50.	40/-	20/-
2. Bindeshri Prasad peon.	55/-	40/-	40/-	20/-
3. Shyam Sunder Lal peon.	.	35/-	25/-	12/8
4. Onkar Nath peon		30/-	25/-	12/8
5. Ram Gopal "	5/-	25/-	25/-	12/8
6/- Bhagwati	5/-	25/-	25/-	12/8
7. Suraj Sin	5/	25/-	25/-	12/8
8. Ram Saran	-	30/+10/- ~~plus 10~~/ of Mahabir ~~4X-~~	30/- ~~30/-~~	15/-
9. Musai peon		70/-	40/-	20/-
10. Sheonath Rai peon.		35/-	25/-	12/8
11. Dwarka Pd. "		60/-	35/-	17/8
12. Gaya Pd. peon		55/-	35/-	17/8
13. Nand Ram "		45/-	30/-	15/-
14. Batuk Nath "	.4/4	30/-	25/-	12/8
15. Ram Kirpal "	7/8	35/-	30/-	15/-
16. Ram Lakhan "	10/8	25/-	25/-	12/8
17. Sheomohan "	40/-	50/-	40/-	20/-
18. Bachchu "		40-	30/ ~~x40~~/-	15/-
19. Ramanand "		35/-	25/-	12/8
	172/4	750/-	575/-	287/8.

For Magistrate.

18/4/30

NOTES AND ORDERS.

DEPARTMENT.

FILE No. 258/1930

Serial No. 1

The Commissioner, Allahabad division, requests the sanction of Government to the writting off of the loss of Government property amounting to Rs. 448/6/- and supports the Collector's recommendation that Rs. 287/8/- half the estimated amount of loss sustained by ~~Mela~~ servants (employed at the last Kumbh mela at Allahabad) may be granted to them as compensation from the Mela Fund.

Deputy Secretary,

Please see the P.U.C. and its accompaniments.

1. Under para 1330 (53) of the M.G.Os a loss of Government property has to be reported to the Head of the department or the Commissioner of the division who is empowered to write off up-to Rs. 200/- but when the loss exceeds Rs. 200/- the sanction of the Government is necessary. In this case the loss amounts to Rs. 448/6/- and the write off may be sanctioned with the concurrence of Finance (A) department under article 227 (a) of the Civil Account Code.

2. The rules regarding compensation for accidental loss of property of Government officers are contained in Appendix X - 5 of the Financial Handbook, Volume V, Part I, and if it is decided to compensate the peons, sanction may be accorded under Appendix X-5 (i) (2) of the Financial Handbook with the concurrence of Finance department.

Submitted for orders.

24.6.30.

24/6/30

F.D.,

Do you agree?

26/6/30

Dy. Secy.

Notes above. There is no audit objection to the proposal. Act section may however see.

30/6

2/7/30

Provl. 107 C9 Provl.—1929.

NOTES AND ORDERS—(continued). | REFERENCES.

DS

Notes overleaf and Serial under note explains the cases.

There is no objection to the proposals in Budget.

[illegible] 4.7.30.

[illegible] 4-7-30

[illegible] 9/7

Genl 9/7 @ 1 pm

Deputy Secy.

Please see the notes from page overleaf. A draft is submitted for approval which Finance (A) Deptt. will see before issue.

R. [illegible] 11.7.30.

[illegible] 11/7/30

[illegible] 14/7/30

F.D. (A) 16/7/30

Dy. Secy.

Notes overleaf. The draft is in adn.

[illegible] 16/7/30

[illegible] 18/7/30

G. A. deptt 21/7 @ 12-40 pm

[illegible] 21/7/30

निर्वाणी अखाड़ा के स्वामी विश्वानन्द द्वारा दिनांक 11 नवम्बर, 1941 को गृह विभाग युनाइटेड प्राविन्सेज के सदस्य को लिखे गये पत्र के क्रम में तत्कालीन कमिश्नर इलाहाबाद द्वारा जारी दिशा-निर्देश।

पत्रावली संख्या- 98(8)/1941

To

The Advisor to
His Excellency the Governor of the U.P.
In charge of the Home Department,
Lucknow.

Sir,

We invite your attention to the Memorandum addressed to The Hon'ble The Home Member, United Provinces Government, in the year 1936, by the Hindus of Bengal headed by Swami Viswanand of the Nirwani Akhara. In reply to that Memorandum Swami Viswanand received a letter dated the 11th January 1936 from H. Bomford, Esq., C.I.E., I.C.S., the Chief Secretary to the United Provinces Government, stating that no licences were issued for gambling carnivals or booths in 1930 and that a licence for one Carnival was granted in 1933 but was cancelled as soon as it was known that it was a den of gambling. The Chief Secretary assured that no Carnival in the Parva area would be allowed the next year and further referred Swami Viswananda to the Commissioner, Allahabad Division for the disposal of other things contained in the Memorandum. The Commissioner, Allahabad Division, on being written to, replied that:-

(1) every effort was being made to prevent annoyance to bathers within the bathing area at the Sangam;

(2) no non-Hindu preaching camps were being allowed in the Mela area below the Bundh;

(3) no restrictions could be imposed on business matters they being independent of religion.

2.

We beg to refer you to one more letter of February 1936 addressed by Swami Viswanand to the Hon'ble The Home Member in which he appreciated the action of the Government in conceding to the requests of the memorialists. In this letter Swami Viswanand said --

" There is a difference of opinion between the Commissioner and myself regarding the restrictions to be imposed for allowing non-Hindu shops to be located in the 'parva' area."

The Kumbha Parva is again going to take place in January 1942. I would like to know what arrangements the Government have made for it. The Government is there to make arrangements for the facilities of the millions of pilgrims who will be visiting Prayag during this great religious congregation. The Government should see that no annoyance is caused to the Hindus within the Sangam area by people of other religions, that no preaching on behalf of religions other than Hinduism is allowed and last but not the least, that no non-Hindu shops or pedlars be allowed to ply their trade within the Sangam area during the Parva. We are confident that Government will see the force of our requests. The Kumbha Parva is a religious gathering of a particular community and not any ordinary fair open to all. Non-Hindus visit the Parva not for any disinterested motives; their pressure is the cause of so many evils which create bad blood. If the Government allows non-Hindus to carry on trade in the forthcoming Parva, the Akharas and the Sadhus wish to make it clear to the Government that it is their duty to make arrangements for the Parva according to all the reasonable wishes of the Hindus.

3.

If the Government does not concede our above requests we will presume that in the management of the Parva, the Government is actuated by commercial motives and that it does not care for the best interests of the Hindus.

We have the honour to be,
Sir,
Your most obedient servants,

November 11. 1941.

Krishna Pal Singh (Raja Kuwar ...)
Raghu... Singh

Dig Vijai Nath
Gorakhpur.

Akhandanand

Shree Mahant Brahmanand Bharti

(6

Register Serial no.	replied to	Genl. Admn. DEPARTMENT

No. 5080/III-98(8)-1941.

Dated Dec 10, 1941.

Sent to Copyist / Press

Copied by

Examined by

REMINDER ON

FILE No. 98(8)/1941.

Serial no. 3/4

For use in Secretariat only: Record in Dep.; Proceeding for Dec. 1941; No.

- Page 1, Correspondence

To

Mahant Harishchandra Giri Sahib,
Sri Panchayati Akhara Mahanirvani,
Head Office, Daraganj,
Prayag.

Sir,

With reference to your petition dated November 5, 1941, addressed to the Advisor to His Excellency the Governor incharge of Home Department, I am directed to reply as follows:-

(1) No Carnival will be allowed in the Mela area,

(2) Every effort will be made to prevent annoyance to bathers within the bathing area at the Sangam;

(3) Non-Hindu preaching camps will not be allowed in the Mela area below the Bundh. and

(4) It is regretted that no restrictions can be imposed on business matters, as they are independent of religion.

I have etc.

Deputy Secretary.

11.12.41

No: 5080(1)/III-98(8)-1941

Copy forwarded to the Comr. Allahabad Divn. for information.

B.O.

Deputy Secretary.

Provl. 108 W— Provl.—1910

Manganlal

Kalyanjani Dutta Purodi

Vishwanath Bhatta
For Varanashram Swaraj sangh.

सन् 1954 में कुम्भ मेला हेतु पुलिस विभाग द्वारा तैयार नोट

पुलिस विभाग द्वारा सन् 1954 में कुम्भ मेला की तैयारी के सम्बन्ध में तैयार किये गये नोट से पता चलता है कि सन् 1942 में कुम्भ मेला के आयोजन में ब्रिटिश सरकार द्वारा अनेक अवरोध उत्पन्न किये गये थे। रेल यात्रा पर प्रतिबन्ध लगाये गये थे तथा मोटर बस आदि को पेट्रोल भी नहीं दिया गया था तथा अनेक अन्य प्रतिबन्ध लगाये गये थे। सन् 1954 में कुम्भ मेला में लगभग 40 से 50 लाख तीर्थ यात्रियों के आगमन का अनुमान निम्न आधार पर लगाया गया थाः-

1. यह स्वतन्त्र भारत का प्रथम कुम्भ पर्व था। 2. रेलवे द्वारा प्रतिबन्धित स्थानों पर अनेक प्रकार की सुविधायें दी जा रही थी।

3. तीर्थ यात्रियों को लाने वाली मोटर बसों को बिना प्रतिबन्ध पेट्रोल दिया जाना था। 4. अनाज की अच्छी कीमत के कारण गांवों में समृद्धता थी।

5. इतने विशाल जन समुदाय के मध्य राजनैतिक दलो को अपना प्रचार करने का अच्छा अवसर था।

पत्रावली संख्या-IVB-1/179/1954 - क्षेत्रीय अभिलेखागार, इलाहाबाद

-2- (88) (2)

(d) On account of high prices of grains, it is said that there is much prosperity in villages and it is expected that people from villages will pore down in this mela in large numbers.

(e) Various political organisations consider the Magh mela as a golden opportunity for coming in contact with large number of peoples at one place and therefore, they are likely to establish their propaganda camps in this mela.

It is expected there will be a gathering of about 40 to 50 lacs of men in this Kumbh Mela. Therefore, the arrangements that are to be made should be based on the principle to cater for a crowd of 40 to 50 lakhs.

The Ganga river has left very little land this year On Baund side with the result that very limited space has been left, so far, for the mela. In making arrangements for controlling the crowd and traffic this will have to be borne in mind. The military authorities of Allahabad Fort have occupied a big area beyond Bund which was formerly used for the purpose of melas. Similarily, rly. authorities have extended the rly. line and brought it near to the mela area with the result that the land which was utilised for purposes of mela has been taken over by the rly.

We will have to consider these factors also while making arrangements for the coming Kumbh mela.

1930KUMBH MELA.

The record that is available to us about 1930 Kumbh mela goes to show that one S.P., 5 A.Ss.P., and 4 Dy.Ss.P. were employed as controlling staff. In addition to this 3 R.Is., and 8 C.Is., were also used in the mela as supervising staff.

There always b... ctive staff, the strength of which ... and wide

NOTE ON ALLAHABAD MAGH, KUMBH AND ARDH KUMBH MELAS. (4) (89)

GENERAL. The Kumbh Mela of Allahabad is held after every 12 years. This mela attracts very large crowds of pilgrims from all over India. The record in our possession shows only the police orders that were drafted for the Kumbh mela for 1930. The complete file of 1930 Kumbh mela was searched for in the year 1942 but it could not be located. We have got the complete file of 1942 Kumbh mela and also a complete record of Ardh Kumbh mela of 1948-

The Kumbh Mela that was held in the year 1942 was not a full-fledged mela on account of restrictions imposed on railway travel, issue of petrol to lorries and various other prohibitory orders on account of the last Great War. Therefore, we could not have the full picture of the arrangements that will be made for the Kumbh mela of 1954, in the file of Kumbh Mela of 1942.

Unfortunately, the file of 1930 Kumbh mela has been destroyed but we have some data in the copy of the police orders for Kumbh mela of 1930.

On account of various reasons it is expected that the Kumbh mela of the year 1954 is likely to attract larger number of crowds from all over the country. Some of the reasons are enumerated below:

(a) This will be the first Kumbh mela after achieving Independence.

(b) There are no restrictions in railway travelling It is expected that many special trains will be run by the railway department which will bring large number of pilgrims from all over the country. For this the rly. authorities are making full preparations from now.

(c) There is no petrol rationing and it is expected that ... uses will be run which will bring pilgrims from far ... by road routes.

My dear Baghel ji. I give you my II note & Appendix A. This is my first note that I prepared about 3 weeks ago. You will get the Budget for SSP. Yours v. Sincerely ... 7/8/?

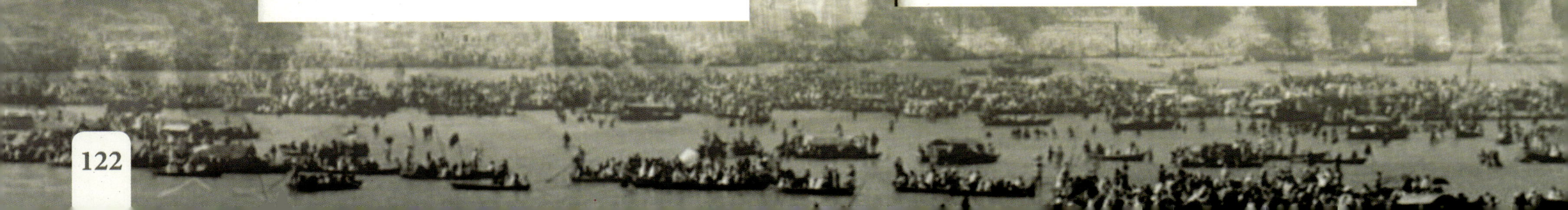

सन् 1954 में कुम्भ मेला की तैयारियों के लिए गठित मेला समिति

पत्रावली संख्या-IVB-1/179/1954 क्षेत्रीय अभिलेखागार, इलाहाबाद

(3) The rules made under the aforesaid Act, called the Allahabad Magh Mela Rules, 1940, *inter alia*, the following provisions :

(i) For the arrest and prosecution of persons found contravening certain specified rules and the provisions of sections 6 and 7 of the Act.

(ii) For the destruction or confinement of any dog or animal suspected to be suffering from rabbies or any other contagious or infectious disease.

(iii) For prevention of entry into the Mela Area of any person suffering from cholera, plague, small-pox or any other infectious disease and for the removal of the same and for removal of such persons to the Infectious Diseases Hospital, if found within the Mela Area.

(iv) That the District Magistrate shall take such steps as may appear necessary to localize and prevent the outbreak of any infectious disease in an epidemic form.

(v) That no person shall throw any dead body or carcass into any river or water within the Mela Area.

(vi) That no person shall take any photograph at bathing places within the Mela Area.

(vii) That no person shall indulge in shooting or fishing within the Mela Area.

(4) Similar provisions have been made by the framing of appropriate bye-laws by the Cantonment or Municipal authorities within whose limits a part of the Mela Area is situated.

(5) *Mela Committee*—The Mela Committee at present consists of the following members :

Chairman

(1) District Magistrate, Allahabad.

Secretary

(2) Office-in-charge, Magh Mela, Allahabad.

Members

(3) Senior Supdt. of Police, Allahabad.
(4) Chairman, Municipal Board, Allahabad.
(5) Executive Officer, Contonment Board, Allahabad.
(6) Asstt. Director of P. H. and M. S., Allahabad.
(7) Divl. Supdt., Northern Rly., Gorakhpur.
(8) Traffic Manager, N. E. Railway, Gorakhpur.
(9) Officer Commanding, the Fort, Allahabad.
(10) Executive Engineer, P. W. D., Allahabad.
(11) President, District Board, Allahabad.
(12) Executive Engineer, L. S.-G. E. D.

Non-Official Members.

(13) Hony. Secy., Hindu Maha Sabha, Allahabad.
(14) President, Prayagwal Sabha, Allahabad.

(15) Organizing Secretary, All India Seva Samiti.
(16) President, Agarwal Seva Samiti, Allahabad.
(17) Chief Scouts, Mahanand Mission, Allahabad.
(18) Head Yogi, Akshaibat Temple, Allahabad.
(19) Sri Amarnath Agarwal, M.L.C., Allahabad.
(20) Sri S. R. Bajpayee, National Organizing Commissioner, Hindustan Scouts Association, Allahabad.
(21) Sri Prasidh Narain Anand, M L C, Allahabad.
(22) Sri Shiv Nath Katju, M. L. A., Allahabad.
(23) Mahant of Hanumanji Temple, Fort, Allahabad.
(24) Sri Masuria Din, M.P., Allahabad.
(25) President, Sanatan Dharam Sabha, Allahabad.
(26) Secretary, Nishad Sabha, Allahabad.
(27) Secretary, Mehtar Union, Allahabad.
(28) President, Traders Association, Allahabad.
(29) Secretary, Harijan Sewak Sangh, Allahabad.
(30) Sri Gangotri Baba.

(6) On the Civil side the following is the Controlling Staff of the Mela :

(1) District Magistrate, Allahabad—Sri J. N. Urga, I.A.S.
(2) Officer-in-charge Mela—Sri A. S. Baghel, I.A.S.
(3) Addl. Officer-in-charge Mela—Sri Babu Ram Gupta, P.C.S.
(4) Mela Manager, Sri Uma Charan Misra.

There are Assistant Managers whose names are as follows :

(1) Sri Sharad Chand Verma.
(2) ,, Hardutt Pande.
(3) ,, Balbir Singh.
(4) ,, Sitla Sahai.
(5) ,, Bhagwati Sahai Verma.
(6) ,, Hira Lal.
(7) ,, Banke Bihari Srivastava.
(8) ,, Ramesh Chandra.

Six magistrates have been asked for by the District Magistrate from the Government for making arrangements in the Mela. These magistrates will arrive in the first week of January and will be posted to various areas.

On the Police side the following will be the Controlling Staff:

(1) Senior Supdt. of Police,—Sri J. P. Tripathi, I.P.S.
(2) Addl. Supdt. of Police, Sri A. M. Shah.
(3) A. S. P., Sri K. L. Chhabra, I.P.S.
(4) A. S. P., Sri S. C. Dikshit, I.P.S.

सन् 1954 में कुम्भ मेला को सकुशल सम्पन्न कराने हेतु पुलिस बल की तैनाती

सन् 1954 के कुम्भ मेले की व्यवस्था हेतु पुलिस बल की तैनाती की गयी जिसमें सिविल पुलिस के अतिरिक्त सी0आई0डी0 स्टाफ, अग्नि शामक दल, यातायात पुलिस, आंसू गैस दल, जल पुलिस की भी तैनाती की गयी।

पत्रावली संख्या-IVB-1/179/1954- क्षेत्रीय अभिलेखागार, इलाहाबाद

APPENDIX 'A'. (15) (78)

Superintendent of Police.	1
Asstt: Supdts. of Police.	5
Deputy Supdts. of Police.	6
Circle Inspectors.	20
Reserve Inspector.	3
A.P. Sub Inspectors.	5
A.P. Head Constables.	25
A.P. Constables.	250
C.P. Sub Inspectors.	50
C.P. Head Constables.	100
C.P. Constables.	2000
Mounted Police Sub Inspectors	2
Mounted Police Hd.Constables.	20
Mounted Police Constables.	120
Chaukidars.	250

DETECTIVE STAFF.

Deputy S.P. C.I.D.	1
C.I.D. Inspectors.	2
CID/DIS Sub Inspectors.	10
" " Hd.Constables.	10
" " Constables.	60

FIRE STAFF.

Regional Fire Officer.	1
ASSTT: Regional Fire Officer	1
Fire Station Officers.	6

and personnel of 6 fire stations with fire engines and water reservior tanks.

Buglers.	6
Trumpeters.	2
Literat~~xxx~~ Constables.	6
Bicycle orderlies.	15

Traffic Police.

Traffic Inspector.	1
~~xxx~~ " Sub "	2
Head Consts.	10
Constables.	60

Prosecuting S.I.	1
Court Moharrir	1

OFFICE STAFF:

Stenographer.	1
Head Clerk	1
Accountant.	1
Asstt: Accountants.	2
Asstt: clerks	2
Despatcher.	1
English knowing Consts.	3

Also for ope

4 Mobile wireless apparatuses fitted in pick-ups or 15 cwt. trucks along with one Control wireless station.

4 Walkie-talkie wireless sets with one control station.

1 temporary wireless station for sending mela messages.

TEAR GAS SQUAD.

Sub Inspector. Hd.Consts. Constables.

-2- (16) (77)

RIVER POLICE.

Head Constables.	2.
Constables	6

from Benaras Police with 2 river boats.

Vehicles.

enough?

2 three tons lorries, 1 pick-up and two jeeps in good working condition with drivers and petrol quota.

MEDICAL.

Police Doctor.	1.	
Compounders.	2.	
Male nurses	3	
Stretcher bearers	36	with 12 stretchers with temporary hospital equipments along with medicines for atleast 20 beds.

सन् 1954 में कुम्भ मेला क्षेत्र में स्थापित पुलिस थाने एवं चैकियाँ

पुलिस थाने -

1. जवाहर लाल नेहरू (फोर्ट) रोड	2. त्रिवेणी रोड	3. कोतवाली परेड	4. कोतवाली संगम
5. गंगा पट्टी	6. कोतवाली झूंसी	7. गंगा पार	8. अरैल

पत्रावली संख्या-IVB-1/179/1954 -क्षेत्रीय अभिलेखागार, इलाहाबाद

(38)

APPENDIX "B"

List of Police Stations and Outposts of the Mela

Sl. No.	Name of P. S.	Sl. No.	Name of the O. Ps.
1.	Jawahar Lal Nehru (Fort) Road	1.	Cemetery Road.
		2.	Exhibition.
2.	Kotwali Parade	1.	Lal Kothi.
		2.	Prayag Ghat Railway Station.
		3.	Naka.
		4.	Alopi Devi.
		5.	Rail.
3.	Tribeni Road	1.	Telephone Exchange.
		2.	Mela.
		3.	Qila.
		4.	Minto Park.
4.	Kotwali Sangam	1.	Dhus.
		2.	Akshaibat.
		3.	Mahabir Jee.
		4.	Bundh.
5.	Ganga Patti	1.	Izat Bridge.
6.	Kotwali Jhusi	1.	Nirmala Akhara.
		2.	Panchayati Akhara.
		3.	Kalap Basi Camp.
		4.	Pragwal Camp.
		5.	Hospital.
		6.	Bazar.
7.	Ganga Par	1.	V. I. P. Camp.
		2.	Bairagi Akhara.
		3.	Sadar.
		4.	Jhusi.
8.	Arail	1.	Naini.

सन् 1954 के कुम्भ मेले में बसन्त पंचमी के अवसर पर तृतीय शाही स्नान हेतु विभिन्न अखाड़ों को क्रम तथा समय का आवंटन

पत्रावली संख्या-186/1954- क्षेत्रीय अभिलेखागार, इलाहाबाद

REVISED TIMINGS IN SUPERCESSION OF THE FORMER ORDERS DATED February 2, 1954 REGARDING TIMINGS OF AKHARA PROCESSIONS ON 8/2/54 ARE AS FOLLOWS:-

****

Akharas.	Departure.	Time of arrival at bridge No.2.	Arrival at Sangam.	Dep. from Sangam.	Time of arrival at bridge No.1.	Arrival at their camps.
SANYASI:						
Maha-Nirwani	530 hrs	545 hrs.	630 hrs.	716 hrs.	735 hrs.	8 hrs.
Niranjani with Juna.	615 "	630 "	715 "	830 "	850 "	935 "
BAIRAGI:						
Nirwani.	945 hrs.	1000 hrs.	1035 hrs.	1105 "	1125 hrs.	1145 hrs.
Digambar.	1020 "	1035 "	1110 "	1200 "	1220 "	1245 "
Nirmohi.	1115 "	1130 "	1205 "	1235 "	1255 "	1315 "
UDASI:						
Chota Panchayati Akhara.	1305 hrs.	1320 "	1355 "	1445 "	1505 "	1525 hrs.
Bara Panchayati Akhara.	1420 "	1435"	1505 "	1605 "	1625 "	1645 "
NIRMALA AKHARA.	1535 "	1550 "	1625 "	1725 "	1745 "	1805 "

Sd/ J.P.Tripathi, IPS.,
Senior Supdt. of Police,(Kumbh Mela)
Allahabad. 7/2/54.

N.B. All the processions will enter by bridge No.2 and return via the Ganga patti return route and not the Jamuna Patti return route and cross back via bridge No.1. Bairagi Akhara will come and return back from the road towards river Ganga in front of Kalapvasi Gata.

Copy forwarded to:-
(1) All Akharas (10 copies each).
(2) A.D.M., Allahabad (10 copies).
(3) All Area Magistrates, Kumbh Mela, Allahabad.(one copy to each).
(4) Officer- in- Charge, (Kumbh Mela) Allahabad, (50 copies).
(5) Deputy Chief Engineer, Kumbh Operations, Allahabad (10 copies).
for information and necessary action.

(J.P. Tripathi) IPS.,
Senior Supdt. of Police, (Kumbh Mela),
Allahabad.

February 7, 1954.

Note: The timings mentioned in my order u/s 30, Police Act (No. V) of 1861 dated 6.2.54 may please be corrected accordingly. Separate revised orders u/s 30 Police Act are being issued to all the Akharas today.

(S.N. Chakravarty)
Asstt Commandant
PAC Forces Kumbh Mela
Allahabad

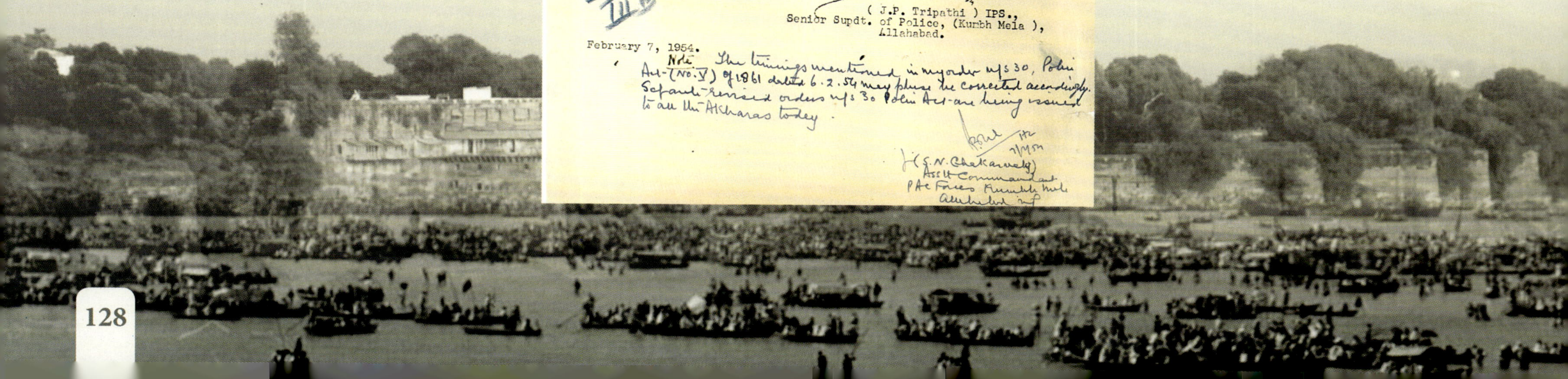

(10) 297

COMMENT ON THE REPORT OF

KUMBH TRAGEDY ENQUIRY COMMITTEE - 1954

GENERAL

In this report the word "Planning" has been used in a much wider sense. It does not relate strictly to the "Preparation of Layout Plan of the available land or land fit for planning'. The comments are listed by me point by point after quoting the page of the report.

I- PLANNING DEFECTIVE (Page 98)

The defects pointed out in Planning are as under:

1(a) Location of Sangam Railway Station was harmful. (Page 97)

1(b) Numerous level crossings of Railway lines and roads in Allahabad harmful. (Page 100).

2(a) Camps and shops should not be placed in Parada area (Page 101).

2(b) Only one road (Triveni Road) was made for "Incoming" traffic. (Page 101). This made the crowd to converge at Ramp No.1. Four roads for incoming and four roads for outgoing traffic have been suggested (Page 102).

2(c) Sangam Area should be left open completely. No shops no camps, no offices should be allowed there and only one flower shop should be permitted (Page 103). Pragwals' Takhats, and barbers may be allowed.

3(a) Routes of Akharas and Pedestrians should be ket separate (Page 103).

3(b) Processions of Akharas should not have elephants, horses, cars etc. Procession should go on foot and at best the Mahant should go in "Tamjhans", "takhats" or palanquins.(Page 105).

5(a) Beggard and pilgrims should not be allowed to sit or remain in sangam area or on roads. They should be given separate areas for their sitting. (Page 107)

6 Watch towers to be manned by more competent officers. The most important watch tower should be incharge of a "Superintendent of Police". Better equipment should be provided. (Page 108).

7 Central control room should be used as a control room only. It should not be accessible to general public because they have nothing to do with "Mela Control".

7(i) Police force inadequate. (Page 109).

7(ii) More police officials of the rank of D.I.G. should be on horseback for traffic control.

7(iii) Treatment of voluntary organizations and their use should be courteous and proper. (Page 111).

-2- (11) 299

7(iv) Work of various official departments not properly coordinated (Page 112).

7(v) Enquiry offices were not functioning properly and men incharge not familiar with mela grounds. They should be manned by volunteer organizations. (Page 112).

7(vi) Faulty sign boards. (Page 112).

7(vii) Encroachments on Bund road should be removed.

7(viii) People should not be allowed to dig out earth to make their huts in Sangam area. This creates many ditches. (Page 113).

7(ix) More than one Agencies (Private) using loud-speakers. This should stop. Only the Mela administration should use them for giving directions to pilgrims (page 113).

It will be seen from the above that the word "Planning" has been used in a much wider sense. It is used in the sense of "Administrative Policies" and "Organizationa work" of Mela. As "Planners" we have no part in all these decisions and we should have no comments to offer in this matter though we can make a few suggestions in these fields.

The "Committee" has pointed out various factors that led to the "tragedy" but one fundamental cause has been overlooked. The real and effective cause of tragedy was that the "length of river shore" available for bathing was the smallest in the history while the crowd was the largest. No doubt the "Sangam Area" was less and some of it was occupied, but this is not the real cause. Even if the Sangam area was twice its size and all was kept open the chances of an accident were there as explained hereunder

(12)
(301)

This diagram shows the situation as existed during the Kumbh of 1954:

(i) Rivershore available for bathing was 1,800ft. in length only.

(ii) The red line shows the rivershore unfit for bathing because water was more than 6ft. deep.

(iii) Area of land below the Bundh was about 80 acres.

The people were ~~hovering~~ "POURING in at a greater rate than the "rive shore" can dispose them off after bathing. The area got over-crowded and the saturation point was reached at 9:00 A.M. when tragedy took place.

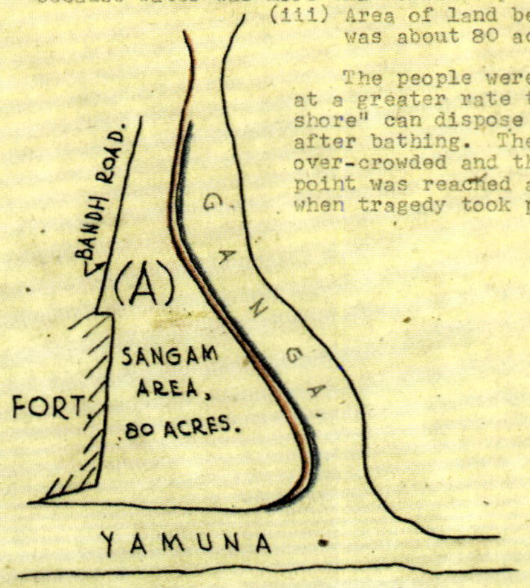

This diagram "B" shows a hypothetical case where all other factors are the same as in "A" except the area of land which is more than twice. Same principle holds good. Since people are coming at a greater rate, the saturation point ~~wi~~ will reach four hours later when the entire area gets crowded. The key factor in the tragedy was the "amount of shore length available for bathing and not the amount of land at "Sangam area" The shore length was a nature's gift and not a man made element.

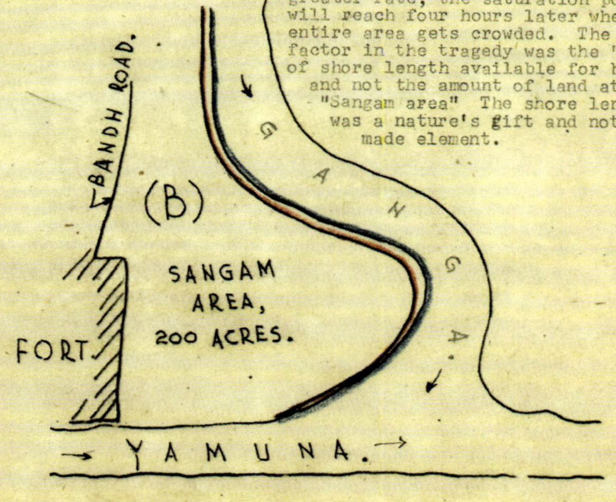

-3-

(13)
(303)

The diagram "A" shows the situation which existed during the Kumbh. The red line shows the river bank unfit for bathing due to deep water. The length of "riverbank available for bathing" was about 1,800 ft. in length. The~~xx~~ people were coming at a greater rate than the river shore could (dispose them off after bath) give them bath. This led to crowding of the Sangam area. The saturation point was reached at 9:00 A.M. when tragedy took place. There were other factors but they were all secondary.

The diagram "B" shows a ~~sketch~~ hypothetical case where the available river shore for bath is the same ~~xkxx~~ while the Sangam area is more than twice.~~tkx~~ The same principle would apply here. The people are coming at a greater rate than the rivershore can dispose them off. The Sangam area being twice, the crowding and saturation point will take place probably after three or four hours. In "B" the tragedy will take place at about 12:00 noon. "How much land was open at Sangam" is not the deciding factor. The deciding factor was "How much rivershore is available".

COMMENTS ON RECOMMENDATIONS FOR FUTURE

6(a) Government Department concerned should start making arrangements well in advance.

Comment — Different Departments have different role, hence their time should change. As far as planning is concerned, we should start work as soon as called by officer-in-charge. I think we should be called as soon as all survey is ready and survey should be ready six months in advance of the starting day of Mela. All required plans of mela should be completed by the ~~end~~ first week of October, i.e. three months in advance of the starting day. This will give enough time for construction of roads, ghats, and other arragements to be done by various departments like Police, Health, Voluntary organisations and private individuals.

After the plans are ready, a guide booklet

should be prepared for the use of police and volunteer organisations who have to give proper information to general public regarding location of various places.

6(d) Whole of Parade and Sangam area should be left open.

Comment

Sangam area--area between the Bandh and the river Ganga has been recommended by Committee to be left open with the exception of the following:

a) Pragwals' Takhats
b) Barbers enclosures
c) Flowers shop

As planners, wex agree with the proposal. But it remains to be seen from the administrative point of view whether the following departments can carry out their functions properly and quickly without some area reserved for their use:-

(1) The Military authorities or those incharge of maintenance of bridges.

(2) The Health Department who have to take care of sanitary arrangements like latrines, urinals, first aid posts for drowned persons.

(3) The L.S.G.E.D. who have to provide light and water facilities.

(4) The Police who have to keep law and order in this area, maintenance of Control towers,

(5) The Mela Administration's Office for Sector Magistrate.

(6) Volunteers Organizations who have to provide proper information and guidance to public.

The Departments require areas for the storage of material and equipment so that the required materials do not have to be brought from outside through the crowds. Bringing the material, in case of failure of some of the installations, will prevent and obstruct traffic flow.

KEEPING PARADE AREA OPEN

Here the Committee recommends that the entire areas occupied by Military authorities and Military Stores, area occupied by Railway, the Agriculture Department etc. be kept open by removing the permanent installa-

tions of these Departments. It amounts to removing the cantonement from this area.

The Committee further recommends that this area be kept vacant i.e. unoccupied by any individual. This recommendation makes the fundamental change in the "Kumbh Snan" and the concept of general public. It may be pointed out here that the popular belief of "Kumbh Snan" gives equal importance to "Staying in the Holy Land" for "kalpwasis". Hinduism is a very liberal religion. The fundamental concept is that one should stay during the "Kumbh" period in the "Holy land" between two rivers for sacrifice, penance and purification. Since all people cannot afford to come at Allahabad and stay at the "Holy land", an important concession has been made in the Hindu philosophy; that those who cannot afford, may take only the "Dip" (snan) during this period and especially on "Amawasya" which is the holiest day in the entire "Kumbh period". The poorer class who cannot afford to stay come for a day's dip while the middle class of the society comes and stays there for "kalpbas". Those who stay for the whole period of seven weeks are called "kapbasis" and they stay in their own camps while those who come and stay for a small period ranging from 3 days to 5 weeks stay with the Pragwals.

Thus keeping the Parade area vacant or unoccupied as suggested by the "Committee" would make the following fundamental change in the popular concept of "Kumbh Mela".

"It takes away the holy land between two rivers from Kalpbasis".

What will be the public reaction if the Committee's recommendation of keeping Parade area vacant, is accepted by the Government, has to be judged. This change would mean changing the agelong tradition, which

does

(16

-6- (309)

does not seem necessary.

It would be better if the Government were to take the following decision with regarding to Parade area

(1) Remove the Military establishments, the Railway Station and the Agriculture Departments installations completely.

(2) Camps for Kalpbasis and "Pragwals" be allowed to be located in Parade area after taking into account the amount of land available in Sangam area at the time o future Kumbh.

(3) Offices of various Departments incharge of Kumbh Mela preparations be allowed in Parade Area if the Officer-in-charge so desires. (Hospitals, Police and fire stations, volunteers' camps, administrative offices of departments, Post Office, Parking areas etc.)

(e) Four roads to be provided for "incoming" and four for"outgoing" traffic in Parade Area.

Comment The recommendation is vague. The "Committee" does not mention the width of these roads. Will each road be 40ft. wide as it used to be in past plans of Kumbh Mela? It would be better to keep fewer roads with larger widths of 120'. This will reduce the number of police required for traffic control. Three roads of 40 ft. width will require three times the number of police required to control the traffic on a single road of 120ft. Similar will be the advantage in volunteers required to provide information to public. So will be the case of cost of providing "public urinals", latrines, sign-posts and facilities of first-aid and drinking water". Similar would be the reduction in manpower required for checking inoculation certificates of pilgrims.

The fundamental recommendation here should be that the width of "ramps on the Bandh" should be the same as the width of the road leading on to it. The ramps prove bottlenecks in traffic if they are not of the same width as the roads leading to it. (this year the ramps were 80ft. wide while the roads leading to it were 120ft.).

Second recommendation should be that in

(17

-7- (311)

the case of "roads for incoming traffic" the width of 120ft. road should be made wider atleast 150ft. after the ramp so that the people while descending on the ramp do not push each other.

The third recommendation should be that the total width of "incoming roads" should be such that more people are "not brought in" than the available rivershore length can accommodate for bathing, otherwise the pressure on the river's bank will increase and drowning or stampede will result.

(f) This recommendation is correct and is to be followed to suit the area available.

(g) This recommendation prescribes separate routes for Akharas and pedestrian traffic. This is the ideal recommendation but it has one defect. Since Akhara routes are to be barricaded, they will remain unused during the whole period. Out of 7 weeks of Kumbh mela, the Akhara processions are taken out on three days only. This will be a waste of useful space. Equally effective will be the routes followed on the day of Vasant Panchmi during this Kumbh. After the tragedy on Amavasya day the routes of Akhara procession were changed and kept along the bank of Ganga for returning. This recommendation actually concerns the Mela Administration and not us.

(h) One flower shop as recommended in Sangam Area will not be enough. Besides a milkshop will be required. In all religious rites, milk is used along with flowers. Shops for "prasad" are equally important.

(i) This would improve the situation.

(j) No comments.

(k) I agree with the recommendation of the Committee.

(l) This concerns the Police Department. We have nothing to say as to who should be placed incharge of Control towers.

(n to v) These concern the Police and the Mela Administration.

K.N. MISRA,
Town & Village Planner to Govt.

सन् 1954 में कुम्भ मेला के अवसर पर तीर्थ यात्रियों की सुविधा हेतु संगम के निकट अस्थायी तौर पर बनाया गया इलाहाबाद संगम रेलवे स्टेशन का मानचित्र

पत्रावली संख्या-H-1201/XXV/1954-क्षेत्रीय अभिलेखागार, प्रयागराज

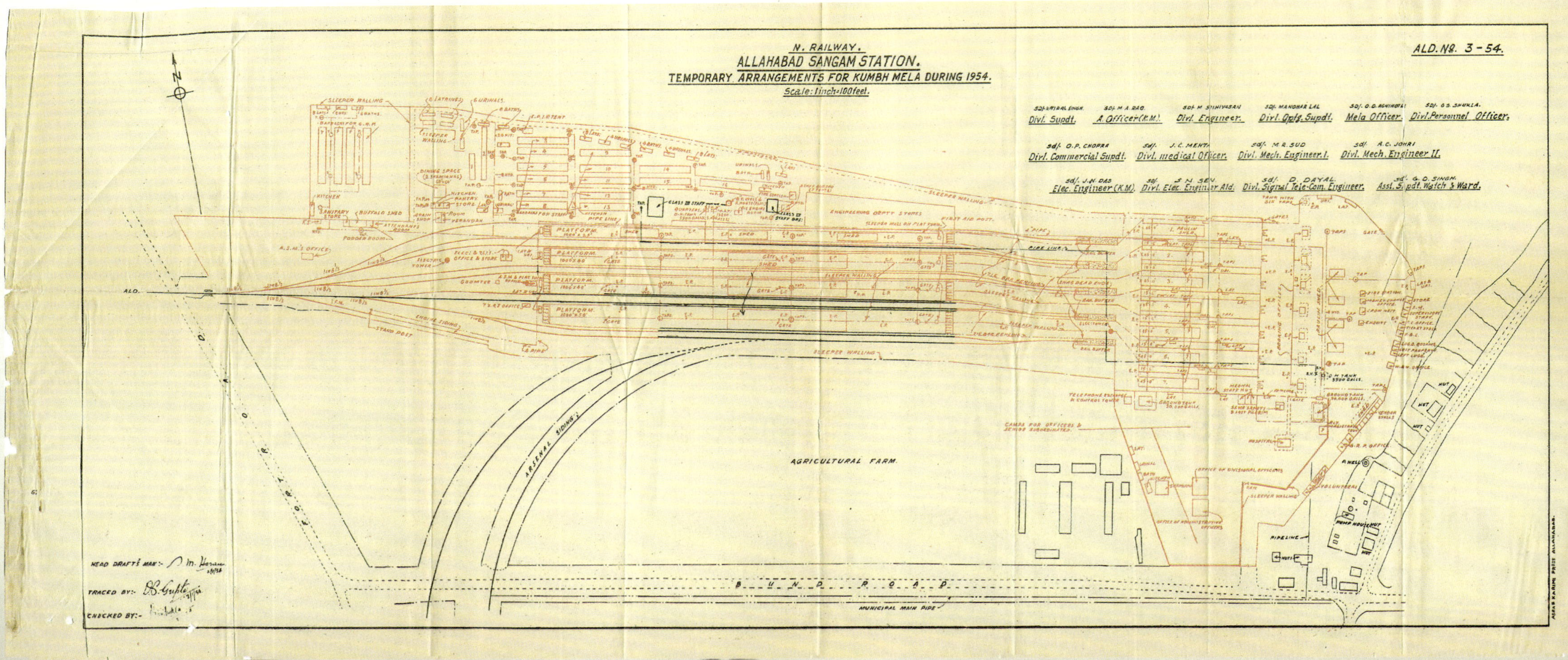
N. RAILWAY.
ALLAHABAD SANGAM STATION.
TEMPORARY ARRANGEMENTS FOR KUMBH MELA DURING 1954.
Scale: 1 inch=100 feet.
ALD. No. 3-54.
Divl. Supdt.
A. Officer (K.M.)
Divl. Engineer.
Divl. Optg. Supdt.
Mela Officer.
Divl. Personnel Officer.
Divl. Commercial Supdt.
Divl. Medical Officer.
Divl. Mech. Engineer. I.
Divl. Mech. Engineer II.
Elec. Engineer (K.M).
Divl. Elec. Engineer Ald.
Divl. Signal Tele-Com. Engineer.
Asst. Supdt. Watch & Ward.
AGRICULTURAL FARM.
ARSENAL SIDING
FORT ROAD
BUND ROAD
MUNICIPAL MAIN PIPE
HEAD DRAFTS MAN:-
TRACED BY:-
CHECKED BY:-

कुम्भ मेला की विस्तृत यातायात योजना - सन् 1954

कुम्भ मेला सन् 1954 के लिए सरकार द्वारा सुगम यातायात हेतु एक विस्तृत योजना तैयार की गयी जिसे मुख्यतः चार श्रेणियों में विभाजित किया गया:-

1. उच्चतम यातायात वाले दिवसों हेतु
2. सामान्य दिवसों हेतु
3. वाहनों के आवागमन हेतु
4. पैदल तीर्थ यात्रियों हेतु

सरकार द्वारा तैयार किए गए यातायात योजना के अन्तर्गत वाहन, रिक्शा, भार वाहन, पैदल तीर्थ यात्रियों, बैल गाड़ियों आदि के लिए पृथक-पृथक मार्ग तथा पार्किंग स्टैण्ड निर्धारित किए गए। उक्त व्यवस्था के साथ-साथ वृद्ध एवं निःशक्त तीर्थ यात्रियों को कुम्भ मेला स्थल तक पहुँचाने हेतु डोली के लिए भी पृथक मार्ग चिन्हित किया गया।

पत्रावली संख्या-186/1954-क्षेत्रीय अभिलेखागार, प्रयागराज

TRAFFIC PLAN KUMBH MELA 1954.

INTRODUCTORY. Broadly speaking the traffic arrangements fall int the following categories.

(1) For Peak days.
(2) For other days.
(3) For vehicular traffic.
(4) and for pedestrian traffic.

Obviously there will be different regulation/for Nos. 3 & 4 on Peak days and on other days.

2. Another important point to remember is that there is (a) City area and (b) Mela area.

3. A yet another feature this time is that the railway line to the Sangam station bars the usual flow of traffic at four level crossings on

(1) Lowther Road (2) Grand Trunk Road

(30 Cemetry Road (4) Fort Road (J.L. Road)

On Peak Days no traffic of any kind can be allowed to pass through these level crossings so as to ensure uninterrupted run of the special trains. However to enable pedestrians to go across without any delay PEDESTRIAN OVERBRIDGES have been provided at each of these level crossings. For vehicular traffic, therefore, on Peak days some detour is inevitable. To ease this problem further recourse has been taken to provide new roads e.g. a rickshaw-worthy road by the side of the railway line over Newal Rai Talab and called hereinafter Talab Newal Rai Road and another road leading from Fatehpur Bochwa to Sardar Patel hospital (Infectious Diseases) near Alopibagh through the underbridge near V. Bichwa and the cultivated and open areas in between the Buxi Bund and railway embankments.

4. It is important to bear in mind that the plan is liable to change under exisgencis of the situation.

CITY PLAN.

FOR PEAK DAYS.

5. Vehicular Traffic. The main flow from outside will be from (1) Kanpur side (2) Phaphamau side (3) Across the Jamuna Bridge from Rewa and Mirzapur and from (4) Banaras

-2-

side to Jhusi.

KANPUR SIDE. Vehicles from Kanpur side will be directed from Kanpur side to Canning Road (Mahatma Gandhi Road) which leads into the Mela area itself.

PHAPHAMAU SIDE. Vehicl es other than bullock carts will go straight on Moti Lal Nehru Road turn on the Lowther Road and join the Canning Road (Mahatma Gandhi Road) flow towards Mela .

For return journey for both these routes Fort Road (J.L.Nehru Road) and Thorn Hill Road will be used.

ACROSS JAMUNA BRIDGE.Vehicles (other than bullock carts) will come for the city across the bridge and turn left on Sir Suleman Road from Gaughat crossing and enter city from K.M. Malviya Road from Katghar. Vehicles with pilgrims will terminate xxxx at Arail where a park and bus stand have been provided. These persons will go to Arail for camping and use the same route for return journey.

BANARAS SIDE. Vehicles coming from this side will terminate at Jhusi parking place and Bus stand and will not be permitted to cross the Pantoon bridge at Daraganj. Persons desirous of coming to the city will take the Phaphamau Road xx and enter city from Phaphamau side. On return journey the same route shall be used.

6. The next flow of traffic is the regular one between places in the city and to the Mela in particular. There will be the following main arteries.

(a) From Junction Station Civil Lines side via Queen's Road and Canning Road on to the Mela.

(b) From Junction Station City side via Leader Road, Hewett Road and onwards. From Hewett Road crossings motor vehicles, Tangas and [ekkas] xxxxxxxx will be diverted on city road to pass on under the Suraj Kund overbridge and join the flow of traffic to the Mela on Canning Road. This traffic will return by Fort and Thornhill Roads. Rickshaws will

-4-

enter Mela area by the Jamuna Bank Road.

10. Pedestrians coming from Phaphamau and Prayag station will turn on Sir Banerji Road from the crossings of Women's hostel, turn on the Annie Basant Road and take the Fatehpur Bichuwa Sardar Patel Hospital Road for the Mela. The same route will be used for the return journey.

11. Buxi Bund Road will also be open for pedestrians who are desirous to go to Prayag station or come from Baghara side.

ON OTHER DAYS.

12. Vehicles will normally take the routes prescribed above but when the traffic rush is reduced to the extent that level crossings can be opened and closed in the normal manner the restrictions will be withdrawn or amended suitably to provide as easy passage as possible.

13. PEDESTRIAN TRAFFIC. It is not proposed to place any restrictions on pedestrians during this time but if necessity arises temporary regulation may be introduced along the lines indicated for peak days.

14. BULLOCK CARTS AND GOODS TRAFFIC. All bullock cart traffic coming from Arail and Jhusi side will be terminated at Arail and Jhusi. Carts coming from Kanpur side will proceed on Kanpur Road turn right on Thornhill Road upto Bharadwaj Crossing on to the Fort Road (Jawahar Lal Nehru Road) and proceed to Kayasth Pathshala Parking ground via Hamilton Road. Similarly carts coming from Phaphamau side will proceed upto Moti Lal Nehru Road and take Hamilton Road for Kayasth Pathshala Parking. Pilgrims from Kayasth Pathshala Parking area will go to Mela by the new road joining the Lowther Road and Parking place to G.T. Road from under the railway embankment at the back of Kayasth Pathshala building.

15. Public carriers, push thelas and bullock carts bringing foodstuffs and merchandise to the Mela and the

-5-

city will be allowed to proceed and unload between 9 P.M. and 4 A.M. on non-peak days and on peak days between 12 midnight and 4 A.M. During the prohibited hours such vehicles carrying merchandise will be detained at the outskirts of the city.

16. Dolies for carrying old and infirm to the Mela will be provided at Canning and Fort Road Parking and Kydganj extension Parking ground in the Mela area.

II

MELA PLAN FOR PEAK DAYS.

17. VEHICULAR TRAFFIC. As already stated in the city Plan, all vehicles entering the Mela area will come either by Jamuna Bank Road or the Canning Road (Mahatma Gandhi Road), Rickshaws will however be allowed to enter the Mela area over Talab Newal Rai Road. Vehicles entering the Mela area from the Jamuna Bank Road will be parked by the side of the Cemetry Road near Minto Park. Those vehicles which pay toll tax will however, be allowed to proceed further on Jamuna Bank Road upto the Parking place at Kydganj extension Road near the Junction of Fort Triveni and Kydganj Extension Roads. These vehicles will take their return journey along the Kydganj Extension Road only, except that rickshaws will go back also on the new Talab Newal Rai Road as described above. Vehicles coming from Canning Road will be parked in the parking place at the crossing of Canning Road and Fort Road. These vehicles will take their return journey by Fort Road (Jawahar Lal Nehru Road).

18 PEDESTRIAN TRAFFIC. The main inlets or the Tribeni Road, Jamuna Bank Road, Canning Road, Buxi Band Road and Fatehpur Bichwa, Sardar Patel Hospital Road as stated above. The return route will be the two side roads ~~xxxxx~~ in the Sangam area, one along the Ganga river edge (a) and the other via the Akshaibat and Mahabirji temple. (b) The former will lead to the Bazar in the Parade area and on to the G.T. Road and Fort Road while the latter will lead to

-5-

city will be allowed to proceed and unload between 9 P.M. and 4 A.M. on non-peak days and on peak days between 12 midnight and 4 A.M. During the prohibited hours such vehicles carrying merchandise will be detained at the outskirts of the city.

16. Dolies for carrying old and infirm to the Mela will be provided at Canning and Fort Road Parking and Kydganj extension Parkin ground in the Mela area.

MELA PLAN FOR PEAK DAYS.

17. VEHICULAR TRAFFIC. As already stated in the city Plan, all vehicles entering the Mela area will come either by Jamuna Bank Road or the Canning Road (Mahatma Gandhi Road), Rickshaws will however be allowed to enter the Mela area over Talab Newal Rai Road. Vehicles entering the Mela area from the Jamuna Bank Road will be parked by the side of the Cemetry Road near Minto Park. Those vehicles which pay toll tax will however, be allowed to proceed further on Jamuna Bank Road upto the Parking place at Kydganj extension Road near the Junction of Fort Triveni and Kydganj Extension Roads. These vehicles will take their return journey along the Kydganj Extension Road only, except that rickshaws will go back also on the new Talab Newal Rai Road as described above. Vehicles coming from Canning Road will be parked in the parking place at the crossing of Canning Road and Fort Road. These vehilces will take their return journey by Fort Road (Jawahar Lal Nehru Road).

18 PEDESTRIAN TRAFFIC. The main inlets or the Tribeni Road, Jamuna Bank Road, Canning Road, Buxi Band Road and Fatehpur Bichwa, Sardar Patel Hospital Road as stated above. The return route will be the two side roads ~~xmxxxx~~ in the Sangam area, one along the Ganga river edge and the other via the Akshaibat and Mahabirji temple. The former will lead to the Bazar in the Parade area and on to the G.T. Road and Fort Road while the latter will lead to

-6-

the Fort gate on the Kydganj extension Road.

ON OTHER DAYS.

19. Vehicular traffic. Some vehicles might be permitted to come as far as the Parking place in the Sangam area along the Triveni Road on payment of Toll tax and to go back along the Parade Bazar Road.

20. PEDESTRIAN TRAFFIC. As in the case of the City Plan, restrictions will be the minimum and according to exigencies of the situation.

Sd/ J.N. Ugra
D.M. Allahabad

Attested.

माघ मेले में तीर्थ यात्रियों हेतु स्वास्थ्य विभाग द्वारा जारी दिशा-निर्देश (एडवाइजरी) - 1967

माघ मेला क्षेत्र में स्वास्थ्य विभाग द्वारा यात्रियों को दी गई सुविधायें

प्रति वर्ष गंगा जमुना के संगम तट पर माघ मास में यह मेला लगता है। इस पवित्र गंगा के तट पर बड़े-बड़े महात्मा, ऋषि मुनि एवं विभिन्न प्रदेशों से आये हुये यात्रीगण भी सत्संग का आनन्द लेने के लिये कल्प वास कर रहे हैं। मेले में आये हुये यात्रियों तथा कल्प वासियों से इस गंगा के पवित्र तट को स्वच्छ रखने के लिये अपने ऋषियों और मुनियों के आदर्शों का अनुकरण करने का निवेदन स्वास्थ्य विभाग करता है क्योंकि:-

,, गंगा के तट पवित्र है ,,

इस गंगा के तट की स्वच्छता के लिये स्वास्थ्य विभाग की ओर से समस्त मेला क्षेत्र में सार्वजनिक शौचालय तथा मूत्रालय की व्यवस्था की गई है। मेले में आये हुये यात्रियों को चाहिये कि वे इधर-उधर बैठ कर मल-मूत्र का [illegible] त्याग न करें। आप मनुष्य हैं? पशु ही सड़क पर इधर-उधर मल-मूत्र का त्याग करते हैं।

स्वास्थ्य विभाग की ओर से मेला क्षेत्र को तीन क्षेत्रों में बांटा गया है। परेड क्षेत्र, गंगा पट्टी और जमुना पट्टी। प्रत्येक क्षेत्र में एक-एक स्वास्थ्य अधिकारी के अंतरगत दो स्वास्थ्य निरीक्षक, स्वास्थ्य नायक और सैकड़ों मेहतर कार्य कर रहे हैं। यह क्षेत्रीय कार्यालय क्रमश: लाल सड़क, काली सड़क तथा त्रिवेणी मार्ग-किले के उत्तर में स्थित है। स्वास्थ्य विभाग का प्रधान मेला-कार्यालय त्रिवेणी मार्ग पर स्थित है।

मेला क्षेत्र में यात्रियों की सुविधा के लिये एक राजकीय चिकित्सालय कार्य कर रहा है। इस अस्पताल में पुरूष एवं महिला चिकित्साधिकारियों की सेवाएं दिन-रात उपलब्ध रहती हैं। आकस्मिक रोगियों को शहर के चिकित्सालयों में भेजने के लिये एम्बुलेंस गाड़ियों का भी समुचित प्रबन्ध है। इस अस्पताल में साधारण रोगों के इलाज की समुचित व्यवस्था है। संक्रामक रोगों की चिकित्सा के हेतु लाल सड़क पर एक संक्रामक रोग चिकित्सालय भी अनुभवी चिकित्सकों की देख रेख में खोला गया है। स्वास्थ्य विभाग मेले में आये हुये यात्रियों के स्वास्थ्य की शुभ-कामना करता है। यदि कोई भी व्यक्ति किसी संक्रामक रोग से पीड़ित रोगियों की जानकारी रखता है तो उसका यह प्रथम धर्म है कि मेले में आये हुये दूसरे यात्रियों के स्वास्थ्य के हित में उस रोगी की चिकित्सा अथवा रोग की रोक-थाम

-२-

के लिये शीघ्र ही अपने निकटतम स्थित स्वास्थ्य विभाग के कार्यालय को सूचित कर दें अथवा टेलीफोन नं० २६८३ पर सहायक स्वास्थ्य सेवा निदेशक को सूचना शीघ्र ही दे देना चाहिये ताकि रोग की चिकित्सा एवं उसकी रोक थाम के लिये तत्कालिक कदम उठाये जा सकें। इसके अतिरिक्त काली सड़क - परेड पर एक राजकीय आयुर्वेदिक चिकित्सालय भी खोला गया है जहां अनुभवी वैद्यों की नियुक्ति की गई है।

माघ मेला क्षेत्र में इधर उधर बैठ कर बाल बनवाना अथवा मुंडन कराना अपने स्वास्थ्य की हजामत बनाना है। इस कठिनायी से बचने के लिये स्वास्थ्य विभाग की ओर से संगम, फूंसी अथवा अरैल में एक-एक नाई बाड़ा बनवाया गया है।

सड़क पर दायें-बायें थूकना महामारी को न्यौता देना है। इसकी रोक-थाम के लिये सड़क के किनारे जगह जगह थूकदान रखे हुए हैं। जनता का धर्म है कि वह सड़क पर जहां-तहां न थूकें केवल थूकदान को ही अपने मुंह की गंदगी दें।

माघ मेला क्षेत्र में जहां तहां नलों के द्वारा पानी की पूर्ति जनता के प्रयोग के लिये की गई है। अत: जन्ता को गन्दे गढ़े व नालों के पानी का प्रयोग भी अपने स्वास्थ्य के हित में न करना चाहिये। केवल जल कल विभाग के द्वारा लगाये गये नलों के पानी का प्रयोग करें।

मेले में आये हुए यात्रियों को चाहिये कि उस हलवाई अथवा अन्य दूकानों की वस्तुओं को जो कि खुली हुई रख कर बेची जा रही हों न खरीदें और न खायें। क्यों कि खुली हुई वस्तुओं पर धूल के द्वारा दूषित रोगों के किटाणु अपना अड्डा जमा लेते हैं फिर वही किटाणु खाने के द्वारा मनुष्य के पेट में जा कर अपने रोगों से उन्हें ग्रसित कर लेते हैं।

मेले में आये हुए यात्रियों को चाहिये कि वे लोग किसी अनजान मनुष्य द्वारा दी हुई वस्तुओं को भूल कर भी न खायें क्यों की बदमाश लोग अपने स्वार्थ हेतु भोली जन्ता को खाने-पीने की वस्तुओं में ज़हर व नशीली वस्तुओं को मिला कर ठगने का प्रयत्न करते हैं।

महात्मा बुद्ध ने कहा हैं :-

मन की स्वच्छता से तन में विकार नहीं रहते।
तन की स्वच्छता से घर में विकार नहीं रहते।
घर की स्वच्छता से नगर में विकार नहीं रहते।।

अत: हम सब तथा मेले के यात्रियों का परम धर्म है कि मेला क्षेत्र को स्वच्छ रखें और गंगा के तट को अपवित्र न करें।

सहायक स्वास्थ्य सेवा निदेशक

SIX

A SALUTE TO AL KALINE

Published by: The Detroit Tigers and Olympia Entertainment

Executive Editor: Michael Bayoff

Managing Editor: Rick Thompson

Author: Dan Ewald

Creative Design: Craig C. Wheeler, CFW Creative Sports, Inc

Produced by: CFW Creative Sports, Inc.

Special thanks: To all of Al's teammates and Hall of Fame colleagues, along with all the Kaline family and friends.

Very Special thanks: Louise Kaline.

ISBN: 978-0-9817729-5-0

Published by the Detroit Tigers and Olympia Entertainment

Printed in the United States

AMERICAN LEAGUE
CHAMPIONS

DETROIT TIGERS

Dear Baseball Fans,

There is a reason that so many of us consider Al Kaline to be Mr. Tiger. He is not only a legend in Detroit and across the State of Michigan, but also with baseball fans around the globe. There are few players that epitomize the true spirit of America's Favorite Pastime the way Al Kaline does.

Al joined the Detroit Tigers in 1953 at just 18 years of age. He never spent a single day in the minor leagues. It did not take long for him to become the youngest player ever to lead the American League in hitting as he won the American League batting title in 1955 at the age of 20 with a .340 average – he was just one day younger than Ty Cobb when he won the same title in 1907! His #6 uniform was retired by the Tigers on August 17, 1980, making him the first Tigers player ever to receive this honor.

I have had the privilege to follow Al through the years – first as a loyal fan rooting for our hometown Tigers and for #6. Then later, having the unique opportunity to work with someone who truly knows and loves the game and brings a quiet passion and remarkable character to the sport he loves. Marian and I are pleased to call his wife, Louise, and him friends, and it has been a special opportunity for us to get to know the personal side of this Hall of Famer.

When we commissioned and erected the bronze statue of Al Kaline at Comerica Park, it was our organization's way of creating an immortal tribute to one of the greatest baseball players of all times. We imagined how baseball fans who were lucky enough to witness Al's amazing feats of greatness in right field and at the plate would point to that statue, recounting his most memorable plays to future generations to keep the memory of this legend alive forever.

But the statue, sitting proudly in the ballpark, also represents more than just one of the greatest to play the game; it represents a truly great man. He loves the game dearly and was grateful just to have the opportunity to play. He is so gracious he once told me he "could never put on another uniform" other than the Olde English D of his beloved Detroit Tigers.

We are truly fortunate that a man with such qualities and character, sportsmanship and athletic ability played for the Detroit Tigers – Al Kaline serves as a wonderful mentor for all who play the game of baseball and all who play the game of life.

Comerica
PARK
Tonight's Game
Big Boy
THINK
FORD
FIRST!
Metro Detroit
Ford Dealers
PEPSI

DETROIT TIGERS

What else can I say about Al Kaline?

Already, generations of fans know him as Mr. Tiger, the ultimate professional.

He is the youngest batting champion. Eighteen-time All-star, first ballot Hall of Famer. Member of the 3,000 hit club. World Series hero. Respected teammate.

Exemplary family man. 26-year TV analyst. A true and treasured friend.

What else can I tell you? Not anything, really, because now you can see everything in these photographs of Al's career, his life on and off the field, his family. Enjoy this well-presented pictorial journey. If a picture is truly worth a thousand words, you've found a real bargain.

Ernie Harwell
August 31, 2009

PHOTO BY

DETROIT TIGERS

No amount of true success comes without the sacrifice and support of family and friends. Without my loving wife, Louise, and my precious sons, Mark and Michael, nothing I accomplished in baseball would mean a thing.

For the love they have shown me and the love I feel for them, I am truly blessed.

I also wish to thank all the owners I played for and the teammates I played with. No individual is bigger than the team.

Tiger fans are special. Their loyalty remains strong in tough times as well as the good. For the support you have always given me and my family, I am forever indebted.

Al Kaline

Al called it a career after the 1974 season and got a standing ovation from the fans.

FOREWORD

Al Kaline is one of those special athletes that comes around only once in a lifetime.

Certainly he's one of just a handful of players to be considered the greatest ever to wear the Detroit Tigers uniform. During his 22-year career, all with the Tigers, he was considered by peers to be among the best in either league.

The wedding was spectacular and the following years sweet.

His achievements, longevity, dedication and loyalty to the Tigers and the game were rewarded by his first ballot election to Baseball's Hall of Fame in 1980.

Like no other sport, baseball thrives on a myriad of facts, figures and statistics large enough to cram every nook and cranny of Comerica Park. And certainly Al posted all the right numbers.

For instance:

- 12th player to be elected to the Hall of Fame on the first ballot.
- One of only 27 players to collect at least 3,000 hits.
- All-time Tigers games played leader.
- Youngest American League player to win a batting title.
- 18 All-Star Games.
- 10 Gold Glove Awards.
- 22 big league seasons, all with the Tigers.

But there's something special about No. 6 that doesn't show up in the record books. And for this, Al and Louise Kaline share a priceless sense of pride.

Two days after graduating from Baltimore's Southern High School and signing a bonus contract, Kaline reported to the Tigers. The following year he married his high school sweetheart, Louise. And now almost six decades later, the couple still chooses to make Detroit their permanent home.

In typical quiet fashion, Kaline has become part of Michigan's fabric as much as the world famous Mackinaw Bridge. Such loyalty to one city by one of baseball's all-time icons probably will never be matched again. It's a quiet distinction that both Al and Louise keep close to their hearts.

When the Kalines arrived in Detroit, the city was the fifth largest in the United States. It was a time when:

- Automobiles were cheaper in Detroit than anywhere else in the country because they were manufactured and assembled here.

- Detroit was the nation's only city where someone could purchase a cold Vernor's soda pop.
- Milk and bread were delivered to homes by truck.

- Milky the Clown was the clown prince for Twin Pines milk.
- Soupy Sales was the clown prince of lunchtime for kids.
- Bob-Lo Island was a daytime fantasy for kids and an evening dating paradise for young adults.
- Electric-powered streetcars stopped at the corner of Michigan and Trumbull where Briggs Stadium sat.
- Hudson's was a one-stop shopping dream for mothers and a Christmas toy land for kids.
- Suburbs hardly stretched farther from the city than Dearborn and Grosse Pointe.

People have come and people have gone. Some traditions have faded and new ones were born.

One that withstood the passing of time, however, is the presence of Al Kaline somewhere in the Tigers organization. First as a player for 22 years…then as a broadcaster on Tigers television…and finally as a special assistant to the president of the club.

The city was made for Al. And he was made for Detroit.

Detroit is a working man's city filled with blue collars, hard hats and lunch buckets. There's nothing fancy about Detroit's work ethic. Workers show up on time, put in a full day's work and don't ask for special favors other than the opportunity to do their jobs.

There's nothing flamboyant about Al. No controversies. No off-field misadventures. No meaningless flashes of bravado.

That's just the way Al did it for the Tigers for 22 years.

When times were good, Kaline was leading the way. When tough times struck, he could lift a team. With his bat, his glove, his legs and his laser sharp arm, Al provided the Tigers an identity.

And he's still providing that identity to the entire state merely by his presence.

Just as it's impossible for any Tigers fan to think of anyone else but Al wearing that famous No. 6, it's impossible to think about the Tigers without him being there.

Unlike numbers, feelings have no place in record books. But not one of his countless record-setting figures means more to Michigan than the loyalty the Kalines have demonstrated for almost six decades.

And isn't that appropriate for the number Al made famous?

Dan Ewald

There's no other place where Al feels more at home than around the batting cage.

It didn't matter if the Tigers lost that day. These youngsters will never forget their day at the park.

After 22 glorious seasons, Al makes a final walk to the dugout.

George Kell did the play-by-play and Al provided expert analysis that made the Tiger TV duo a dynamite tandem.

Al celebrated winning a pennant as a player in 1968. In 2006, he joined the clubhouse frenzy as a club executive when the Tigers won the American League crown. Justin Verlander looks proud to spray the champagne on the Hall of Famer.

AMERICAN LEAGUE
CHAMPIONS

6 SIX

The Prospect

At 18 months, just look at that smile and sparkle in his eyes. No question Al was born to be a Tiger.

BALTIMORE

The house at 2222 Cedley was similar to all of the other row houses that lined the streets near Baltimore's Inner Harbor.

After several years, however, the house assumed a distinction that few homes anywhere in America enjoy. It was the first home for a future Hall of Famer and one that still fills Al with countless warm memories.

Now who wouldn't want to take this Baltimore cutie home?

Visitors to the Inner Harbor today are dazzled by the array of boutiques, restaurants and entertainment centers that make the downtown site a Baltimore destination stop.

That's far from its profile when Al was a youngster and small manufacturing plants, vacant buildings, shacks and fishing enterprises filled the area with a distinctive odor before massive renovation.

Nicholas and Naomi Kaline lived in the blue collar neighborhood with daughters Margaret and

Caroline and son Al. Dad worked in a broom making factory only a handful of blocks from home. On weekends he earned extra money by fishing in the harbor. Mom earned a little by cleaning offices on weekends.

Workers at a few of the nearby factories often spent their spring and summer lunch breaks playing softball in the parking lots. Before reaching his teens, Al liked to watch them and once in a while was asked to play when a team needed an extra player.

"Obviously, they were all older than me, but once I got in there, I was able to hold my own," he said.

Standing in front of his neighbor's house, Al always was ready for a game of ball.

Southern High School, which no longer exists, was the fortunate school to land the Hall of Fame bound player and Al created a lot of memories for those fortunate enough to see him play. He earned all-state honors in baseball all four years and three times in basketball.

"I loved both sports," he said. "I really enjoyed basketball because the whole school got behind the

This is the way a high school baseball team should look. Of course, few ever have a player with the talents of Al (front row, far left).

Al (middle row right, next to boy in sweater) was an All- State basketball player for Baltimore's Southern High.

Check out the follow through...and basketball shorts the way they used to be.

"I really enjoyed basketball because the whole school got behind the team. The gym was always packed."

ALBERT KALINE
2222 Cedley Street
GENERAL TECHNICAL

V. Baseball 1, 2, 3; Vice-Pres. 1, 2; J. V. Basketball 2; V. Basketball 3, 4; Pres. Homeroom 3; Student Aide 3, 4; Senator 4.

Al leaves his favorite Ted Williams size "36" bat to Mr. Anderson . . . Wants to play pro baseball . . . Baseball, basketball . . . Chicken . . . "Let's go, Dad."

Al is among the happy 1953 senior class getting ready to leave Southern High.

One of the happiest nights in Al's life was the evening his old high school buddies shared time together at Baltimore's Camden Yards.

team. The gym was always packed. In baseball, only the parents showed up whenever they could."

Dad loved baseball and spent countless hours driving Al to the various sandlot games he played. It was at those games that Dad struck a friendship with Tigers scout Ed Katalinas who wound up signing Al after feverish competition with scouts from other teams.

It was also at Southern High that Al met Louise. The two married a year out of high school and still share memories of all the good times before their permanent move to Detroit.

And all Tigers fans throughout Michigan are grateful for that move.

Judging by the look on Al's face, he must have come up with the right answer in this junior class.

"The rules at that time didn't allow a scout to talk directly to a high school player. Dad trusted Kat and made a promise I wouldn't sign until he listened to the Tigers offer."

Al (kneeling far left) let his hair grow for one season at Southern High.

THE SIGNING

It took Al just one day to rectify his first setback in baseball. And then he made the most of his opportunity.

Like all freshmen at Baltimore's Southern High School, Al did not make the cut for the varsity baseball team. The day after the cuts were announced, an upperclassman suffered a broken leg and Al was elevated to the team.

Not only did Al make the starting lineup, he earned all-state honors four straight years. He also was an all-state basketball player, but it was clear which direction he was headed.

Al played in a 10 to 12-year-old league before moving up to American Legion baseball. Although the youngest player on any team, he started to play in a semipro league when he was just 16 years old.

"That's when I really learned to play baseball and matured as a player," Al said.

The league was filled with players aged all the way to 27 years old. Many had played in the minor leagues or college. They worked for companies who paid them $25 per game.

"They were a lot more advanced than me, but once I got on the field I felt pretty relaxed," Al said. "I had certain skills. I knew I could play the outfield and run and throw. I didn't know how I would

How about this sporting goods salesman? Al worked the off-season in Baltimore before winning the 1955 American League batting championship.

Only days out of high school and Al found his way into Yankee Stadium.

Ed Katalinas made his mark in scouting by signing Al out of high school in 1953. Katalinas went on to become the head of Tigers scouting.

hit against such mature players, but I was able to hold my own."

Obviously he did because major league scouts from all teams regularly attended his games to see one player – Al Kaline. Al's father drove Al to all of his games and wound up developing a good relationship with Tigers scout Ed Katalinas.

"Kat got pretty close to my father and talked to him all the time," Al said. "The rules at that time didn't allow a scout to talk directly to a high school player. Dad trusted Kat and made a promise I wouldn't sign until he listened to the Tiger offer."

Al wound up receiving offers from several teams. The Philadelphia Phillies and Boston Red Sox actually offered more of a signing bonus than the Tigers. During that time, a player signing for more than a $6,000 bonus was forced to stay in the big leagues at least two years.

"We studied the rosters of the Phillies and Red Sox and determined I would probably have to sit on the bench for two years," Al said. "Dad and I decided it might be best to sign with Detroit. I knew about the great Tiger tradition, but I felt I would get a chance to play a little quicker. I didn't want to sit on the bench for two years. I wanted to play. It worked out."

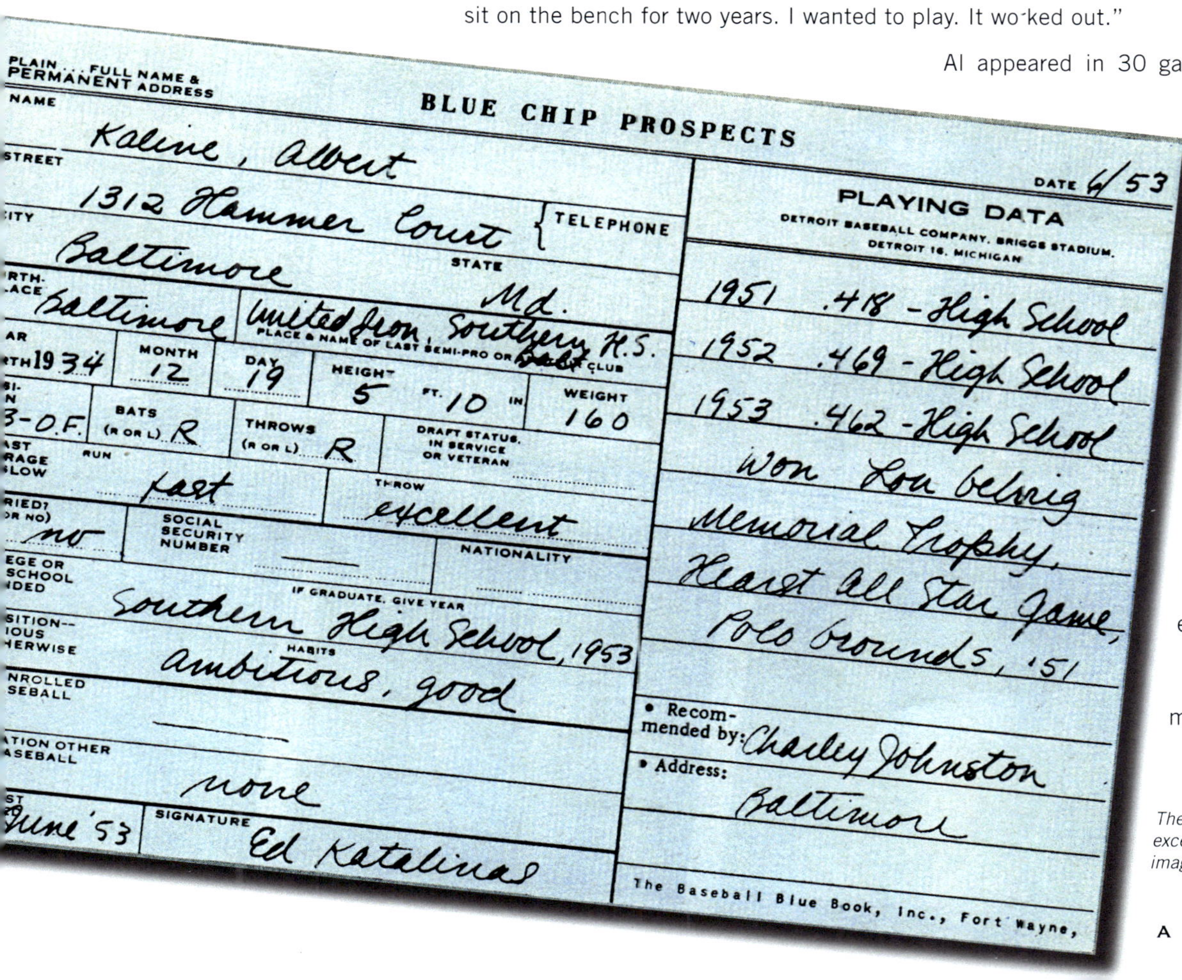

PLAIN . . . FULL NAME & PERMANENT ADDRESS

BLUE CHIP PROSPECTS

NAME Kaline, Albert

STREET 1312 Hammer Court TELEPHONE

CITY Baltimore STATE Md.

BIRTHPLACE Baltimore

United Iron, Southern H.S. PLACE & NAME OF LAST SEMI-PRO OR BALL CLUB

YEAR OF BIRTH 1934 MONTH 12 DAY 19 HEIGHT 5 FT. 10 IN. WEIGHT 160

POSITION 3-O.F. BATS (R OR L) R THROWS (R OR L) R DRAFT STATUS, IN SERVICE OR VETERAN

RUN fast THROW excellent

MARRIED? (YES OR NO) no SOCIAL SECURITY NUMBER NATIONALITY

COLLEGE OR SCHOOL ATTENDED IF GRADUATE, GIVE YEAR Southern High School, 1953

HABITS ambitious, good

June '53 SIGNATURE Ed Katalinas

DATE 6/53

PLAYING DATA

DETROIT BASEBALL COMPANY, BRIGGS STADIUM, DETROIT 16, MICHIGAN

1951 .418 – High School

1952 .469 – High School

1953 .462 – High School

Won Lou Gehrig Memorial Trophy, Hearst All Star Game, Polo Grounds, '51

• Recommended by: Charley Johnston

• Address: Baltimore

The Baseball Blue Book, Inc., Fort Wayne,

The scouting report on Al was excellent...but who could have imagined the Hall of Fame?

Al appeared in 30 games in 1953 after graduating from high school. In 1954 he made the most out of an opportunity that arose within the Tigers. Outfielder Steve Souchak broke his hand playing winter ball. Al batted .400 during his first spring training and wound up being the regular right fielder. He played 138 games and batted .276 without making an error.

The verdict is unanimous. Al made the right choice.

There's nothing to be embarrassed about being tagged out by Yogi Berra.

Al learned a lot from old-timers like Schoolboy Rowe and Goose Gosl'n.

Fresh out of high school and ready to play at Briggs Stadium.

6 SIX

The Fan

Pat Mullin was proud to present the No. 6 he had worn. Now it belonged to Al and it will never again be worn.

NUMBER 6

Like so many boys growing up in America when he was a youngster, Al had two baseball idols – Ted Williams and Stan Musial.

Unlike almost all of those boys, however, Al was fortunate to befriend both.

"Ted was probably the greatest hitter ever to live," Al said. "Stan actually was my favorite because he was more of an all-around player – good hitter, runner and outfielder. I really admired him as a player. I tried to play the game the same way he did."

Tigers fans felt comfortable with Al on deck.

"Stan actually was my favorite because he was more of an all-around player – good hitter, runner and outfielder. I really admired him as a player. I tried to play the game the same way he did."

"Stan the Man" Musial was Al's boyhood idol and the reason he loved the No. 6. Playing against him in spring training was a dream come true.

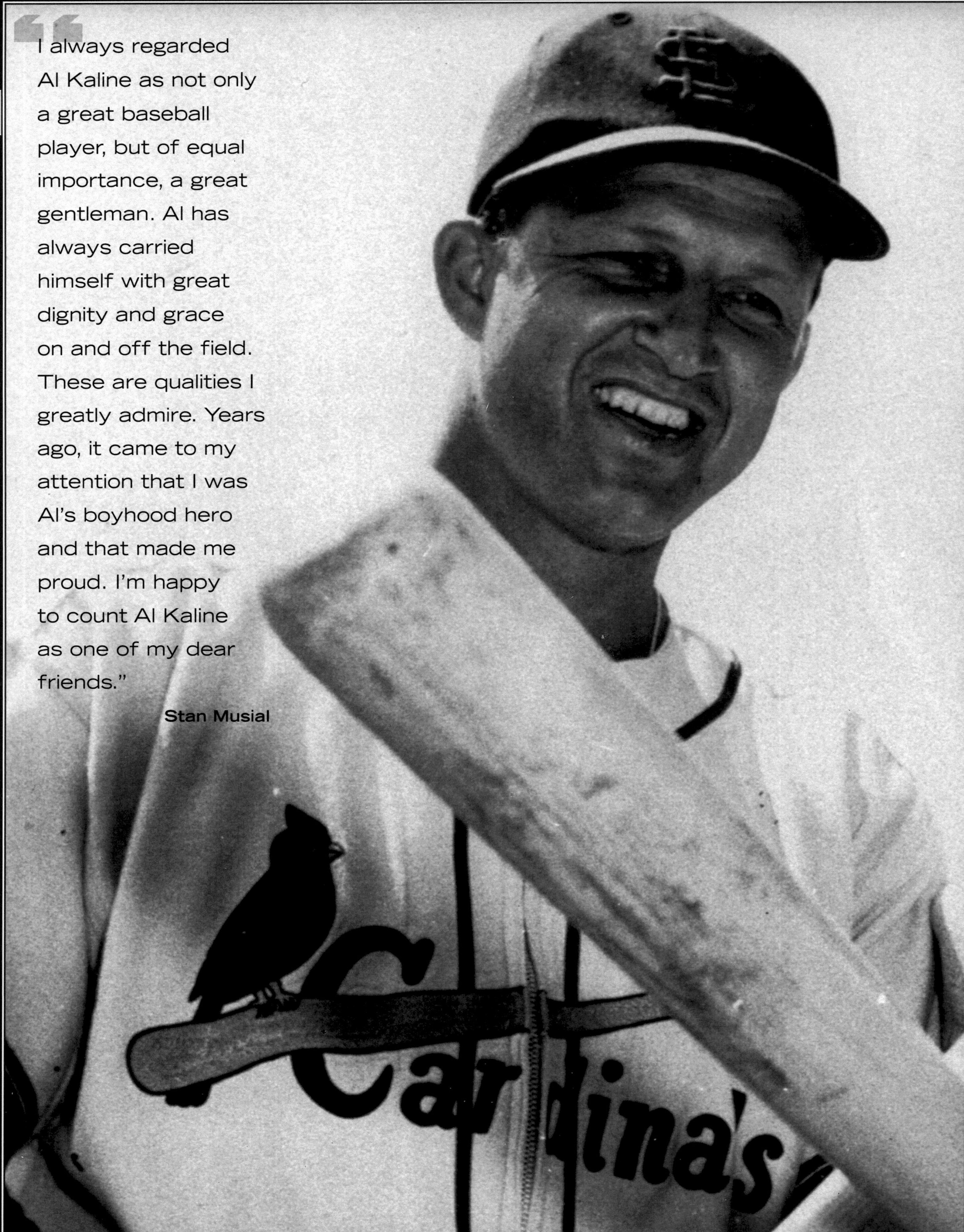

"I always regarded Al Kaline as not only a great baseball player, but of equal importance, a great gentleman. Al has always carried himself with great dignity and grace on and off the field. These are qualities I greatly admire. Years ago, it came to my attention that I was Al's boyhood hero and that made me proud. I'm happy to count Al Kaline as one of my dear friends."

Stan Musial

Detroit

It's fairly obvious that after signing with the Tigers, Al was hoping to be assigned the No. 9 Williams wore or the No. 6 worn so proudly by Musial.

That's not the way it happens, though, when breaking into the big leagues at just 18 years old. Al was assigned No. 25 and wore it throughout his first season in 1953.

Longtime Tigers outfielder Pat Mullin wore No. 6 at the time. He had played for Detroit from 1940 through 1953, with the exception of serving three years in the military during World War II.

When Mullin retired after the 1953 season Al asked him if it would be alright for him to wear No. 6. Recognizing the potential in Al from his lengthy tenure with Detroit, Mullin told Al: "It would be an honor if you do."

That was the beginning of the No. 6 legend and certainly Mullin and Musial are proud of what that number has come to mean in Detroit Tigers history.

The famous number that all Detroit youngsters scrambled to wear while playing on the sandlots now is retired forever. And even those not privileged to have seen Al play appreciate the fact that the number belongs to him.

There was nothing more identifiable in Detroit than the number six or that classic Kaline swing.

Now forever Al's.

Framed and ready for hanging.

Whenever the Tigers played Boston early in Al's career, he always tried to spend some time talking hitting with Ted Williams. The Splendid Splinter absolutely loved Al's swing.

TED WILLIAMS

One of Al's most precious memories occurred at Boston's Fenway Park, but a long way from the diamond.

Before a night game with the Red Sox while serving as a Tigers TV broadcaster, Al was enjoying a pre-game dinner in the media hospitality room when word spread that Ted Williams was in the park. Any visit by Williams was treated as a royal appearance and the Boston media was scurrying to talk to him.

Williams was returning from a fishing trip in New Hampshire and showed up at Fenway for a single, simple purpose.

"Get away from me," he ordered the writers. "I came up here for one reason. I want to talk to my friend, Al Kaline."

Al, of course, was honored. Only a handful of people in baseball were blessed by such a visit.

"He came over, shook my hand, asked about my family and then walked out," Al said. "This was the man I idolized when I was a kid. When our visit was over, I felt 10-feet tall."

Since almost the time Al had broken into the American League, Williams befriended Al like he did so few others. He was fascinated by Al's swing and the way he carried himself on the field.

Al will never forget meeting Williams on his first trip to Fenway Park fresh out of high school. The Tigers realized the gem they had signed. And Tigers manager Fred Hutchinson wanted Al to meet the man many consider the greatest hitter ever to live.

"Hutch knew Ted well," Al said. "He took me to the Boston dugout after batting practice. In a baseball sense, talking to Ted Williams was like talking to God."

That was the start of a relationship that lasted for the rest of Williams' life.

The Tigers stayed at the Kenmore Hotel on their visits to Boston. Williams had an apartment in the Somerset only blocks away.

Here's what Ted Williams loved about Al's swing – everything. All parts are in proper place. The shoulders, arms, hands, hips, feet and especially the eyes. Ted loved it.

Even as he advanced in age, Ted Williams always welcomed a visit from Al and Louise.

"He called me one time and told me to visit him in his room," Al recalled. "Of course, I dropped what I was doing and got over there quickly."

When Al arrived, Williams was in the living room making fish flies for the fishing trips he so loved. Upon Al's arrival the conversation quickly turned to hitting.

> "He talked about getting your hands and wrists strong and being patient for a good pitch to hit. He maintained that 'pitchers are dumb.' Be patient and you'll get a good pitch to hit. Don't swing at their pitches."

"What are you looking for off Early Wynn?" Williams would challenge his young protégé.

"I'd say something and then he would say: 'You dumb so-and-so...you know he's gonna throw you this or that. You have to learn to be patient.' Just for him to think about having me come over is something I'll always remember."

Al made the most out of the personal tutelage he was honored to receive from the all-time master.

"He never mentioned how to swing or anything like that," Al said. "He talked about getting your hands and wrists strong and being patient for a good pitch to hit. He maintained that 'pitchers are dumb.' Be patient and you'll get a good pitch to hit. Don't swing at their pitches."

Williams was known throughout the game for his keen eyesight that allowed him to pick up the spin of a pitch better than most hitters.

"I think I was lucky that way," Al said. "For some reason I think I was able to pick up a pitch a fraction of a second sooner than most."

In retirement, Al and Louise visited Williams in Florida several times. Al feels particularly honored to have been chosen as a member of Williams' Hitters Hall of Fame Museum, also located in Florida.

Al's respect for the heritage of the game of baseball is unquestioned as he holds a precious part of his personal collection.

The spirit of Tiger tradition through the generations – Hank Greenberg, Charlie Gehringer, Mickey Cochrane and Al.

Al got his first opportunity to meet Willie Mays before a spring training game.

"Baseball is a game where you must respect history ... I've been blessed to have met so many of the greats who are legends forever."

Age made no difference. They all loved Al.

Al salutes teens before a home game.

Long hair was popular in the 60s and so was Al with the fans.

This Boys Club youngster will always remember his special moment with Al.

In uniform or street clothes, Al drew the fans.

6 SIX

The Fielder

Detroit

DEFENSIVE PRIDE

Al took pride in never taking any aspect of his game for granted.

He took particular pride in his ability to play defense at a level that made the rest of the American League simply marvel.

"I took great pride in making a good defensive play," he said. "I knew I couldn't get the big hit every time up. No player can. That's impossible. I made a point, though, that if I made an out, I was going to make a great play in the field. I was out in that field to help the pitcher make a living, too. If I could make a play and save a big inning, then I was helping to save that pitcher's job. That's the way I looked at it."

Al made the game-saving catch in Yankee Stadium, but paid the price with a broken collarbone.

Even at a young age before signing professionally, Al knew that he could run, catch and throw the ball better than anyone he competed against.

"I may not have had the best arm, but I was accurate," he explained. "I threw straight from the top so my throws wouldn't sail much and I was on line. I could see at a distance well and was able to pick up the ball quickly."

When he joined the Tigers in Philadelphia after signing, Al knew he could compete with the big leaguers, at least defensively.

Early in his career, Al kept crashing into the stands while chasing foul flies. The Tigers removed some seats and named the area "Kaline's Corner" much to the dismay of enemy hitters who wound up making more outs.

"I'll take that," Al seems to say to silence a Yankee Stadium crowd.

"I knew right then I could run, catch and throw with those guys," he said. "Hitting wise I didn't know what I could do. Nobody does at that age."

While he made playing defense look as easy as picking cherries, Al was relentless with his work ethic in the field.

"I studied hitters and pitchers a lot," he said. "I got to know what our pitchers could do and how they would work on hitters," he said.

And rarely did he fail. Al's relentless preparation and basic instincts wouldn't allow him to miss a cutoff man or throw to the wrong base. He knew when to go for a ball in the gap and when to play it safely.

And he was fearless playing the walls.

"Once I learned to play in enclosed stadiums with stands and fences I knew I could catch and throw in the big leagues," he said.

Ernie Harwell and George Kell presented Al with his 1962 Gold Glove and a plaque commemorating his 200th home run.

Always ready and always with two hands.

The enemy learned quickly not to challenge Al's accurate arm.

Al considers modern players to be bigger and stronger than those when he played. He's concerned, though, that they're more concerned with hitting than playing fundamentally sound in the field.

"I don't think all of them take playing the outfield as seriously," he said. "Everyone wants to get a base hit. Everyone wants to hit that big home run to win a game."

Certainly, Al wanted those same things. But that's not the way he approached the game.

Early in his career, the Tigers decided to make an adjustment in their right field seating area to accommodate Al's ability to cover so much space with reckless abandon. The club eliminated a number of seats behind the right field foul line to keep Kaline from crashing into the wall to make spectacular grabs. The area became popularly known as "Kaline's Corner."

Because of the pride he took in defense, Al never suffered what he calls a "fielding slump."

And everyone in baseball took notice.

During his career, Al collected 10 Gold Gloves signifying defensive excellence for the position. A couple of them came when only one award for each position was given to the combined members of both the American and National Leagues.

"I'm very proud of those Gold Gloves because they prove I was a fairly good all-around player," he said. "Playing defense helps a club as much as driving in a run."

The proof is in the gold. And Al has lots of that to back it.

Former Tigers center fielder Billy Bruton is proud to stand with Al and his 1967 Gold Glove Award and All-Star plaque.

One of Al's long-time teammates is Willie Horton. Both are honored with statues at Comerica Park.

During a 22-year career, Al spent plenty of time in this locker room preparing for his next opponent.

WILLIE HORTON

The old saying of "if you want to make someone listen just whisper" has a special meaning for Willie Horton and his long-felt admiration for Al.

Al had established himself as a legitimate major league star by the time Horton broke in with the Tigers in 1963. As a rookie and having grown up in the shadows of Tiger Stadium, Horton was quiet and studied his new teammates trying to learn how to act in the big leagues.

> "As soon as he stepped through the door, he had his game face on. He started preparing before he reached the park... That set the tone for me and all the other young players."

He paid particular attention to Al who always seemed to have everything under control without having to say too much.

"I always had so much respect for Al," Horton said. "I always called him Mr. Kaline. He was a quiet leader. He didn't go around yapping his opinions. But if you paid attention to him and everything he did, you learned how to play the game the right way."

One of the most critical lessons Horton came to appreciate was the preparation Al made for each game.

"I used to watch him when he walked into the clubhouse," Horton said. "As soon as he stepped through the door, he had his game face on. He started preparing before he reached the park. He knew the pitcher who he would be facing and all the rest of the pitchers on the other team. That set the tone for me and all the other young players. I learned that if you wanted to stick around and play the game right, you had to prepare yourself. You had to know what to do in every situation."

Horton quickly understood that Al was more concerned with winning a game than how many hits he

Let the 2006 World Series begin as Willie Horton and Al fire out the ceremonial first pitch.

might get in any certain game.

"Young players have to learn that winning is what it's all about," Horton said. "Sometimes a situation calls for a bunt or a hit-and-run instead of swinging for a home run. Al did whatever it took to help the team win."

Horton also admired Al's determination to stay in the lineup even when hurt.

"People don't realize he played half of his career in pain," Horton said. "I could see the pain on his face, but he never complained."

Horton believes he became a good outfielder by watching Al attack an opposing team from his right field position.

"The key to playing the outfield is knowing your own pitching staff," Horton said. "Al knew what each one of his pitchers was going to do. He made adjustments. And I never saw a more accurate arm than his. Al took great pride in his defense. It made me work hard."

Through their years as teammates and now serving the Tigers as Special Assistants to the President, Horton considers Al part of his family.

"I used to call him Mr. Kaline, but now he's closer to me than a brother," Horton said. "I'm very fortunate just to be around him. Al and Louise are such a big part of my family's life."

How about these two All-Stars – Willie Horton and Al – throwing out the first pitch?

Al regularly got a better jump on the ball than any American League outfielder.

DICK TRACEWSKI

Al was not intimidated playing at Yankee Stadium. He saved a game by snagging this almost certain home run.

As much as he appreciated all of the records Al accumulated with his bat and glove, Dick Tracewski particularly admires Al for something he never did.

"He never short cut his work," said Tracewski, former Tigers player and long-time coach. "He never missed throwing from the outfield during infield practice. Not during the season and not even in spring training. He could have done whatever he wanted. He was the man. But he always worked on fundamentals. He did it to show people you had to work hard to be good in this game.

"He was never a loud guy. He was a quiet leader. He led by example. All great players are like that."

> "You never saw him do one of those fake dives to catch a ball like the players do today. He didn't have to. He caught the ball at his knees without going to the ground. And he never shied away from any wall.

Having spent several years with the Los Angeles Dodgers in the National League before joining the Tigers, Tracewski had the opportunity to evaluate all the great players during a 33-year-professional career.

"Defensively, Al was outstanding," Tracewski said. "His arm wasn't as strong as Roberto Clemente's. No one's was. But Al was so accurate. He never missed a cutoff man and never short hopped an infielder or catcher with his throws.

"You never saw him do one of those fake dives to catch a ball like the players do today. He didn't have to. He caught the ball at his knees without going to the ground. And he never shied away from any wall.'

At the plate, Tracewski was equally impressed.

"Al was an outstanding breaking ball hitter," Tracewski said. "One of the best I ever saw. He would take a nasty slider from one of those tough right-handers and rifle a line drive to right field. That's why he was such a good two-strike hitter. He could hit the breaking ball. He wasn't the strongest hitter, but he had such good quick hands."

Most importantly, he wasn't afraid to work.

BILL FREEHAN

No one had a better seat for watching the grace of Al's magic in right field than Bill Freehan from his catcher's position behind home plate. Playing 15 seasons for the Tigers, he had plenty of opportunities to watch Al's brilliance.

Freehan knew when a ball was hit to right field it would either be caught or swiftly cut off with the throw going precisely to the right base or relay.

"I never saw him make a mistake in right field," Freehan marveled. "He was the textbook for making the right play all the time."

As an 11 time All-Star catcher, Freehan appreciates the value of sparkling defense. He also understands that such brilliance doesn't simply just happen.

"Al was the consummate professional," Freehan said. "He was always prepared. Not just before a game, but as it unfolded one batter at a time."

Besides all the Gold Glove Awards the two All-Stars earned, the pair shared a lot of memorable moments on and off the field.

The two often shared rides to the park for a game so that Louise and Pat Freehan could drive together to the park a little later. Freehan recalls many of those rides being made in silence as they prepared for the opponent of the day.

Of course, they played in many All-Star Games together and shared their happiest professional moment as teammates on the World Champion 1968 team.

"We've shared jobs, families, happy times and some difficult times together over 47 years," Freehan said. "Al was a great player and a great teammate. Louise was a great help to him, too."

That's high praise from a man who saw all those games over the years from the unique perspective of a catcher.

And it didn't come by accident. Al earned it by always being prepared.

Manager Bob Swift must be the Secretary of Defense with his 1965 Tigers who collected three Gold Gloves. That's Mickey Stanley, Bill Freehan and Al.

6 SIX

The Ambassador

On the Tigers' 1962 trip to Japan, Al was the biggest attraction.

JAPAN TOUR

In 1962, Al, Louise and the entire team were treated to a special trip once the regular season ended.

The Tigers were one of the early major league teams invited to play in a goodwill tour of Japan. It was good for the players, good for Major League Baseball and good for the team to represent its city on the other side of the globe.

Japan was excited to host a team so rich in baseball tradition. Japanese fans were familiar with Detroit's power punch featuring Al, Norm Cash and Rocky Colavito. They were particularly anxious to watch Al who was well on his way toward Hall of Fame status.

Al didn't disappoint them. He flashed that classic swing and demonstrated his fury and finesse in the outfield. During the two-week trip, Al led all hitters with nine home runs. The Japanese immediately placed Al into that country's version of the Hall of Fame.

For everyone on the trip, it was a Hall of Fame experience. And the Tigers made everyone feel proud.

The Kalines and Cashes enjoyed the Japanese dining experience in true native fashion on the trip to Japan.

The Tigers traveled to Japan in 1962. The Japanese had heard of Al's great talents and didn't have to wait long to enjoy them in person.

Tigers
6

3
DETROIT

A STAR AMONG STARS

Hollywood star Tom Selleck grew up a Tigers fan. His favorite player? Al, of course.

Al was invited to participate in several celebrity golf tournaments. This one in LaCosta, California also drew NFL Hall of Famer Ray Nietschke, who is standing next to Al.

Pillars of Detroit – Al, Louise and homegrown rock star Bob Seger.

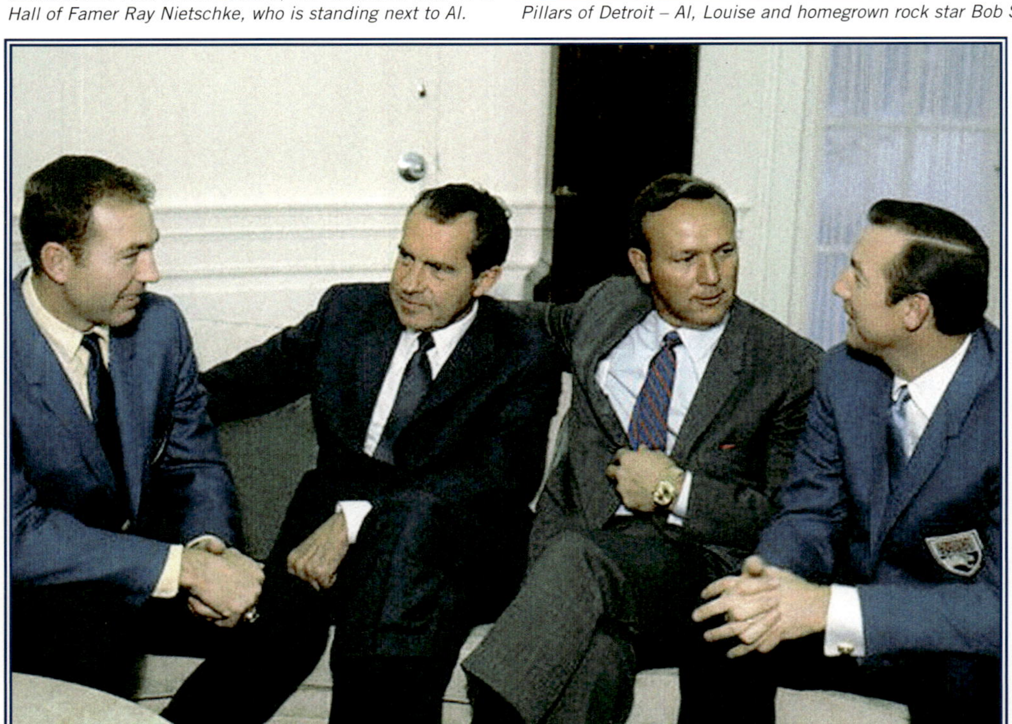

President Nixon knew how to pick an All-Star team from all sports. That's Bart Starr, Arnold Palmer and Al.

Al has had the privilege to meet countless sporting greats. Here's The Greatest – Muhammad Ali.

Looks like Olympian Jessie Owens and race car driver Dan Gurney are looking to Al for some baseball insight.

Al was an all-state basketball player in Maryland when he attended Baltimore's Southern High. Michael Jordan once tried out for the Chicago White Sox. Seems like each picked the right sport.

Two-barreled toasts of the Detroit sports scene – Al and Gordie Howe.

Al and Louise have made a few White House visits Not many, though, get photographed with George and Laura Bush.

Rubbing shoulders with President Ford.

Former University of Michigan great and Heisman Trophy winner Tom Harmon pictured with Al before a game.

Owner Spike Briggs was quite proud of these prized youngsters. Surrounding the owner (from the left) are Bill Tuttle, Al, Frank House (godfather to Mark) and Reno Bertoia. Seated are Frank Bolling and Bob Miller.

Al's admiration for Tigers Owner John E. Fetzer can be seen in his eyes.

A star-studded lineup – Al, Bo Schembechler, Cardinal Adam Szoka and then Tigers Owner Tom Monaghan.

Al and Louise were invited to President Nixon's inauguration.

SOME BASEBALL PALS

Billy Martin had played for the Yankees. When he became Tigers manager, he appreciated the fact that Al was good enough to have played for any team.

"I would have paid for the chance to see Al Kaline play," said all-time Tigers great Alan Trammell.

Old-timers games can be lots of fun. Especially sharing stories with All-Stars like Tony Oliva and Whitey Ford.

Roger Maris and Al find time to talk before a spring training game

Al and former Tigers slugger Hank Greenberg on the day the Tigers honored Hall of Famers Greenberg and Charlie Gehringer.

Fantasy Camp in Lakeland brings smiles and warm memories.

The "K Boys" – Harvey Kuenn and Al Kaline – simply killed American League pitchers.

Wouldn't it be nice to share a laugh with Mickey Mantle? He and Al shared the greatest respect for each other.

6 SIX

The Hitter

Two Tigers icons shaking hands. That's the immortal Ty Cobb with Harvey Kuenn looking on.

BATTING TITLE

Everything happened quickly in Al's 22-year Tigers career.

Only days out of high school, he joined the Tigers in mid-season. Two weeks after his first full season in 1954, he married high school sweetheart Louise. Following an off-season of Louise's delicious home-cooking, Al added some much needed weight. At just 20 years old in 1955 he set a record for the youngest player to win the American League batting championship with a .340 average. Al was one day younger than Ty Cobb who had held the record since 1907.

"It was a magical year," Al said humbly in gross understatement.

And it also jumped to a sizzling start.

In the frigid season opener against Cleveland, the Tigers faced Mike Garcia. The freezing April temperature coupled with the right-hander's heavy fastball and wicked slider made every enemy batter uncomfortable to dig in at the plate.

In spite of the conditions, Al ripped Garcia for a pair of triples. And the rest of the season snowballed from there.

"I got so much confidence by getting those triples off Mike," Al said. "It seemed

Al became the youngest American League player to hold the silver bat that represents the batting championship.

Al studied hitting even during batting practice.

Al touching the plate after a home run was a familiar sight at Tiger Stadium.

The heart of the Tiger lineup in the 50s was ruthlessly imposing. That's Harvey Kuenn, Al and Ray Boone. No rest for enemy pitchers.

like everything I hit somehow found a hole. It went on and on."

Al credits Ray Boone who batted behind him in the lineup for much of his success.

"I was just a kid and Ray was a good RBI man," Al said. "The pitchers didn't want to face him with men on base so early in the season I got a lot of good pitches to hit."

As the season progressed, pitchers had to worry about Al as much – or even more – than any veteran hitter they faced. By August he was getting brushed back off the plate and pitched to carefully.

"They started to pay me a little more respect," Al said. "They started playing games with me and I had to adjust."

Obviously the adjustments worked. Al led the league with 200 hits and a .340 average. He also hit 27 homers and knocked in 102 runs.

Quite a season for the youngster who didn't turn 21 until December 19, 1955.

Even as a kid out of high school, Al's swing was classic.

Al and Mickey Mantle each won a silver bat for winning a league batting title.

There's a lot of hits loaded in that lumber.

Detroit
Detroit

Pardon my dust, but I'm coming in. Al not only had speed, but was considered to be a crafty runner. He knew when to take the extra base and what to do when he got there.

Al was always a student of the game.

Hardening a bat on a hambone to perhaps get an extra hit goes all the way back to Ty Cobb. And if it was good enough for him, why not?

3,000 HITS

There are certain milestones reached that no player forgets.

Not the game. Not the opponent. Not the day. Not even the precise moment it occurred.

For Al, all the magic surrounding his 3,000th hit is alive today as it was on September 24, 1974. It wasn't just that hit that put him into the Hall of Fame. It was merely the exclamation mark to a first ballot election. At the time, Al became only the 12th player in major league history to accumulate at least 3,000 hits.

"I really wanted to wait and get the hit in Detroit," Al said. "But I talked to Jim Campbell (Tigers General Manager) and he said to do it wherever it may be."

And if not Detroit, what more appropriate place than Baltimore where Al was raised?

"It was beautiful with my mom, my dad, my sisters and a whole lot of friends there," Al said.

It came in the fourth inning with Dave McNally on the mound. McNally was a 20-game winning left-hander who cracked off a wicked two-strike breaking pitch on the outside corner of the plate. It was a beautiful pitcher's pitch. Al fought it perfectly and sliced a line drive down the right field line. As he neared first base, he watched the ball clearly fall into fair territory and wound up at second base with a ground rule double.

When he reached the bag, Al bowed his head to deal with the millions of thoughts bouncing around in his mind and emotions darting throughout his body as the Memorial Stadium crowd erupted with a standing ovation.

Even at Dodger Stadium, Al made the big board.

"I had so many people to thank," Al said. "So many things to be grateful for. McNally made a good pitch. He had to because the Orioles were fighting for a pennant."

The irony of Al getting No. 3,000 off McNally, though, was uncanny.

During spring training that year, McNally called Al for a little help on a project he and his brother were undertaking. They were trying to obtain a Ford dealership in Montana and wanted to know if Al had any connections with the company.

Not only did he have a connection, but Ford President Lee Iacocca happened to be a personal friend. Al placed a call and the McNally brothers were able to purchase the franchise.

Early in the season, McNally called Al to thank him for the favor.

Al always wanted to take a lineup card to the plate. He got his chance with Hall of Fame compatriot George Brett.

3,000 HIT CLUB

PLAYER	DATE OF 3,000TH HIT
Cap Anson	unknown
Honus Wagner	June 9, 1914
Nap Lajoie	September 27, 1914 (first game)
Ty Cobb	August 19, 1921 (second game)
Tris Speaker	May 17, 1925
Eddie Collins	June 3, 1925
Paul Waner	June 19, 1942
Stan Musial	May 13, 1958
Hank Aaron	May 17, 1970 (second game)
Willie Mays	July 18, 1970
Roberto Clemente	September 30, 1972
Al Kaline	**September 24, 1974**
Pete Rose	May 5, 1978
Lou Brock	August 13, 1979
Carl Yastrzemski	September 12, 1979
Rod Carew	August 4, 1985
Robin Yount	September 9, 1992
George Brett	September 30, 1992
Dave Winfield	September 16, 1993
Eddie Murray	June 30, 1995
Paul Molitor	September 16, 1996
Tony Gwynn	August 6, 1999
Wade Boggs	August 7, 1999
Cal Ripken Jr.	April 15, 2000
Rickey Henderson	October 7, 2001
Rafael Palmeiro	July 15, 2005
Craig Biggio	June 28, 2007

A trainload of hits between Al and Pete Rose.

From above, side or any angle, the swing remains sweet.

JIM PALMER

Jim Palmer was just 19 years old when he made his first major league start for the Baltimore Orioles against Denny McLain and the Detroit Tigers in 1965.

He had heard all the stories about how Al had turned hitting into an art form during the previous dozen years with the Tigers. But at 19 and with a Hall of Fame arm, Palmer relished the challenge.

Palmer won the first volley by striking out Al in the first inning. Now, however, Al knew what to expect.

"I got two strikes on him and then tried to fool him with a change-up," Palmer smiled.

Big mistake. Al timed it perfectly and sent the ball soaring over the fence for a home run.

"The next time up I threw him my best fastball on the outside corner of the plate," Palmer said.

Another mistake. Al sent it sizzling to right field for a single.

"That was my first big league start and suddenly I realized, this guy was better than me," Palmer smiled.

Of course, Al and Palmer wound up in the Hall of Fame. And Palmer knows precisely why Al made it on the first ballot.

"There wasn't a whole lot of tension in Al's swing," Palmer said. "His swing was simple and relaxed. When you have a sound swing like that, you become a great two-strike hitter. He could cover the whole plate."

Palmer still remains impressed with Al's entire approach to the game.

"Al made everything look so easy," he said. "A lot of players are maximum effort guys. Al always gave maximum effort but made it look so easy. He played the game the way you're supposed to play. He never lost his composure."

Palmer learned that lesson early and respected it for the rest of his career.

Al and Brooks Robinson were keen competitors throughout their careers. "We were friends then and even closer friends now," Robinson said.

BROOKS ROBINSON

Al was busy putting the finishing touches on claiming the 1955 American League batting championship when Brooks Robinson made his debut with the Baltimore Orioles.

Now more than a half century later, the two Hall of Famers remain close friends.

"When I came up it seemed like everyone in Baltimore was talking about Al Kaline," Robinson said. "They talked about the long home runs he hit when he played around the city and how he was an all-state basketball player. Al made Baltimore proud. And he was proud of his hometown, too."

He cast that same magic on Detroit, his adopted home since signing with the Tigers.

> "Al was such a great all around player ... And he's a great all around guy. I am proud to call him a friend."

The catcher doesn't have a chance to grab this pitch.

Bending like a pretzel, Al made it back safely to first.

And the umpire says so.

Those unforgiving wind sprints remain part of spring training.

"Al came from a blue collar part of Baltimore," Robinson said. "You could tell immediately from the way he acted that his parents raised him well."

That discipline under which Kaline developed was demonstrated in every major league ball park.

"He was the consummate right fielder," Robinson said. "He never made a mistake. Always caught the ball the right way. Always threw to the right base. Knew when to play it safe and when to take a chance. A lot of people never realized that right field, with that upper deck overhang, was a tough position to play in Tiger Stadium. It was something like left field in Fenway Park. Kaline owned it."

Robinson was treated to a special thrill the evening of September 24, 1974, even though it came at the expense of his Orioles.

"I felt real fortunate to see Al get his 3,000th hit in Memorial Stadium," he said. "I can still see the ball slicing down the right field line for a double. What a thrill for him to get that hit in his hometown."

As impressed with Kaline's career on the field, Robinson is equally impressed with the way Kaline still conducts himself off the field today.

"Al was such a great all around player," Robinson said. "And he's a great all around guy. I am proud to call him a friend."

6 SIX

The Champion

ENTER GATE 8
45 AA 17
SEC. ROW SEAT
AMERICAN LEAGUE vs. NATIONAL LEAGUE
Detroit TIGERS
DETROIT BASEBALL CLUB Agents
GAME 4
TIGER STADIUM
UPPER DECK RES. PAVILION
$6.00
1968 World Series
RAIN CHECK
RETAIN THIS CHECK
W. D. ECKERT
Admit To UPPER DECK RES. PAVILION

"I was so fortunate to play on that team... Great team and great bunch of characters."

1968 WORLD SERIES

Al waited...and waited...and waited.

Who could have blamed him for thinking that he might have been one of those rare great players unfortunately never to have played in a World Series?

"After 15 years of not making it, you start to wonder if your time is running out," he said.

From above, side or any angle, the swing remains sweet.

In 1967, the Tigers found themselves in one of the tightest pennant races in baseball history. On the last weekend of the season, four teams had a shot to win the American League pennant.

The Tigers missed on the final day. The feeling was devastating.

"We thought we had the best team, but it didn't work out that way," Al said. "In 1968, everybody came to spring training with a tremendous attitude. It was win at all cost. We were a team. No individual records mattered. The only thing that counted was getting to the World Series."

The 1968 Tigers were a collection of magnificent talent sprinkled with characters whose memories still are alive.

Bill Freehan. Mickey Lolich. Norm Cash. Willie Horton. Dick McAuliffe. Mickey Stanley. Jim Northrup. Gates Brown. And Denny McLain who rocked the baseball universe by winning 31 games.

"I was so fortunate to play on that team," Al humbly said. "Great team and great bunch of characters."

Of course, Al was a major contributor on his way to the Hall of Fame. But it didn't come easy.

Al missed five weeks of the regular season with a broken right arm. Northrup replaced Al in right field and became an offensive force in the lineup. When Al returned from the disabled list in September, the media began to speculate about how Manager Mayo Smith was going to work him back into the lineup.

"I talked to Mayo and told him he couldn't sit Northrup down," Al said. "He was hitting the ball too hard and the team was going well."

The manager told Al to start working out at third base to see how things unfolded.

Soon after, Horton got hurt and Northrup moved to left field with Al returning to right. Al went on a hitting frenzy that created a pleasant problem for the manager to handle. Before the regular season ended, Mayo concocted a plan perhaps unmatched in World Series history.

"Mayo called me and a few other players into his office one day to tell us he was thinking about moving Stanley from center field to shortstop for the Series," Al said. "Mickey was the best athlete on the team and we all felt that if anyone could do it, Mickey could."

Now with added punch in the lineup, the Tigers were more formidable for the St. Louis Cardinals who featured Hall of Fame bound Bob Gibson, arguably the most intimidating pitcher ever to take the mound.

The Cardinals threatened to end Detroit's dream early by winning three of the first four games. In Game 5 at Tiger Stadium, Al delivered a clutch single to right center field to put the Tigers ahead and send the Series back to St. Louis.

The Tigers hammered the Cards, 13-1, to force Game 7. Behind Lolich's third straight complete game victory, the Tigers defeated the Cardinals, 4-1, to complete the comeback miracle.

Kaline's patience was richly rewarded. For the Series, he collected 11 hits and batted .379 with two home runs, eight RBI and six runs scored.

"I was fortunate to have a good Series," Al said. "But none of us cared about any individual numbers. Our only goal was to make it to the Series and then to win it."

In 1967 when the team endured its greatest disappointment, the City of Detroit suffered its deepest wound with the summer civil riots whose scars are still felt.

No one can say that the Tigers' magical ride of 1968 healed the city. But it certainly shed some critically needed spirit that, perhaps, only a team like the Tigers could provide.

"We got off to a great start," Al said. "Suddenly all the people shared something in common. Maybe it did help a little to pull the city together. I don't know how, but it did seem to have a positive effect on the city."

And certainly Al made sure he did his part during his one shot in baseball's ultimate test of excellence.

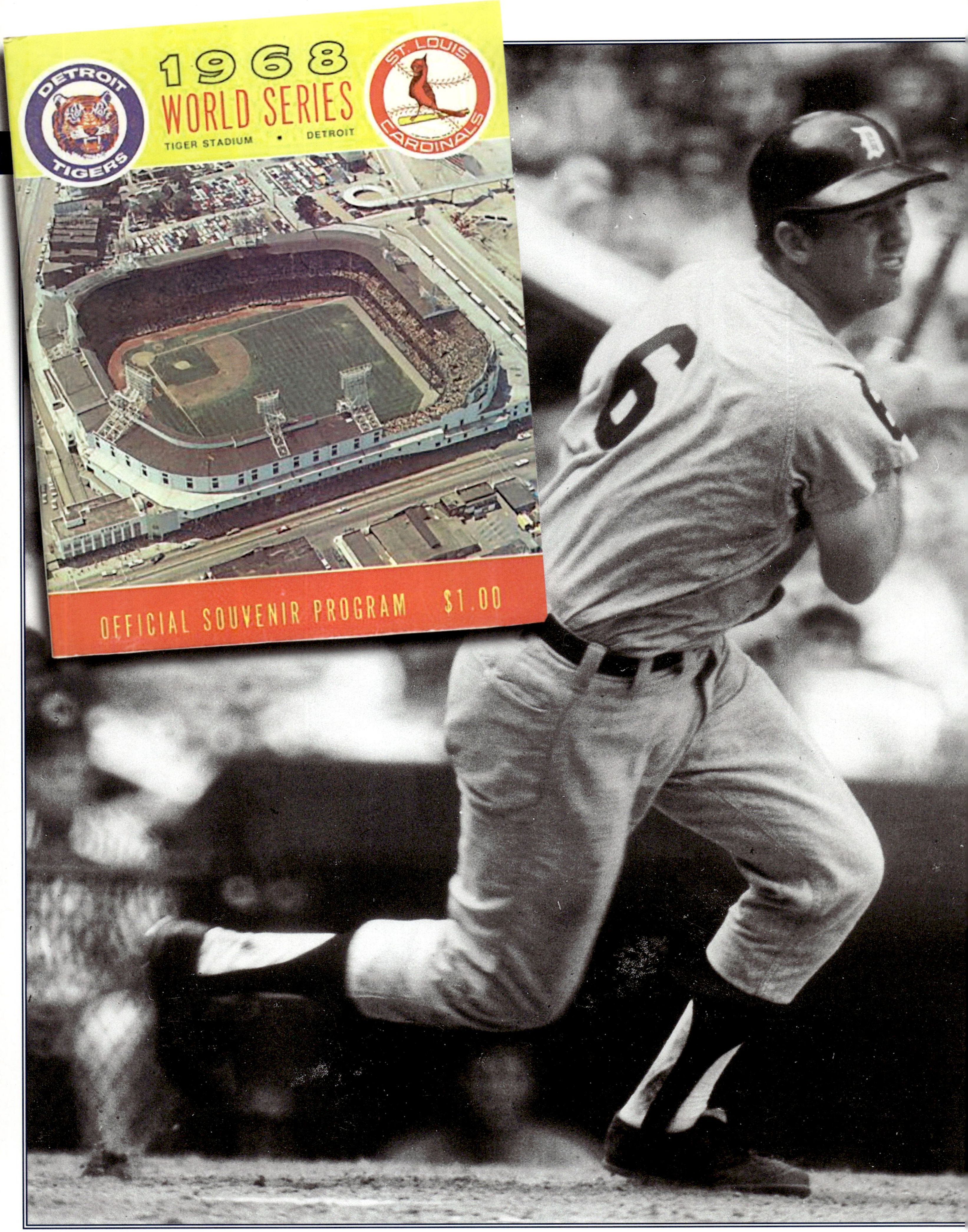
1968
WORLD SERIES
TIGER STADIUM • DETROIT
DETROIT TIGERS
ST. LOUIS CARDINALS
OFFICIAL SOUVENIR PROGRAM $1.00

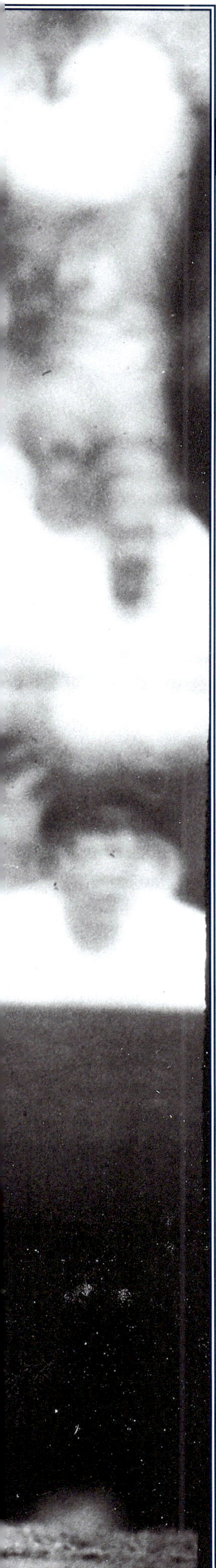

WORLD SERIES STATISTICS

YEAR	CLUB	G	AB	R	H	2B	3B	HR	RBI	BB	SO	BA	E	FA
1968	Detroit	7	29	6	11	2	0	2	8	0	7	.379	0	1.000

Look at those shirts! That's Al with Jim Northrup and Mickey Stanley making one youngster deliriously happy.

PAIR OF "MICKEYS"

A pair of Tiger "Mickeys" who spent many seasons together with Al remain as impressed with some of his personal traits as accomplishments on the field.

"Al was never flamboyant," said popular pitcher Mickey Lolich. "You never saw him running around trying to grab the headlines. In fact, on road trips you usually only saw him at the park. He didn't run around. He was always quiet and reserved."

On the field, Al let his baseball tools do the talking.

"Outstanding player," Lolich said. "Great in the outfield. Clutch hitter."

Mickey Stanley was one of the most popular players ever to play for Detroit and, arguably, the franchise's best defensive center fielder.

"It was definitely an honor to play with Al," Mickey said. "Smartest player I ever played with and also the most honest. If you asked him a question, he'd tell you exactly what he thought."

Al was the Tigers' Secretary of Hitting. Mickey Lolich served as Secretary of the Mound. Between the two there were plenty of thrills.

6 SIX

The Hall of Famer

AL KALINE
COOPERSTOWN
COOPERSTOWN
AUG
3
1980
NY
USA 15c
IN HIS FIRST YEAR OF ELIGIBILITY, SLUGGING
TIGER OUTFIELDER AL KALINE WAS INDUCTE
INTO BASEBALL'S HALL OF FAME WITH 3,00
BASE HITS, 399 HOME RUNS, AND A .297 LIFE
TIME AVERAGE.

AL: THE PROTOTYPE

The batting averages are impressive. The number of home runs and the distances they traveled are awesome. The ERAs and strikeout totals are enough to make a grown man shiver.

Every player – regardless of position – enters Baseball's Hall of Fame with a trunk full of sizzling figures. Their separation from so many other talented major leaguers, however, is as distinct as the Marines are from the Boy Scouts.

While no statistical standard other than superior consistency over an extensive period are specified for consideration for induction into the Hall of Fame, one significant requirement is clearly stated.

And it's not measured in numbers.

As stipulated by the Hall of Fame, each candidate is expected to be of good moral character that has been demonstrated over a long period of time.

And that's one area in which Al helps to set the standard.

"Al Kaline exhibits exactly what a Hall of Fame player should be," said Bill Haase, senior vice president of baseball's holiest hall. "Certainly, he has all the statistical qualifications necessary to earn his rightful place. But the intensity, the integrity, the honesty and professionalism he has displayed throughout his playing career and his whole life makes him particularly worthy of enshrinement."

> "Certainly, he has all the statistical qualifications necessary to earn his rightful place. But the intensity, the integrity, the honesty and professionalism he has displayed throughout his playing career and his whole life makes him particularly worthy of enshrinement."
>
> **Bill Haase**
> **Senior Vice President**
> **National Baseball Hall of Fame**

Haase should know. He's followed a peculiar path that has paralleled Al's career and his whole life.

Having been raised in Detroit, Haase skipped a few days of school and was quite a regular at Briggs Stadium – later Tiger Stadium – soon after Al broke in with the Tigers. Following his Marine tour in the Vietnam War, Haase returned home and wound up as a vice president with the Tigers where he spent 18 seasons. He joined the Hall of Fame administration in 2001.

Just taking time to say hello made the kids smile.

"You can judge a person's character by the consistency of his actions," Haase said. "That's the beautiful part about Al. He's the same person today as he was years ago. He does things in a quiet way, but always does the right thing. He's always ready and willing to do what he can so that the character and integrity of the game is always placed ahead of everything else. He's soft-spoken and lets actions do the talking. He's the consummate professional."

Since his childhood, Haase treasures so many memories of Al's graceful playing career. There were so many clutch hits. So many spectacular catches.

One of his most precious memories, however, comes from when teams always took infield practice before all games.

"I loved to watch that even more than batting practice," he said. "It was a ritual and Al turned it into an art form. He had such a fluid motion in the outfield. His arm was so accurate and strong. He always came within inches of his target even from the deepest part of right field. He knew precisely how to go after a ball and exactly what to do once he got it."

Above all of Al's baseball's skills, however, Haase still regards character as his most endearing characteristic.

"Al was a player that could do it all," he said. "He was one of the best and one of the smartest. He was a team player and winning was more important to him than any individual honors. That's a sign of character."

And that's one of the main reasons for Al's enshrinement in the Hall of Fame.

"You can judge a person's character by the consistency of his actions ... That's the beautiful part about Al. He's the same person today as he was years ago."

Bill Haase
Senior Vice President
National Baseball Hall of Fame

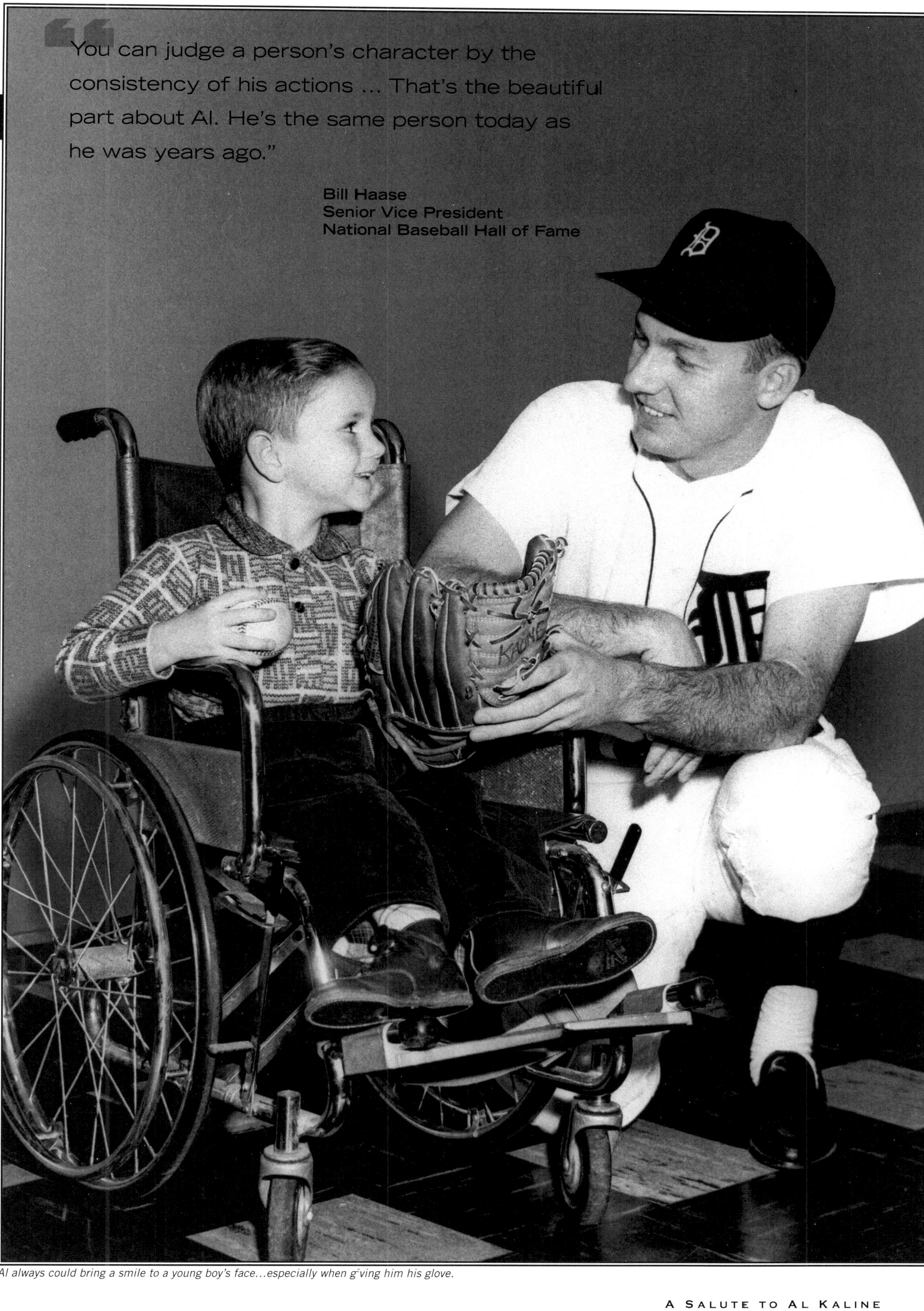

Al always could bring a smile to a young boy's face...especially when giving him his glove.

The plaque is permanently mounted now, but Al got a real close up.

What a moment to have Mom and Dad standing by the plaque.

THE INDUCTION

Al thought playing all those games and traveling across the country at insane hours was the toughest part of making it to the Hall of Fame.

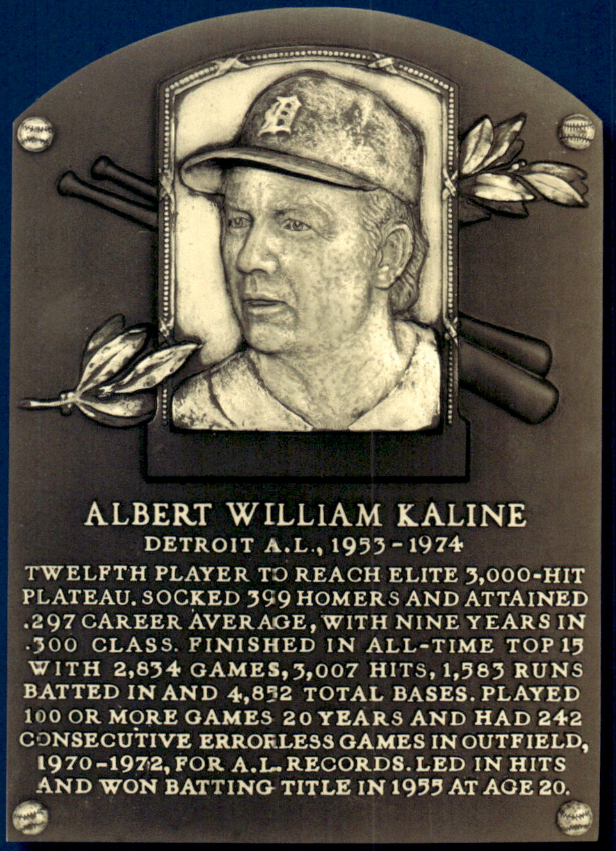

But when he went behind the stage before being inducted at Cooperstown in 1980, he was struck by the realization that he hadn't seen anything yet.

"I looked around at all the guys gathered there," he said. "There's Ted Williams, Stan Musial, Mickey Mantle, Yogi Berra and a bunch of other Hall of Famers. Suddenly I asked myself – what am I doing here?"

And the real test was yet to come.

Every Hall of Fame member emphatically believes that the toughest part of being inducted is the acceptance speech that is nastier than a Nolan Ryan fastball.

"I looked out in the crowd and there was my mom and dad, my sisters, Louise and Mark and Mike and so many friends that it was hard to keep everything together," he said.

But he did and managed to acknowledge all for the contributions to his success from so many.

At the time of his induction, Al was only the 10th player in history to be elected on the first ballot of eligibility.

"That's a tremendous honor," Al said. "There are a lot of good players who get passed on the first ballot and eventually make it. I thought there was a chance, but I tried not to get my hope too high."

When he did receive the call to confirm his election, Al and Louise hurriedly booked a flight to New York where the press conference was to be held the following day. To avoid any leaks to the press prior to the announcement, airline reservations were made in the name of Hamilton, Louise's maiden name.

Al and Louise return to Cooperstown each summer for the annual induction ceremonies.

"We love going to Cooperstown," Al said. "The honor of being a member is tremendous. It means that as long as there is baseball, you'll always be remembered."

Every Hall of Famer says the acceptance speech is the toughest. Al made sure to credit all the right people who helped him on his lifelong journey.

Front row seats for the Kaline Family that day.

Al receives a replica of his plaque that hangs in Cooperstown from Commissioner Bowie Kuhn in 1980.

KALINE CAREER STATISTICS

YEAR	CLUB	G	AB	R	H	2B	3B	HR	RBI	BB	SO	BA	E	FA
1953	Detroit	30	28	9	7	0	0	1	2	1	5	.250	0	1.000
1954	Detroit	138	504	42	139	18	3	4	43	22	45	.276	0	.971
1955	Detroit	152	588	121	200+	24	8	27	102	82	57	.340+	7	.979
1956	Detroit	153	617	96	194	32	10	27	128	70	55	.314	6	.984
1957	Detroit	149	577	83	170	29	4	23	90	43	38	.295	5	.985
1958	Detroit	146	543	84	170	34	7	16	85	54	47	.313	2	.994
1959	Detroit	136	511	86	167	19	2	27	94	72	42	.327	4	.989
1960	Detroit	147	551	77	153	29	4	15	68	65	47	.278	5	.987
1961	Detroit	153	586	116	190	41+	7	19	82	66	42	.324	4	.990
1962	Detroit	100	398	78	121	16	6	29	94	47	39	.304	4	.983
1963	Detroit	145	551	89	172	24	3	27	101	54	48	.312	2	.992
1964	Detroit	146	525	77	154	31	5	17	68	75	51	.293	3	.990
1965	Detroit	125	399	72	112	18	2	18	72	72	49	.281	3	.985
1966	Detroit	142	479	85	138	29	1	29	88	81	66	.288	2	.993+
1967	Detroit	131	458	94	141	28	2	25	78	83	47	.308	4	.983
1968	Detroit	102	327	49	94	14	1	10	53	55	39	.287	7	.977
1969	Detroit	131	456	74	124	17	0	21	69	54	61	.272	7	.974
1970	Detroit	131	467	64	130	24	4	16	71	77	49	.278	6	.989
1971	Detroit	133	405	69	119	19	2	15	54	82	57	.294	0	1.000*
1972	Detroit	106	278	46	87	11	2	10	32	28	33	.313	1	.994
1973	Detroit	91	310	40	79	13	0	10	45	29	28	.255	1	.997
1974	Detroit	147	558	71	146	28	2	13	64	65	75	.262	0	.000
		2834	10116	1622	3007	498	75	399	1583	1277	1020	.297	82	.987

+ Led League

And how about the rush in pride for Michael, Mark, Louise and Al smiling by the plaque?

1980

Al shares his Hall of Fame selection with family and friends.

DICK MCAULIFFE

Dick McAuliffe was a scrappy middle infielder who spent many seasons with Detroit at both shortstop and second base.

He was the relay man for many of Al's throws from deep in the outfield and had first-hand experience with the quality of his teammate's arm.

"Very accurate arm," McAuliffe said. "He never sailed a ball. He was always on target. I never saw Roberto Clemente that much because he was in the other league. But Al was definitely one of the best right fielders I ever saw."

Even more impressive to McAuliffe was Al's ability to stay tuned to the game.

"He never threw to the wrong base," McAuliffe said. "In fact, I can't remember him ever making a mistake."

McAuliffe certainly didn't make a mistake when he had Al as a guest on a radio show he hosted for a small station near his Connecticut home during spring training.

"I remember telling him on the show that he was going into the Hall of Fame on the first ballot," McAuliffe said.

That prediction was as accurate as one of Al's throws.

Al kept rolling into the 70s and was greeted by Norm Cash and Dick McAuliffe after another home run.

HARMON KILLEBREW

Since the first day he laced his spikes for the old Washington Senators, Harmon Killebrew was considered to be one of the greatest home run hitters in history.

And he carries a special regard for Al who has become one of his closest Hall of Fame buddies.

"There was a 10-year period in his career when I thought he was the best all-around player in the American League," Killebrew said. "Al did everything so smoothly. There was nothing he couldn't do. He was a great hitter, a great runner and a great right fielder. I know there must have been a couple of times he made a mistake in the outfield, but I can't remember one. Not only did he make all the physical plays, he had a tremendous awareness of the situation at all times. That's the difference between a good fielder and a great one. And believe me – he was a great one."

Killebrew also respects the work ethic that Al displayed throughout his career.

"Detroit is a working class city and that's exactly the way Al played," he said. "This was a young man coming to the city right out of high school and wound up staying there for the rest of his life. That's a tribute to him, the Tigers and the city."

Because of the low key personality that Al and Killebrew share, the two are proud of a friendship that now is more than a half-century old.

"We were friends when we played against each other," Killebrew said. "Now he's even a greater friend. When I think of the Detroit Tigers, I think of Al Kaline."

When the President calls, the Hall of Famers answer.

6 SIX

The Broadcaster

Spring training brings the boys out of men. In 1981, Al and George Kell donned uniforms and were the talk of the camp.

THE DYNAMIC DUO

Not even Al could have guessed that his venture as a Tiger TV broadcaster in 1976 would wind up as a 26-year run that made him the most popular color analyst in the history of the franchise.

The station carrying the Tiger telecasts contacted Al about giving the job a shot. Reluctant at first, Al suggested a 10-game trial to determine if he liked the position and, more importantly, if the station liked his work.

> "I really loved working with George...We got so close. We did everything together on the road. In the booth we could just read each other before anything was said."

Obviously, the results were mutually unanimous. After a Hall of Fame career in Tiger Stadium, Al had found a new home in the booth behind home plate.

"I struggled at first," Al admits. "A lot of the guys playing at that time were my friends. When they made mistakes, it was tough to criticize them. A former player sees mistakes on the field easier than the fans. On almost every play, something goes wrong. So I just kept quiet."

And that's where fellow Hall of Famer turned broadcast giant George Kell carefully stepped up to help his long-time partner.

"George was a tremendous help," Al said. "He was such a great announcer

Al and George Kell comprised a Hall of Fame TV broadcast duo that many Tiger fans grew up watching.

and such a great man. He told me that you've got to stay upbeat. You don't have to criticize a player, but it's important to point out exactly what's going on."

With that simple piece of advice and encouragement, Al began to feel more comfortable and the Hall of Fame duo became one of the most distinguished broadcast teams in the game.

"I really loved working with George," Al said. "We got so close. We did everything together on the road. In the booth we could just read each other before anything was said."

While many players today strive to land a broadcasting job after their playing careers end, Al never envisioned becoming a broadcaster. He is quiet by nature and rarely engaged in long discussions with members of the media.

"When I was a player, I probably made some of the writers mad because I didn't have much to say," Al said. "They always wanted me to talk about myself. If they wanted to talk about the game, I could talk all day. But when it was about me, I had a hard time."

Instead, Al let his bat and his arm and his glove and his legs do all the talking. If that wasn't enough he couldn't be concerned. That was the best he had to offer.

But his experience and insight into the nuances of the game prepared him well for his quarter century of service to Tiger telecasts.

And a generation of Tiger faithful is happy with the decision Al made to give the broadcast booth a shot.

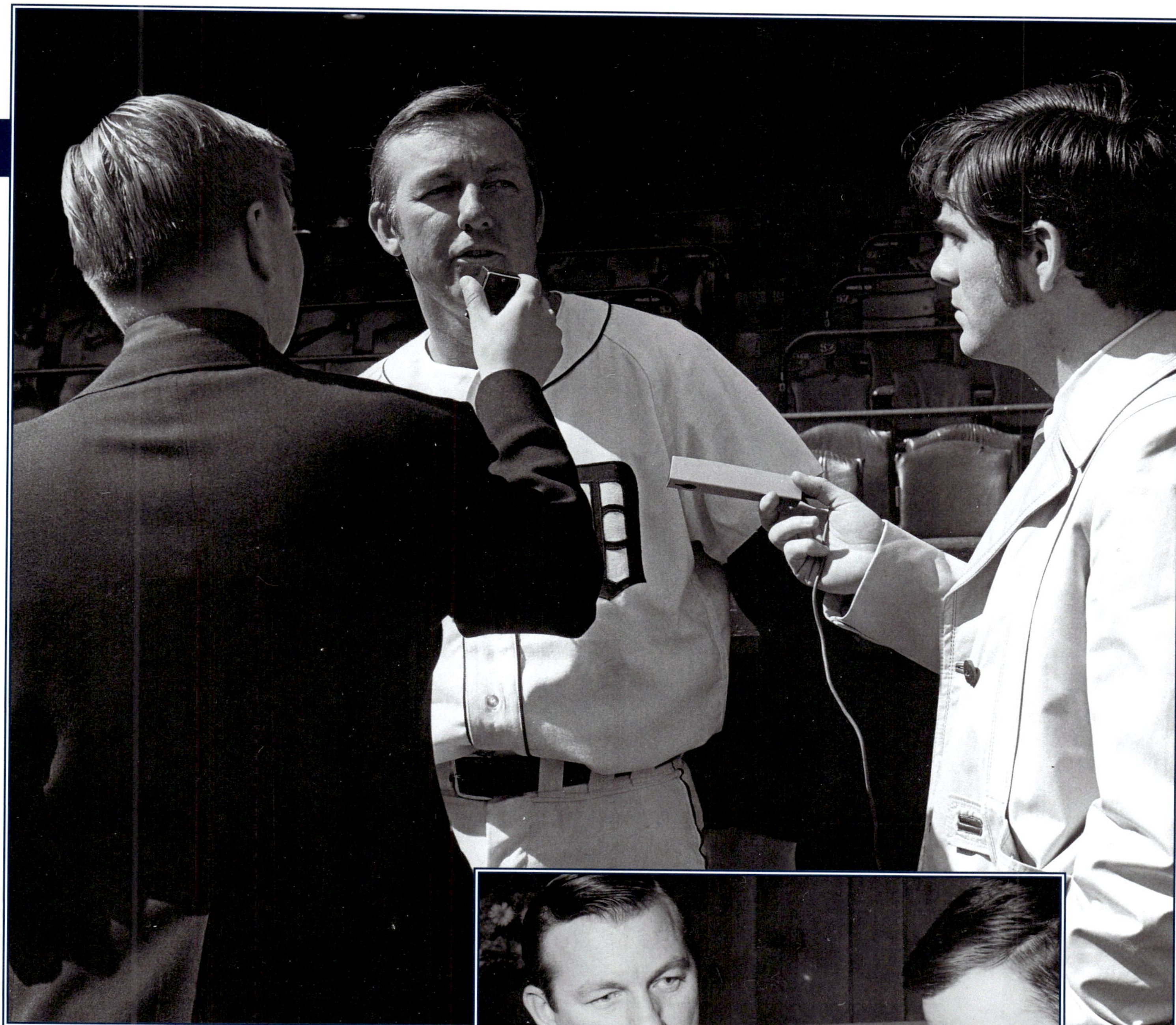

When you reach the heights Al did, it's impossible to avoid the media

"When I was a player, I probably made some of the writers mad because I didn't have much to say...They always wanted me to talk about myself. If they wanted to talk about the game, I could talk all day. But when it was about me, I had a hard time."

6 SIX

The Family Man

Al and Louise during Al's retirement at Tiger Stadium

LOUISE KALINE

No one more than Louise has a deeper level of respect for Al's dedication and loyalty to the only organization he's served throughout his professional career.

Not any of the four owners Al has served. Not any of the general managers, managers or former teammates.

Al and Louise have been a team since their marriage in 1954, a year before Al rewrote baseball history by becoming the American League batting champion before turning 21. And Louise has shared every moment...both the highlights and the trials along the way.

Al and Louise during 1954 honeymoon.

And the best part of the day – a big smooch from Louise.

"I feel blessed to have been part of this gentleman's life...He's a wonderful husband and wonderful father."

Come on Michael, you can do it.

The three Kaline men.

Al shows three-year-old Mike and eight-year-old Mark where Daddy works.

How come the kids always win the Fathers/Sons Game?

These smiles are the real deal.

The travel and relentless demands of interminably long seasons in baseball are tests for even the strong of heart. Louise did her part by making home life less stressful so that Al could practice his unforgiving persistence on the field.

"I tried to keep Mark and Michael busy while Al was away," Louise said. "There was little league and cub scouts and a variety of other activities that we all enjoyed. We did a little traveling ourselves. Trips always made for good book reports."

Louise still smiles at the memory of the boys standing outside of Al and Louise's bedroom pounding their fists into their mitts so that Al would get up and play catch with them before going to the park.

"He always tried to oblige them," Louise said proudly. "And both boys made us proud graduating from college."

Mark is a graduate of Michigan State and Michael graduated from Miami of Ohio.

"I know Al appreciates whatever help I could give him," Louise said. "I also know how much we love our home here and how much I love the man for far more than all the records he set on the field."

At home with the family.

6 SIX

The Legend

SPARKY ANDERSON

Sparky Anderson summed up Al's place in Tiger history in typical Sparky fashion before a spring training workout early in his legendary tenure as manager of the Tigers.

"There ain't no bigger Tiger than you," Sparky told Al.

The occasion arose when the pair was sitting in Sparky's office and left Al slightly tongue-tied. As usual in spring training, Al was helping outfielders polish their defensive skills.

"I kept watching him the first few days as he went about his business," Sparky recalled. "He kept his mouth shut and just went about working hard. He walked around the clubhouse like he was just somebody who had walked in from the street."

Sparky was impressed with the way Al carried himself and finally had to pose a question.

"Do you know who you are?" Sparky asked. "I mean do you really know who you are?"

Unsure how to answer, Al merely smiled.

Sparky then proceeded to recite a litany of accomplishments in Al's distinguished playing career.

"There ain't no bigger Tiger than you," Sparky summed it up.

Sparky was always impressed with Al's professional demeanor. When he came to the park, he came to work. He never found the need for the spotlight to shine on him.

Except for spring training games when he managed Cincinnati and played exhibitions against the Tigers, Sparky didn't have a lot of first-hand experience competing against Al. But he certainly held great respect for him. The record books tell that story.

"I do know this," Sparky said. "Anyone who got as many hits as he did deserves to be in the Hall of Fame. And I know all about how he played right field. He had one of the most accurate arms in the history of the game."

What continues to impress Sparky more than anything, however, is Kaline's approach to the game and his personal rules of conduct.

"He doesn't have to go around bragging about himself," Sparky said. "He can let the record books do all the talking. Talk to anyone in baseball. When you talk about the Detroit Tigers, you immediately think about Al Kaline. I don't know how much higher any player can get."

And that's from a man who also is in the Hall of Fame and managed a long line of greats in Cincinnati and Detroit.

How many basbeball stories can a threesome like George Kell, Al and Sparky Anderson tell?

Riding around the perimeter of the park gave Al and Louise the opportunity to thank the fans.

Marquis

When a club and a city throw a day to honor you, sometimes the words are tough to get out.

Master of Ceremonies Ernie Harwell had to pause for a moment while Daddy gave a hug to Michael.

None of the 1970 players were with Al from the beginning, but discovered quickly what Al means to the city.

Al played most of his career under the watch of General Manager Jim Campbell. In 1964, Campbell and Manager Charlie Dressen were ecstatic to have Al in the lineup.

Al always received plenty of fan mail to read.

A CLASS ACT

Negotiations for Al's 1971 contract with the Tigers were more than simple.

There weren't any.

After receiving the contract by mail in December, 1970, as per baseball rules, Al reviewed it, signed it and returned it to the Tigers to get ready for spring training. The contract called for the same amount of money he had received the previous season.

A day later, Al received a call from General Manager Jim Campbell who told him the offer was merely preliminary. Any player not receiving a contract in December was declared a free agent. Campbell fully expected regular negotiations and wanted Al to become the club's first $100,000 player.

"I thought the money you offered was fair," Al told the boss. "Maybe I'll have a good year and I'll get it next year."

Al, indeed, had a good year in 1971 to reach the now completely obsolete figure that always went to a team's best player. The difference had been a mere $3,000, but to Al it was a matter of principle.

Al's integrity to his team, his family and the game resulted in a significant number of awards, including the prestigious Joseph E. Cronin Trophy awarded by the American League to its player of the year in 1974 and the Roberto Clemente Award presented by Commissioner Bowie Kuhn to the player "best exemplifying baseball on and off the field."

Despite having played his last game in 1974, Al still leads the Detroit franchise in games played (2,834) and home runs (399). He's in the top three of nine of 11 key categories. Following was his standing at the time of his retirement:

AL KALINE'S FINAL TOTALS AND RANKING

(Among all-time major league leaders, Tiger career leaders)

	Kaline Totals	Major League Ranking	All-Time Tiger Ranking
Games	2,834	5th	1st
At Bats	10,116	8th	2nd
Runs	1,622	24th	3rd
Hits	3,007	11th	2nd
Doubles	498	22nd	3rd
Triples	75	---	6th
Home Runs	399	16th	1st
Extra Base Hits	972	16th	2nd
Total Bases	4,852	13th	2nd
Runs Batted In	1,583	14th	2nd
Batting Average	.297	---	12th

"Al is truly Mr. Tiger. He has been invaluable to me as a special assistant, sharing his vast knowledge of baseball, Detroit, and the Tigers. What he has meant to the game of baseball is beyond words. Al is a man of great humility and total class. He's truly a Hall of Fame person."

David Dombrowski
President, Chief Executive Officer and General Manager

From ground up, Al's statue is as imposing as his presence was felt in right field.

THE TIGER

From the president's box where he sits for home games, Al can look past the Comerica Park field and see the No. 6, representing his retired number, displayed on the wall. Nearby is a handsomely sculpted statue of Al that captures the graceful fury of his defensive prowess.

As a Special Assistant to the President, Al's career with the Tigers has come full circle from that beautiful June afternoon when he reported to the team in Philadelphia in 1953.

> "I enjoy what I do now more than I expected ... I still see the beauty of the games and I want to help the Tigers be as good as they can be."

From player to broadcaster to his executive advisory position, Al begins his 58th season of association with the Tigers in 2010. Al was promoted to his executive position before the start of the 2001 season.

So where has all that time gone?

Thinking about the Tigers without Kaline is impossible. He's part of the franchise fabric. A living tradition. He's the essence of what being a Tiger is all about.

He's served and known four men privileged to have been guardians of one of sports' most sacred franchises going from Walter O. Briggs, John E. Fetzer, Tom Monaghan and Mike Ilitch.

"All good men," Al says. "I just wish I would have had the opportunity to play for Mr. Ilitch."

Even more importantly, he's served the game's most faithful fans with dignity and integrity.

Al spends little time, though, reflecting upon the past. In his position, he's too busy with the present helping to shape a ball club whose tradition is more than a century old. The Tigers are wise to capitalize on Al's experience and loyalty to the storied franchise.

"I enjoy what I do now more than I expected," he said. "I wanted to be involved, not just a figurehead. I study the way players perform. I like to anticipate what's going to happen. I still see the beauty of the games and I want to help the Tigers be as good as they can be."

Louise merely smiles at the start of each new season.

44
Detroit
6

To celebrate their 50th anniversary, Al and Louise took the entire Kaline family on a Caribbean cruise

Al's grandchildren. From left to right the girls are Kelsey and Brittney. And left to right the boys are Branden and Colin

"I can't believe it," she muses. "We've been married 55 years and I still have to check the Tiger schedule to see what my life's going to be."

Al's presence not only makes the Tigers stronger, but also serves as reassurance to loyal fans across the state.

"This is our home," Louise said. "We don't even consider Maryland our home. We were so young when we came here."

Fortunately for Al and Louise, their two sons and have chosen to remain in the Detroit community and reside in the immediate area where their parents live. It provides the Kalines the opportunity to play proud grandparents.

Mark and Jill are the parents of Brittney and Branden. Michael and Marcia are the parents of Kelsey and Colin. Mark is a graduate of Michigan State University and Michael graduated from Miami of Ohio.

The Tigers without Al Kaline would be like a Detroit uniform without the Olde English "D." Michigan without the Kalines would be like a highway without one Ford on the road.

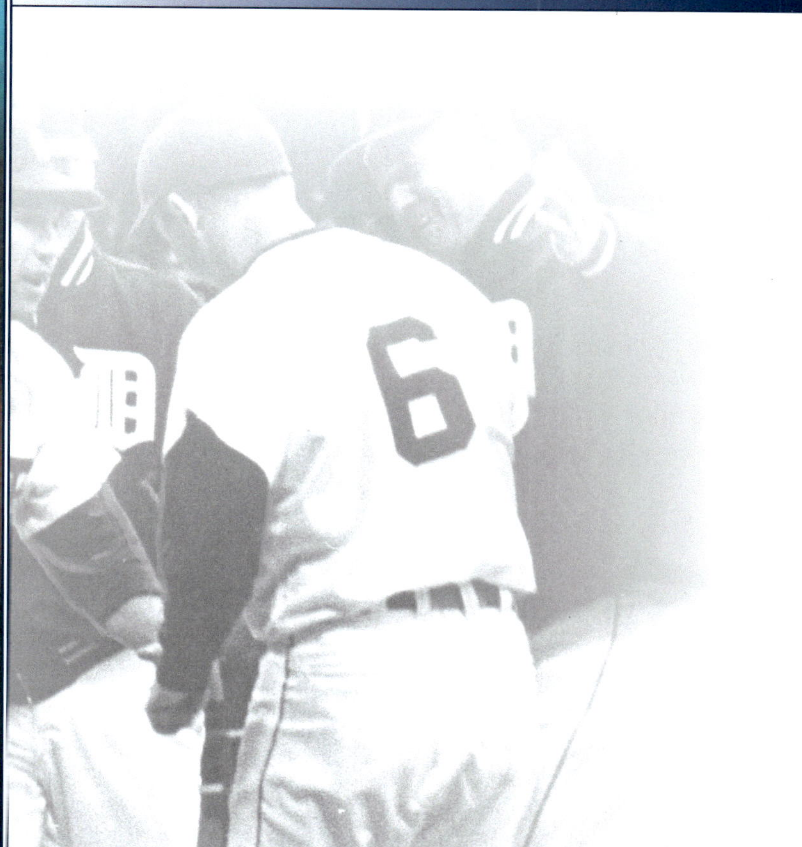

SIX